CRIMINAL JUSTICE ACT 2003

A Guide to the New Procedures and Sentencing

Criminal Justice Act 2003
A Guide to the New Procedures and Sentencing

Published 2004 by

WATERSIDE PRESS

Domum Road
Winchester SO23 9NN
Telephone 01962 855567
Fax 01962 855567
E-mail enquiries@watersidepress.co.uk

345 GIB

ISBN 1 904 380 07 7

Printing and binding Antony Rowe Ltd, Chippenham and Eastbourne.

Cover design © Waterside Press. Collage of contemporary clippings mainly from British broadsheet newspapers including *The Guardian*, *The Times* and *The Telegraph*.

CRIMINAL JUSTICE ACT 2003

A Guide to the New Procedures and Sentencing

Bryan Gibson

With the assistance of **Michael Watkins**

WATERSIDE PRESS

Acknowledgements

My thanks are due to Michael Watkins for his help in piecing together, at relatively short notice, this overview of the CJA 2003. Michael has written (or co-written) four editions of *The Sentence of the Court*, and this experience allowed him to make a number of suggestions in relation to matters covered by the new legislation. I am also grateful to David Faulkner of the Centre for Criminological Studies at Oxford University for looking over the proofs. Many people will remember David at the Home Office where he was one of the architects of the first comprehensive statutory sentencing framework - that contained in the Criminal Justice Act 1991 - on which the 2003 Act in part builds. It was invaluable to receive support from two such informed perspectives.

I must also acknowledge the Home Office 'Explanatory Notes' to the 2003 Act. Whilst, for the most part, it was a relatively straightforward (if sizeable and sometimes complex) task to work from primary sources - the Criminal Justice Act 2003 itself, other statutes as amended by it and existing law in general - there are certain changes which, but for some 'clues' to the minute reconstruction of other statutes, seemed to defy comprehension in their raw state as 'amendments'. Given the timescale for publication, I have thus, on occasion, taken a lead from those notes - on the assumption that the Home Office and the Parliamentary draftspeople did a sound job. Any residual errors are, of course, my own.

Finally, my thanks are due to my in-house editor Jane Green, for not only straightening out some of my English, but also for pointing to things that people might not readily understand.

Bryan Gibson

March 2004

Criminal Justice Act 2003
CONTENTS

Acknowledgements *iv*
Preface *vii*

CHAPTER

The authors

Bryan Gibson is Editor-in-Chief at Waterside Press. His publications include *Introduction to the Magistrates' Court* (1989, 1995, 1999, 2002), *Introduction to the Criminal Justice Process* (1995, 2002) (with Paul Cavadino/David Faulkner) and the *Waterside A to Z of Criminal Justice* (2004) (forthcoming). He is a barrister and a former Clerk to the Justices who served on the council of the Justices' Clerks' Society, as legal adviser to the Magistrates' Association Sentencing of Offenders Committee and co-editor of *Justice of the Peace*.

Michael Watkins is Director of Legal Services and Justices' Clerk for Warwickshire. He has contributed to training programmes for magistrates for the Judicial Studies Board and at the Universities of Birmingham and Cambridge. He is a former member of the Executive Committee of the Magistrates' Training Forum. He is a solicitor, a member of the Justices' Clerks' Society's Criminal Law Network and an original co-author of *Introduction to the Youth Court*. His previous publications include four editions of *The Sentence of the Court*.

Preface

The Criminal Justice Act 2003 (CJA 2003) stands at the centre of a range of developments that are serving to create the 'Brave New World' of criminal justice alluded to in the final chapter of this book. They affect all aspects of the criminal process from the discovery of an offence to sentencing by courts and beyond. At the forefront of this process are technological advances that are transforming the detection and investigation of crime. Police, local authorities and the Crown Prosecution Service are being given enhanced powers and responsibilities. Once an offender has received his or her sentence there is from the summer a National Offender Management Service (NOMS) with separate arms to commission and provide accommodation, facilities and programmes in prisons and in the community.

Through a combination of legislation, exhortations and sometimes directions from central government, 'crime reduction', 'crime prevention', 'fear of crime', 'public perception of crime' and 'public confidence' have become points of focus for the criminal justice system as a whole. The creation of Criminal Justice Boards (nationally and locally) means that the relevant agencies now jointly discuss strategies and arrangements linked to achieving these ends. To a large extent, daily practice depends on meeting targets that have some connection with such objectives. The CJA 2003 introduces a Sentencing Guidelines Council (SGC) which will become a key factor in efforts to link courts more closely with such objectives.[1] The next few years will also see the abolition of the ancient office of Lord Chancellor, the creation of a Supreme Court, revised approaches to judicial training, changes of jurisdiction, common Criminal Procedure Rules and implementation of the Courts Act 2003 that should streamline administrative arrangements. Further legislation includes the Anti-Social Behaviour Act 2003, the Sexual Offences Act 2003, and the Domestic Violence, Crime and Victims Bill which was introduced at the end of last year. Even without the CJA 2003, this is quite an agenda.

According to the White Paper, *Justice for All* (2002) (which preceded the Act) a central purpose is to 'rebalance the system' in favour of victims and the community whilst ensuring the fair treatment of suspects and offenders.[2] The new Act seeks to do so through radical reforms, including changes to various time-honoured procedural and other rules - as described in the chapters that follow. What is striking is the sheer scale of the CJA 2003 and the extent to which the changes will demand certain fresh ways of thinking, including in relation the new sentencing framework described in *Chapters 7* to *10*. Without doubt, it is the most wide-ranging measure of its kind in modern times, running as it does to 339 sections, 38 schedules (some highly detailed) and almost 500 pages.

To 'make sense' of such extensive change within a slim volume is no easy task, and naturally involves a degree of reduction and selection - but this book is offered as a straightforward guide (or as straightforward as can be in the circumstances) in the hope that it will allow readers to gain an understanding of

---

[1] The SGC is described in *Chapter 7* and further comments about its key role appear in *Chapter 14*.
[2] Critics might suggest that the system is being rebalanced in favour of the State.

the changes without having to face the daunting prospect of starting with the Act itself. There is no way around some of its complexities, or the dynamics of its 'delivery' as noted in *Chapter 14*. But it *is* possible to simplify information, present it in manageable portions and to 'decipher' events - which is the main aim of this book.

If there is one further thought by way of introduction it concerns whether the Act will 'deliver' - whether it will lead to more offenders being brought to justice, reliable convictions, appropriate sentences and ultimately a reduction in crime and a smaller proportion of people who re-offend. As with any attempt to redirect the way an institution operates, a great deal will depend on the thousands of individual decisions taken each day by individual practitioners: in the present context by judges, magistrates, Crown prosecutors, police officers, prison and probation staff and others. Quite considerable effort has gone into creating the CJA 2003 and a corresponding 'investment' is now about to be made in its implementation, through training, guidance and the provision of materials. As can be seen from the final chapter of this work, the essential structures are in place (or are emerging). But as will become evident from the text that follows, there will need to be a high level of professionalism both in understanding and in applying the new measures.

Bryan Gibson

March 2004

CHAPTER 1

Overview of the Criminal Justice Act 2003

The Criminal Justice Act 2003 (CJA 2003) represents a landmark in the evolution of crime and punishment in England and Wales. Conceived in the White Paper, *Justice for All* (2002),[1] it is by far the most wide-ranging statute of its kind of modern times. It contains measures that will transform the actions of judges, magistrates, the police, prosecutors, probation officers, prison governors and other people involved in the provision of criminal justice. The changes are directed principally towards:

- **processes and procedures of criminal justice:** from those affecting the earliest stages of an investigation to those bearing upon a criminal trial, including in relation to juries, witnesses and the law of evidence; and

- **sentencing:** where the Act creates a new framework based upon statutory 'purposes' and criteria, fresh legal considerations, new-style sentences and revised release arrangements; and a Sentencing Guidelines Council.

This chapter describes the Act in outline, its overall structure, topics and approach to 'rebalancing the criminal justice system'[2] as a prelude to more detailed treatment in later chapters.

THE OVERALL SCHEME OF THE ACT

The CJA 2003 includes provisions of a general kind - potentially affecting every criminal case as it progresses through the system - and of a specific or targeted nature, like those in relation to 'double jeopardy' (generated, in part, by the Stephen Lawrence case), anxieties about 'jury nobbling' and concerns about protecting the public from dangerous offenders. Certain of the changes, such as the new rules on disclosure of evidence and the 'allocation and sending' of either way cases to the Crown Court[3] are designed to 'streamline' the management of cases generally, and are aimed at constructing a more flexible approach. Some changes are quite fundamental, including those to the law of evidence which replace common law and statutory rules that have served for over a century.

Strategically placed decision-making
In broad terms, the legislation seeks to make criminal trials and sentencing more 'effective'[4] and to reduce the scope for abuse of the system. It introduces enhanced and more strategically placed decision-making, e.g. by involving the Crown Prosecution Service (CPS) in decisions about charging and cautioning (as

---

[1] The changes also stem from earlier recommendations in Lord Justice Auld's *Review of the Criminal Courts* (2001) and John Halliday's *Making Punishments Work* (2001).
[2] See the *Preface*.
[3] For an explanation of 'allocation and sending' see *Chapter 4*.
[4] E.g. by reducing the number of 'cracked trials', delays and costs, and the number of reconvictions.

well as allowing police officers to grant 'street bail' pending an investigation), by the new system of 'allocation and sending' (already mentioned above) and by increasing magistrates' sentencing powers so that fewer cases need to be sent to the Crown Court purely on the basis that those powers are insufficient. A raft of measures supports better and more timely information and decision-making; and there are various new situations in which reasons or explanations must be given for decisions made by courts and other people, and many processes - including the sentencing provisions - are intended to be clearer to understand and more adaptable.

Implementation

The new measures will come into force at different times under a series of commencement orders from 2003 onwards, with certain provisions being tested ('piloted') in selected areas of England and Wales first. Shortly after Royal Assent, certain provisions were brought into force by the Criminal Justice Act 2003 (Commencement No. 1 Order) (SI 2003, No. 3282), including in order to allow 'intermittent custody' in 'pilot' areas. The new 'generic community sentence' is anticipated late in 2004. The total impact of the Act may not occur until late-2006/early-2007. Information is being issued periodically by the Home Office and an extensive 'updated list' of projected start dates has been circulated to courts by the Judicial Studies Board[5] (which is to play a key role in relation to implementation).

What the changes cover

Simply listing the areas of change is a substantial enough task. The Act contains 14 Parts, 339 sections and 38 schedules and makes extensive changes to many existing statutes - so that what appears in this book represents an 'editing down' from some 500 pages of legislation, but hopefully one that will be of use to readers in getting to grips with the essentials, including new terminology and shifts of thinking. In basic outline the main changes affect:

- the **investigation** of offences, **detention** of suspects and other Police and Criminal Evidence Act 1984 (PACE) matters (Part 1 CJA 2003): as to which see *Chapter 2* of this book;
- **bail** (Parts 1 and 4) In particular police officers will be able to grant 'street bail' unless there is some other reason to take suspects to a police station following their arrest: *Chapters 2* and *4*;
- **cautions** There is a new scheme of 'conditional cautioning' for adults (Part 3): *Chapter 3*;
- **charging** of accused people where the CPS, rather than the police, will become responsible for decision-making except in straightforward or urgent situations (Part 4): *Chapter 3*;
- **disclosure** of evidence by the prosecution and defence (Part 5): *Chapter 4*;
- **allocation** and **'sending'** of cases to the Crown Court (Part 6): *Chapter 4*;
- **trial without a jury** (or 'judge alone trials') including where there are fears of jury intimidation (Part 7): *Chapter 5*.

---

[5] Letter to courts of 21 November 2003.

- **evidence** Fundamental and wide-ranging changes to the rules about evidence of 'bad character' and concerning the admissibility of hearsay evidence in criminal proceedings - in effect the abolition and replacement of existing and longstanding rules (Part 11): *Chapter 5*;
- **'live links'** between courts and other locations (Part 8): *Chapter 5*;
- **prosecution appeals** (Part 9): *Chapter 6*;
- the **retrial** of certain serious allegations following an earlier acquittal (i.e. exceptions to the 'double jeopardy' rule) and associated measures (Part 10): *Chapter 6*;
- **sentencing** A new framework which is sumarised below and further described in *Chapters 7 to 10* (Part 12); and
- **release from custody** and **post-custody supervision** where a fresh scheme is introduced linked to new varieties of custodial sentence (Part 12): *Chapter 11.*

The CJA 2003 also affects juveniles at various points: either from a general standpoint - when adult rules are frequently applied in a modified form - or, in some instances, via provisions that apply exclusively to juveniles (such as parenting orders and a new 'individual support order'). These aspects are drawn together in *Chapter 12.* Parts 13 and 14 CJA 2003 deal with various 'other', 'supplementary', 'miscellaneous' or 'general' provisions. These extend from terrorism to outraging public decency; and from assessing the risk posed by certain offenders to criminal records certificates. The main strands are drawn together in *Chapter 13.*

Scope of the book
This book is designed to allow busy practitioners, students and other people who are interested in the impact of the CJA 2003 to grasp its essentials without the need to grapple, at the outset, with its inner complexities. Clearly, in a book of this size it would be impossible to deal with every detail that appears in a statute which is itself three times that length - still less to describe all existing Acts as amended. The approach has thus been to:

- summarise and explain changes to existing law;
- 'focus in' on key provisions, especially those central to the day to day work of the criminal courts and other agencies; and
- reproduce statutory extracts in their full form where these seem to be essential to an understanding of the new legislation or the best way of describing the new law.

Generally, speaking, references to the relevant provisions of the CJA 2003 and other Acts as amended are provided within the text of subsequent chapters so as to allow those readers who wish to do so to trace or further explore the changes. The Act can be downloaded from the Internet free of charge.[6]

Key questions
The essential questions the book seeks to deal with are: 'How will the CJA 2003 change things?', 'What problems might arise when it is put into effect?' and 'What may need rethinking?' Greatest attention has been paid to those items that

---

[6]   Go to http://www.hmso.gov.uk/acts/acts2003/20030044.htm

are entirely novel rather than areas where existing law is substantially restated. The main changes are summarised below and each detailed in a later chapter.

Reasons for decisions
A feature of the CJA 2003 is the extent to which - human rights considerations apart - it adds to the situations in which reasons or explanations must be given for particular outcomes. These situations are mentioned in the text. Due to their key nature in identifying areas where legislators have placed an extra burden on courts and other decision-makers they are also collated in the *Appendix*.

Setting the Act in context
As already intimated in the *Preface*, the CJA 2003 comes at a time of widespread change in relation to criminal justice. In *Chapter 14*, an attempt is made to place the Act within the context of what can be described as the 'Brave New World' of criminal justice in which there is increasing reliance on technology and the components of the criminal justice system, especially the courts, police, prison and probation services are being re-marshalled, re-packaged and in some cases 're-branded' as never before.

INVESTIGATION AND DETENTION (PACE)

Part 1 CJA 2003 overhauls various aspects of the investigation of offences, detention of suspects and associated items by amending PACE and related Acts of Parliament. These changes are dealt with in *Chapter 2* of this book.

Prohibited articles, 'sus'[7] and warrants to search premises
Section 1 CJA 2003 extends the definition of 'prohibited article' in section 1 of PACE so as to include articles made, adapted or intended for use in causing *criminal damage*. The effect is to provide a police officer with additional powers to stop and search people on reasonable suspicion that they are carrying such an item. Section 2 CJA 2003 makes provision for warrants to enter and search premises. Under existing law, people who accompany police constables bearing search warrants can do so only in an administrative or advisory capacity. The changes allow such people to actively assist in the search. Amongst the changes, section 3 CJA 2003 also extends Schedule 1A of PACE which lists specific offences that are 'arrestable offences', including possessing cannabis or cannabis resin (see *Chapter 2*).[8]

Review of detention and the recording of a suspect's belongings
Section 6 CJA 2003 enables PACE reviews of the continuing need for detention of a suspect without charge to be conducted by telephone, rather than obliging the senior reviewing officer to be present in person at the relevant police station. However, if video conferencing facilities are available these must be used instead. Section 7 CJA 2003 widens the PACE provisions under which a suspect

---

[7] 'Sus' is the common tag for 'stop and search' by police officers, sometimes called 'the sus law'.

[8] Certain media coverage has implied that people cannot now be arrested for possession of cannabis: this is not so, in view of section 3 CJA 2003.

may be detained without charge under the authority of a police superintendent for up to 36 hours (i.e. by way of extension to the standard 24 hours) to an 'arrestable offence' rather than a 'serious arrestable offence' (the existing, higher criterion). Whereas a custody officer must, under existing law, record everything that a detained person has upon him or her on entering custody, section 8 CJA 2003 relaxes this so that - whilst the officer will still have a responsibility to ascertain the items involved - choice of details is left to his or her discretion.

PACE codes
At a more general level, section 11 CJA 2003 relaxes the Parliamentary and other procedures for creating and amending codes of practice under PACE thereby allowing the Secretary of State greater flexibility and more direct controls. The existing codes, which are also affected by this provision, are noted in *Chapter 2*.

Fingerprints
Section 9 CJA 2003 extends police powers to take fingerprints without a suspect's consent whilst in police detention following arrest in relation to a recordable offence; and section 10 does the same in relation to DNA (or 'non-intimate') samples. A brief note of developments in relation to this area of 'forensics' is contained in *Chapter 2*.

CHANGES TO THE LAW OF BAIL

Changes to the law of bail are dealt in *Chapter 2* in so far as they relate to Parts 1 and 2 CJA 2003 and in *Chapter 4* in so far as they relate to Part 4 of the 2003 Act and the charging of suspects. Overall, the changes can be summarised as follows:

Street bail
Under novel procedures aimed at streamlining the bail process at street level, section 4 CJA 2003 amends the Bail Act 1976 so as to enable instant bail to be granted by a police officer at the scene of someone's arrest where there is no obvious or immediate need to convey the arrested person to a police station. The non-statutory label 'street bail' has been attached to this power. The police are given an element of discretion, e.g. as to when and where an arrested person should be required to attend at a police station for interview and there are provisions whereby the requirement can be varied or cancelled. It is important to note that *the Bail Act 1976 does not apply to street bail, that bail conditions cannot be added to such bail, and that the only sanction for failure to surrender at the police station specified in a street bail notice is re-arrest by the police.*

Offences committed whilst on bail and absconding
Part 2 CJA 2003 deals generally with other bail-related matters, including the situation where offences are committed on bail and absconding (failure to surrender to bail). The existing Bail Act 1976 provision seeking to create an exception to the right to bail based on the fact that an offence appears to have been committed whilst the defendant was already on bail for another offence or offences is repealed.[9] This is replaced by a new presumption of law, i.e. that bail

---

[9] Seemingly due to the fair trial provisions of Article 6 ECHR.

may not be granted to an adult in such circumstances unless the court is satisfied that there is no significant risk of his or her re-offending on bail (section 14 CJA 2003 amending Schedule 1 to the 1976 Act). A similar presumption - that an adult who without reasonable cause fails to surrender to custody *may not be granted* bail - is also created, in this instance unless the court is satisfied that there is no significant risk that he or she would fail to surrender to custody if released (section 15).[10] In each situation, existing discretionary powers are over-ridden.

Drug users and bail

As part of the Government's strategy to target drug use,[11] the CJA 2003 creates a similar presumption to those already noted that bail *may not be granted* to an adult - charged with an imprisonable offence - who:

- tests positive for a specified Class A drug; or
- refuses to undergo assessment as to his or her dependency or propensity to misuse such drugs; or who
- following assessment, refuses relevant follow-up action

unless, in whichever case, the court is satisfied that there is no significant risk of his or her re-offending while on bail (section 19 CJA 2003 amending section 3 and Schedule 1 to the Bail Act 1976). These provisions can be seen as in line with court powers to order a drug test before sentence and the fact that failure to comply with such an order becomes an additional, new basis for imposing custody (see *Chapter 7*).

Appeals following bail decisions

Section 16 CJA 2003 gives effect to recommendations in Lord Justice Auld's *Review of the Criminal Courts* for simplifying bail appeals, including by removing the High Court's bail jurisdiction where this runs concurrently with that of the Crown Court. In a sweeping move, the right of a prosecutor to appeal to the Crown Court against a decision by magistrates to grant bail is extended to *all* imprisonable offences. Various other new appeal rights are conferred on the prosecutor by other provisions of the Act (see within *Chapter 6*).

THE NEW SCHEME OF CONDITIONAL CAUTIONS

Part 3 CJA 2003 builds upon existing (non-statutory) arrangements in relation to cautioning by the police of adult offenders. Instead of prosecution, under section 22 CJA 2003 a caution can be given to which conditions are added concerning:

- the rehabilitation of the offender; or
- reparation to a victim of the offence.

There are 'five requirements'[12] before a conditional caution can be given, including the existence of evidence 'that the offender has committed the offence', and the offender must admit the offence and agree to the caution.

---

[10] In relation to either presumption the exception allowing bail differs for juveniles: see *Chapter 12*.

[11] As to which see further in *Chapters 13* and *14*.

[12] The expression 'the five requirements' is used by the CJA 2003 as a shorthand way of cross-referring to these. They are set out in *Chapter 3*.

Under a realignment of functions, it will in future be for the CPS (not the police) to decide whether a conditional caution is appropriate, and in the normal course of events for the police to carry it into effect - although the CPS can authorise other people to do so. If a suspect fails to comply with a condition attached to a caution under the CJA 2003, he or she becomes liable to prosecution for the underlying offence. At that stage, again by way of a fresh departure, the admission document that the offender is obliged to sign before a conditional caution can be given becomes admissible in that prosecution (see section 24(3)) and the conditional caution ceases to have effect. Already, the Home Office has issued a draft Code of Practice and this (and its links to restorative justice) together with other matters relating to conditional cautions is discussed in *Chapter 3*.

PREPARING FOR THE COURT HEARING

Part 4 CJA 2003 in conjunction with Schedule 2 to the CJA 2003 gives the Crown prosecutor a more central role in framing charges against accused people. It also reforms the rules on advance disclosure of evidence and creates a new - and in most cases replacement - method of instituting proceedings. The changes are summarised below and further outlined in *Chapter 4*.

Charges and bail
Schedule 2 CJA 2003 amends PACE so as to provide that, where a custody officer is deciding whether or not there is enough evidence to charge a suspect who is in police detention, he or she must have regard to guidance issued by the Director of Public Prosecutions (DPP) concerning whether the suspect should be:

- released without charge but *on bail;* or
- released without charge and *without bail* or
- charged with an offence.

Where, under the DPP's guidance, a case is referred to the CPS to determine whether proceedings should be instituted (and, if so, the nature of the charge), the defendant must be released on police bail with or without conditions.

New forms of process
Section 29 CJA 2003 provides for a more streamlined method of initiating *public* prosecutions, to replace that of laying an information and issuing a summons. The police, CPS and other named 'public prosecutors' (defined by way of a list in section 29(5)) will instead issue a written charge accompanied by what is called a 'requisition'. The requisition repeats the charge and tells the defendant when and where he or she is to appear in court to answer the allegation. The CJA 2003 does not abolish informations and summonses as such, which will continue in the case of a 'non-listed' prosecutor. Neither does it prevent conventional charges against someone in custody where this is the appropriate way to start

the proceedings in the circumstances (see section 30(4)) (otherwise, e.g. the police might sometimes be faced with releasing a dangerous offender).

Advance disclosure by prosecution and defence
Part 5 CJA 2003 amends the Criminal Procedure and Investigations Act 1996 concerning defence case statements and disclosure by the prosecution to the defence of 'unused material'. The provisions are further explained in *Chapter 4*.

Disclosure by the defence
Section 33 CJA 2003 amends the defence disclosure requirements in section 5 of the 1996 Act so that the accused will be obliged to provide a more detailed defence statement than under existing law. In summary, the accused person:

- must set out the nature of his or her defence including any particular defences on which he or she intends to rely; and
- must indicate any points of law that he or she wishes to raise, including those concerning the admissibility of evidence or abuse of process.

There are further requirements for an updated defence statement - ahead of the trial - to assist the management of the trial, and the accused person must serve details of the witnesses he or she intends to call (other than himself or herself), and of any experts consulted.

Associated provisions require the court to warn the accused about the consequences of failure to comply with the requirements. In the Crown Court, the judge will have a discretion to disclose the defence statement to the jury (e.g. where what the accused person puts forward in court differs from what was originally notified) and there are provisions about when comments can be made by the judge or prosecutor regarding defence faults in complying. Magistrates or a jury will, as under existing law, be able to draw inferences from certain faults in disclosure by the accused when deciding if he or she is guilty of the offence charged, but they cannot convict solely on the basis of such an inference.

Unused material
Under further amendments in Part 5 CJA 2003, the existing two-stage process affecting disclosure by a prosecutor to the defence of any material not used for the purposes of the prosecution is replaced by a new, single test. This requires the prosecutor to disclose material that has not previously been disclosed and which might reasonably be considered capable of undermining the case for the prosecution or assisting the case for the accused. The prosecutor will have to review prosecution material on receipt of the defence statement (above) and make disclosure as appropriate under a continuing duty.

MODE OF TRIAL AND CONNECTED MATTERS

Following implementation of Part 6 CJA 2003 and in relation to 'either way' offences the terms 'mode of trial' and 'committal for trial' are likely to fade away, or at least will not be used in their existing senses. In their place, Part 6 CJA 2003 establishes a system for the 'allocation' of cases as between the Crown

Court and magistrates' court and of 'sending' cases to the Crown Court for trial or sentence. In conjunction with this, committal for sentence - in its conventional sense of a decision made *following summary trial by magistrates* - is replaced by provisions that will normally prevent committal for sentence *once magistrates have themselves assumed jurisdiction.*[13]

Again, these changes are perhaps best viewed in the light of a general streamlining of procedures, and parallel moves to create common Rules of Criminal Procedure and seamless administrative arrangements under the Courts Act 2003 - bringing the Crown Court and the magistrates' court within what Lord Woolf, Lord Chief Justice, has dubbed 'the same criminal justice family'. Both legally and administratively, transferring cases from one court to the other is set to become more straightforward.[14] The provisions also need to be understood in the light of a general increase in magistrates' own sentencing powers and allocation guidelines to be issued by the Sentencing Guidelines Council (*Chapter 7*).

In summary, Part 6 CJA 2003 together with Schedule 3 CJA 2003 alters the procedure in the Magistrates' Courts Act 1980 which to be followed by magistrates' courts in determining whether either way cases should be tried summarily (i.e. in the magistrates' court) or on indictment (by a jury in the Crown Court), and for the sending to the Crown Court of those either way cases that do need to be sent there for trial. The underlying purpose is to allow cases to be dealt with in the level of court appropriate to their degree of seriousness and to ensure that they reach that venue as soon as possible. The changes - which do not take away a defendant's own basic right to elect to be tried (normally) by a jury in the Crown Court in relation to any either way offence - are dealt with in *Chapter 4*. They give effect to certain recommendations in Lord Justice Auld's *Review of the Criminal Courts* (2001), including:

- that magistrates should be made aware, when determining allocation, of any previous convictions of the defendant;
- removing the option of committal for sentence in cases that magistrates decide to hear themselves (as opposed, e.g. to those where they commit for sentence following indication of a guilty plea under the 'plea before venue' arrangements; or in relation to public protection situations and extended sentences for dangerous offenders (see *Chapter 7*);
- allowing defendants in circumstances where summary trial is considered appropriate to seek a broad indication of the sentence they would face if they were to plead guilty at that point (section 20 MCA 1980 as amended by Schedule 3 CJA 2003, paragraph 6); and
- replacing committal proceedings (and transfers for trial in serious fraud and child witness cases) with a common system for sending cases to the Crown Court.

---

[13] The relevant changes to the Magistrates' Courts Act 1980 and Powers of Criminal Courts (Sentencing) Act 2000 appear within Schedule 3 to the 2003 Act. They are explained in *Chapter 7*.

[14] Following patterns set in relation to family cases (allocation) and indictable only matters (sending). The latter have for some years reached the Crown Court straightaway following an initial remand appearance by the accused person before magistrates.

The CJA 2003 also makes provision for juveniles to give an 'indication of plea' in relation to certain offences along the lines of the 'plea before venue' procedure that applies in relation to adult cases. Provision is also made for juveniles charged with certain firearms offences to be sent to the Crown Court for trial. For these and juvenile matters generally, see *Chapter 12*.

BROAD-BASED JURIES AND JUDGE-ALONE TRIALS

The CJA 2003 aims to ensure wider involvement in juries of members of the community as a whole by reforming the rules about jury service, albeit that one suggestion in *Review of the Criminal Courts* that juries should be weighted in favour of minorities in certain cases was not followed. The new arrangements are outlined in *Chapter 5*.

Trials without a jury[15]
Part 7 CJA 2003 deals with Crown Court trials without a jury, i.e. what have been dubbed 'judge only' or 'judge-alone' trials, i.e. where:

- the prosecutor applies for this in relation to certain fraud charges (section 43 CJA 2003);
- the prosecutor applies for this where there is a danger of jury tampering (section 44 CJA 2003); or
- a trial collapses because of jury tampering and the jury has to be discharged, e.g. due to intimidation or bribery (section 46 CJA 2003).[16]

Further rules are set out in the 2003 Act. Thus, e.g. where a trial has begun and a jury has been discharged due to tampering, that trial will continue without a jury unless the judge considers it necessary in the interests of justice to terminate it. In that event, he or she *may* order a retrial, and if the judge does so he or she will have a further discretion to order that the retrial take place without a jury.

Appeals and reasons for decisions
Section 47 CJA 2003 provides a right of appeal to the Court of Appeal for both prosecution and defence against the determination of a Crown Court judge to continue a trial in the absence of a jury, or to order a retrial without a jury because of jury tampering. Under section 48, where a trial is conducted or continued without a jury, and a defendant is convicted, the judge is required to give his or her reasons for that conviction.

---

[15] It should perhaps again be stressed - since the author is aware of confusion from several sources - that the CJA 2003 (whilst it makes considerable alterations to the penalties for certain summary offences and increases magistrates' powers generally) does not alter or 'take away' rights to elect trial in the Crown Court in respect of an either way offence. What it does do, in certain cases where that right is exercised, is allow a judge-alone trial in prescribed situations.

[16] In Parliament and elsewhere, the 'judge-alone' provisions were amongst the most hotly debated, and only settled at the eleventh hour in the House of Lords. A proposal to allow such a trial if the defendant requested it was conceded and significant modifications made to surviving provisions.

EVIDENCE, WITNESSES AND 'LIVE LINKS'

Part 11 CJA 2003 makes sweeping changes to the rules of evidence and consequently the giving of evidence by witnesses, principally in relation to:

- evidence of **bad character**; and
- the use of **hearsay evidence.**

There are also important further provisions concerning confessions, evidence at a retrial following an earlier acquittal and evidence by way of a video recording - as well as in relation to 'live links' (under Part 8 CJA 2003): all outlined more fully in *Chapter 5.*

Bad character, previous convictions etc.

In relation to evidence of bad character (whether of the accused, a co-accused or a 'non-defendant'), Part 11 CJA 2003 abolishes the existing legal rules in favour of a new code which also encompasses matters such as: evidence to correct a false impression, the situation where the accused attacks another person's character in court, stopping cases where there is contaminated evidence and the court's duty to give reasons when admitting certain categories of evidence. It also allows evidence of the accused person's bad character which may be of probative value in establishing his or her guilt in certain situations, though in a diluted form compared with highly controversial proposals in the original Bill.

It should be noted that 'bad character' and previous convictions are relevant in two other contexts, i.e. 'allocation' (*Chapter* 4) and sentencing (*Chapter* 7).

Hearsay evidence

Normally, hearsay (sometimes called 'second hand' or 'reported') evidence is not admissible, especially in a criminal trial, although it has become widely admissible in relation to civil matters including, e.g. applications before 'criminal' courts in relation to anti-social behaviour orders. However, under existing law the hearsay rule has been subject to certain well-established 'exceptions'. The CJA 2003 abolishes these exceptions and enacts a new code under which hearsay evidence may be admissible under certain statutory heads. These extend the scope of hearsay evidence in criminal proceedings and, in part, mirror (but do not simply reproduce) certain of the former exceptions to that rule. The most significant extension to existing law, perhaps, is that hearsay will be admissible where there is a sound, statutory reason why the person who originally made a statement cannot be present at court, or the court otherwise considers that to admit the hearsay evidence would be appropriate in the interests of justice. Beyond these few simple points, the complexity of the provisions makes it essential to deal with the changes within an overall context in *Chapter 5.*

'Live links' to a courtroom

Part 8 of the CJA 2003 deals with 'live links' in criminal proceedings, meaning a live television link from some other location, beyond the court premises. Under section 51 CJA 2003, a court will have power to authorise evidence by way of such a link where it believes this to be in the interests of the efficient or effective administration of justice. Existing law does provide for the use of live links in limited situations, such as where there are young, disabled, vulnerable or intimidated witnesses (see the Youth Justice and Criminal Evidence Act 1999). Much of this 'special measures' legislation is still under piloting and only limited parts of it apply at present in magistrates' courts. The new provisions extend the potential of live links to any witnesses - other than the accused person.

SENTENCING

Part 12 CJA 2003 - one of the most substantial parts of the Act - concerns sentencing. It creates a new sentencing framework to replace that introduced by the Criminal Justice Act 1991. Whilst the new law retains certain features of the 1991 framework such as the threshold tests for community sentences and custody, the CJA 2003 creates a largely new approach based on statutory purposes and new-style sentences. There are also special measures dedicated to particular aspects of sentencing such as life sentences, deferment of sentence, offenders who are considered to be dangerous, drug treatment and testing and firearms offences. The new framework - described more fully in *Chapters 7 to 10* - is intended to be clearer and more flexible than before.[17]

The CJA 2003 identifies various situations in which, when assessing the seriousness of an offence, certain factors *must* be treated by the courts as aggravating factors, i.e. factors that increase the seriousness of the offence and thus, *prima facie*, the severity of the offender's sentence. This will be the case where the offender has, in effect, recent and relevant previous convictions, or (as under existing law) the offence involved 'racial' or 'religious' motivation.

Key sentencing changes
The following key aspects of Part 12 CJA 2003 can be noted at this stage:

- **general purposes** of sentencing are introduced for the first time in relation to adults, namely (in summary)
  —punishment
  —crime reduction (including deterrence)
  —reform and rehabilitation
  —public protection; and
  —reparation.

- **community orders** assume a new shape in the form of the 'generic community order' for offenders aged 18 and over.[18] This replaces all existing community orders. In a sense, the existing, separate community orders are transformed into individual components (called 'requirements') out of which the single new generic order can be constructed according to the decision of the court and considerations of the extent to which certain requirements are suitable for the offender and the overall outcome restricts his or her liberty. The generic community order is described in *Chapter 8*.

---

[17] As to which there is room for opinion concerning the first of these objectives.
[18] See *Chapter 12* for the position in relation to juveniles.

Under the CJA 2003, there are no longer certain provisions limiting the use of some community orders or requirements to situations where the offence is 'punishable by imprisonment'.

- **custodial sentences** in relation to sentences of less than 12 months are replaced by three new varieties of custody for adults: 'custody plus'; 'custody minus' (the new-style suspended sentence) and 'intermittent custody'. These new-style sentences, each with its own new rules concerning the actual time to be spent (or in the case of a suspended sentence 'potentially spent') in custody, and requirements which can be attached during periods when the offender is in the community, are outlined in *Chapter 9.* These sentences, in particular, need to be considered against the background of a general increase in the sentencing powers of magistrates as noted in *Chapter 7.*

- **dangerous offenders** are dealt with under special provisions designed to protect the public from such offenders generally, and also to ensure that all violent or sexual offenders are subject to supervision so long as they remain a threat, by way of an 'extended sentence'. Dangerous offenders are dealt with in *Chapter 10.*[19]

- **release and post-custody supervision** where fresh arrangements are introduced in relation to sentences of 12 months or more or where the terms of post-custody supervision are not an integral part of the original sentence. This is explained in *Chapter 11.*

An intention of Government is that courts will be equipped to provide every offender with a sentence that best meets the need of his or her particular case, and at whatever level of seriousness. Sentences will, it is claimed, be 'more effectively managed' by a National Offender Management Service (NOMS), with separate arms for commissioning and providing services that were previously arranged by the National Probation Service and HM Prison Service.[20] There is also a general emphasis on electronic monitoring both in relation to the generic community sentence and post-custody supervision.

The Sentencing Guidelines Council
A quite significant development of the CJA 2003 is the creation by section 167 of a Sentencing Guidelines Council (SGC) to be made up principally of members drawn from various strata of the judiciary together with a minority of 'non-judicial' members. The remit of the SGC and its relationship to the existing Sentencing Advisory Panel (which will continue alongside it) is outlined in *Chapter 7.* The creation of an authoritative body that can issue statutory guidelines to all criminal courts and which will be in line with judicial thinking at the highest level - since the Lord Chief Justice is designated by the CJA 2003 to chair the council - represents a major step forward.[21] Courts will be required to

---

[19] See also the arrangements for longer-term detention of certain juveniles noted in *Chapter 12.*

[20] See *Managing Offenders, Reducing Crime* (the 'Carter Report') and the Government's accompanying statement *Reducing Crime, Changing Lives* (both published in January 2004).

[21] Following proposals in the independent Carter report (January 2004), the council should also be required to take account of the capacity of prison and probation: see *Chapter 14.*

have regard to definitive guidelines (section 172 CJA 2003) and the council must make an annual report to Ministers on the exercise of its function (section 173).

APPEAL AND RETRIAL ('DOUBLE JEOPARDY')

Part 9 of the CJA 2003 deals with appeals by the prosecutor. Also, included in that part is the controversial provision under which certain suspects will be able to be arrested, charged and tried a second time by way of exception to the rule against 'double jeopardy'. These provisions are further explained in *Chapter 6*.

Prosecution appeals

As already indicated, there will, under the CJA 2003, be prosecution rights of appeal in relation to decisions by a judge to deal with a case without a jury in the Crown Court, and extra prosecution rights of appeal concerning grants of bail. Part 9 CJA 2003 confers a right of appeal on a prosecutor against a judge's decision in a trial on indictment to direct or order an acquittal before the jury has been asked to consider the evidence, so as 'to balance the defendant's existing right of appeal against conviction and sentence'.[22]

Under section 58 CJA 2003, leave to appeal must be obtained either from the trial judge or the Court of Appeal and the ruling terminating the trial will not take effect while the prosecutor is considering whether to appeal, or until the conclusion of any appeal or its being abandoned. The prosecutor must agree to an acquittal if leave to appeal is not granted or the appeal is abandoned.

Double jeopardy

Part 10 CJA 2003 deals with the retrial of certain serious offences by way of exception to the existing and longstanding common law rules against 'double jeopardy', i.e. the idea that no-one should be tried twice for the same offence. The principal provisions are contained in sections 75 to 97 CJA 2003 (whilst Schedule 4 lists the qualifying offences). These provisions stem partly from the acquittal of the defendants in the Stephen Lawrence murder case. They make a retrial possible provided that there is 'new and compelling' evidence of guilt.

PROCEDURES

The Department of Constitutional Affairs has indicated that a new Criminal Procedure Rule Committee is being set up under the CJA 2003 to replace the existing and separate committees for Crown Courts and magistrates' courts. The intention is that 'there will no longer be separate sets of criminal procedure rules governing different parts of the procedure and supplementing different Acts'.[23] The department anticipates that the first of these new rules will be in existence by late spring 2005.

---

[22] There is no comparable new provision in relation to a finding by magistrates of 'no case to answer', but such a ruling can be challenged under existing appeal mechanisms in the High Court and, seemingly, there is no bar to a 'second trial' by magistrates where the original acquittal was not 'on the merits', i.e. not following a determination on the facts.

[23] Letter circulated by the Criminal Procedure Rules Secretariat in March 2004.

CHAPTER 2

Investigation, Detention and Bail

The CJA 2003 contains a range of provisions designed to enhance 'the front end' of the criminal process - the investigation of crime, arrest and detention of suspects and decisions concerning release on bail. The provisions appear in:

- Part 1 CJA 2003 and Schedule 1 CJA 2003 in so far as they relate to the Police and Criminal Evidence Act 1984 (PACE) and associated provisions;
- Part 2 CJA 2003 in so far as they relate to changes to the Bail Act 1976.

None of these changes concern any matters of broad principle or overriding purpose. Rather, as part the Government's wider strategy to 'rebalance the system', they focus on perceived deficiencies in specific situations which are affected by PACE and the Bail Act 1976 - although there are certain new departures such as 'street bail', greater freedom to take fingerprints or 'non-intimate' samples from a suspect whilst he or she is in detention, and a heavier onus is placed on people who commit further offences whilst on bail or who abscond if they then seek to avoid being remanded in custody in future. The relevant provisions are outlined below.[1]

STOP AND SEARCH

Section 1 CJA 2003 extends the power of a police officer to stop and search suspects for 'prohibited articles' by adding offences of destroying or damaging property contrary to section 1 Criminal Damage Act 1971 to the PACE list of offences in respect of which such powers can be exercised. The effect is to allow a police officer to stop and search someone on reasonable suspicion that that he or she is carrying an article made, adapted or intended for use in causing such damage. Examples given during Parliamentary and other debates concerning the type of articles potentially caught by the provision have ranged from aerosol paint sprays intended for use in creating graffiti (where the new powers will operate alongside others to deal with anti-social behaviour) to petrol cans carried by would-be arsonists.

WARRANTS TO ENTER AND SEARCH

Section 2 CJA 2003 makes provision for warrants to enter and search premises. Under existing law, people who accompany police constables bearing search warrants can only assist in an advisory or administrative capacity. An amendment to section 16 of PACE allows authorised people who accompany such an officer actively to participate in the search. A newly inserted section

---

[1] Except for certain provisions of Part 1 concerning the drug-testing of juveniles which are dealt with in *Chapter 12*. Note also that section 20 CJA 2003 makes supplementary amendments to the Bail Act.

16(2A) states such a person has 'the same powers as the constable whom he accompanies in respect of (a) the execution of the warrant, and (b) the seizure of anything to which the warrant relates' whilst section 16(2B) makes it clear that that person 'may only exercise those powers in the company, and under the supervision, of a constable'. In the light of the Police Reform Act 2002 whereby civilians can be authorised to carry out certain policing functions and the emergence of police community support officers this extension should prove expedient in terms of allowing police officers to deal more speedily with searches and thus concentrate on moving an investigation forward.

NEW ARRESTABLE OFFENCES

Section 3 CJA 2003 extends Schedule 1A of PACE which lists specific offences that are 'arrestable offences' - by adding three further offences to that list:

- making an untrue statement for procuring a passport under section 36 Criminal Justice Act 1925;
- possessing either cannabis or cannabis resin under section 5(2) Misuse of Drugs Act 1971;
- making a false statement or withholding material information etc. to obtaining a driving licence or other driving documents (and analogous offences) under section 174 Road Traffic Act 1988.

POLICE DETENTION

Part 1 CJA 2003 contains various provisions concerning police detention, i.e. the situation where arrested people, usually suspects, are detained without charge.[2]

Telephone review of police detention
A new section 40A(1) and (2) of PACE is substituted by section 6 CJA 2003 so as to enable reviews of the continuing need for detention without charge to be conducted 'by means of discussion [by the senior reviewing officer] . . . by telephone, with one or more persons at the police station where the arrested person is held' rather than obliging the reviewing officer to be present in person at the police station in question. But where video conferencing facilities are available these must normally be used instead. A new section 40A(2) of PACE provides that the telephone review provisions will not apply if '(a) the review is of a kind authorised by regulations under 45A [of PACE] to be carried out using video-conferencing facilities; and (b) it is reasonably practicable to carry it out in accordance with those regulations'.

Detention without charge: time limits
Section 7 CJA 2003 amends section 42(1) of PACE by lowering the threshold of the PACE provisions under which a person may be detained without charge

---

[2] For the position in relation to charging and afterwards see *Chapter 4*.

under the authority of a police superintendent for up to 36 hours (rather than the standard maximum 24 hours). In future such an extension will be possible where the offence for which the suspect is under arrest is an '*arrestable offence*' rather than a '*serious arrestable* offence', the existing criterion.

Property of detained people

Whereas under the existing provisions of section 54 of PACE a police custody officer is required to ascertain and record everything that a detained person has with him or her on entering custody, section 8 CJA 2003 relaxes that provision so that in future - whilst the custody officer still has a responsibility to ascertain what a suspect has on him or her under section 54(1) of PACE - the recording of details is left to the discretion of the individual officer who '*may* record or cause to be recorded all or any of the things which he ascertains . . . ' (section 54(2)(a) (italics supplied); and, to avoid duplication or disparate records, 'any such record may be made as part of his custody record' (section 54(2)(b)).

FINGERPRINTS AND 'NON-INTIMATE' SAMPLES

Part 1 CJA 2003 contains two provisions concerned with the forensic detection and investigation of crime - and which can be seen as part and parcel of the unprecedented advances in relation to the detection and investigation of crime using new technology that have been happening in recent years. Fingerprints can now be taken electronically and the police can confirm within minutes the identity of a suspect if his or her fingerprints are already stored on the National Fingerprint Database. Similarly, the DNA profile of an arrested person can be input into the National DNA Database and subjected to a similar, virtually instantaneous, search. Fingerprints and DNA can also be subjected to a 'speculative search' against the Scenes of Crime Database to establish whether they produce a match (or 'hit') against samples from unsolved crimes. The arrangements are designed, among other things, to prevent people 'getting away' with giving false details, and to assist in identifying fugitives of various kinds. Some 40 'old' murders and a significant number of other serious offences have been re-investigated and solved since this type of technology became available. The changes noted below serve to increase that potential.

Fingerprints

Section 9 CJA 2003 extends police powers to take fingerprints without a suspect's consent. The principal changes are contained in a substituted section 61(3) and (4) of PACE which provides as follows:

   (3) The fingerprints of a person detained at a police station may be taken without the appropriate consent if -
      (a) he is detained in consequence of his arrest for a recordable offence; and
      (b) he has not had his fingerprints taken in the course of the investigation of the offence by the police.
   (4) The fingerprints of a person detained at a police station may be taken without the appropriate consent if -
      (a) he has been charged with a recordable offence or informed that he will be reported for such an offence; and

(b) he has not had his fingerprints taken in the course of the investigation of the offence by the police.

'Non-intimate samples'

Similarly, section 10 CJA 2003 amends section 63 of PACE so that DNA (or 'non-intimate') samples can be obtained without the appropriate consent from someone in police detention following arrest in relation to a recordable offence. The person must not have had a non-intimate sample *of the same type and from the same part of the body* taken in the course of the investigation of the offence by the police, or where such a sample has already been taken 'it proved insufficient'. There are comparable amendments affecting the situation where the suspect has been charged.

PACE CODES OF PRACTICE

The CJA 2003 makes significant changes to the processes for establishing and amending codes of practice under PACE. Currently, PACE codes cover: 'stop and search', 'searches of premises', 'detention of suspects', 'identification' and the 'recording of interviews'. Issuing a new code or revising an existing one has required extensive consultation and active Parliamentary deliberation. Section 11 CJA 2003 amends section 67 of PACE so as to provide for a more limited consultation process outside Parliament and to place more straightforward requirements on the Secretary of State in terms of bringing a new code, or revised version of an existing one, into force. The principal rules will be as follows:

- a code, or revised code will only come into operation if and when the Secretary of State by order so provides;
- this power to bring a code into force will be exercisable by statutory instrument;
- an order bringing a code into operation will necessitate a draft of the order being laid before Parliament and its being approved by a resolution of each House;
- an order bringing a revised code into operation will need to be laid before Parliament if the order has been made without a draft having been so laid and approved by a resolution of each House;
- when an order or draft of an order is laid before Parliament, the code or revised code to which it relates will also need to be laid; and
- no order or draft of an order can be laid before Parliament until the required statutory consultation has taken place.

Under the new section 67(4) of PACE, the Secretary of State must consult: persons who he or she considers to represent the interests of police authorities; persons who he considers to represent the interests of chief officers of police; the General Council of the Bar; the Law Society of England and Wales; the Institute of Legal Executives; and 'such other persons as he thinks fit'.

BAIL

Part 1 CJA 2003 includes provision for 'street bail' amongst the changes it makes to PACE (above). Part 2 deals with further bail-related matters, including the situation where offences are committed on bail and absconding, and so as to give effect to a Law Commission recommendation that minor amendments should be made to the Bail Act 1976 to ensure compliance with the European Convention On Human Rights and Fundamental Freedoms. All of these changes are described below. In addition, there are a number of new bail provisions in relation to the charging of suspects. These are noted in *Chapter 4* in relation to that aspect of police and - in future - CPS responsibilities.

Street bail

Under novel procedures styled 'bail elsewhere than at a police station' which are aimed at streamlining the bail process at street level, section 4 CJA 2003 amends section 30 of PACE so as to enable instant bail to be granted by a police officer at the scene of someone's arrest, and where there is no obvious or immediate need to convey the arrested person to a police station for him or her to be dealt with. For obvious reasons, this has attracted the label 'street bail'. The idea is that the arrested person will be required to attend later at a police station for the investigation to continue. With this in mind, the arresting police officer is given an element of discretion, e.g. as to when and at which police station the arrested person should be required to attend for interview.

The new provisions apply where someone is arrested by a constable for an offence or is taken into custody by a constable following the suspect's arrest by someone else. In either case, the arrested person must then be taken to a police station as soon as practicable, except:

- where the constable is required by law to release that person without bail because there are no grounds for keeping him or her under arrest or for releasing him or her on bail (the effect of new section 30(7) and (7A) PACE summarised: see section 4(4) CJA 2003); or
- where the presence of that person at a place other than a police station is necessary to carry out such investigations as it is reasonable to carry out immediately. In this instance 'nothing prevents' the constable delaying taking the person to a police station or releasing him or her on bail, but the reason for any such delay must be recorded when the person first arrives at the police station (the effect of new section 30(10), (10A) and (11) of PACE: see section 4(5) CJA 2003); or
- where the new street bail provisions apply.

In their full form, the street bail provisions in the new section 30A of PACE are as follows:

(1) A constable may release on bail a person who is arrested or taken into custody . . .
(2) A person may be released on bail under subsection (1) at any time before he arrives at the police station.
(3) A person released on bail under subsection (1) must be required to attend a police station.

(4) No other requirement may be imposed on the person as a condition of bail.

(5) The police station which the person is required to attend may be any police station.

Thus street bail will be inapplicable and the person will need to be taken to a police station if conditional bail is in the constable's mind (this can be granted at a police station under existing powers); and the purpose of street bail is that the person concerned will attend at some later time at a police station for the case to be further progressed, not at court to answer a charge (as to which see the separate procedures described in *Chapter 4*).

A new section 30B of PACE states that someone who is allowed street bail must be given a notice in writing before his or her release setting out the offence for which he or she has been arrested and the ground for that arrest. The notice must inform him or her that he or she is required to attend at a police station, and give details of the time and place (failing which he or she must 'subsequently be given a further notice which contains that information'). But the suspect can later be required, by written notice, to attend at a different police station or at a different time (below).

It should be emphasised that a new section 30C(3) of PACE categorically states that 'Nothing in the Bail Act 1976 applies in relation to [street bail]'. There would thus appear to be no statutory right to bail (though a right to fair and proper treatment as a matter of general principle), nor any tying of decision-making by the constable to statutory grounds and reasons for 'refusing' street bail and taking the suspect to the police station instead. Beyond this, it is difficult to envisage the further import of excluding the Bail Act: but the practicalities of allowing bail on the street appear to have resulted from a pragmatic legislative approach.   This may result in the police being 'back on the street or job' sooner but it remains to be seen whether this will adversely affect the gathering of fresh, immediate and reliable evidence.

Variation and cancellation of street bail
Further provisions of section 30C allow for subsequent cancellation by written notice of the requirement to attend at a police station, for release or transfer to a 'designated' police station within the meaning of PACE where the one in the notice is not such (so that other PACE procedures can continue), and make clear that nothing in the street bail provisions prevents re-arrest 'if new evidence justifying a further arrest has come to light' (a provision that emphasises the point that the power to grant street bail should not be abused).

Failure to surrender to 'street bail'
A new section 30D of PACE provides for the situation where a person allowed street bail fails to attend at a police station as required. No offence is committed, but the police are given a power of arrest without warrant tied to that failure, and the person must then be taken to (any) police station as soon as practicable after his or her arrest. It remains to be seen whether such events will be satisfactorily recorded and the details made available and readily accessible in relation to future decisions by constables or courts dealing with remand hearings.

Grant and conditions of bail: general changes

Section 13 CJA 2003 makes a number of changes to the Bail Act 1976. Section 13 (1) alters section 3(6) of the Bail Act 1976 to enable bail conditions to be imposed for a defendant's own protection or welfare, in the same circumstances that he or she might have been remanded in custody for that purpose. Section 13(2) makes comparable changes to section 3A(5), and section 13(3) to paragraph 8(1) of Part 1 of Schedule 1 to the 1976 Act.

Section 13(4) amends paragraph 5 of Part 2 of Schedule 1 to the Bail Act 1976 so that, where a defendant charged with a non-imprisonable offence is arrested under section 7 Bail Act 1976 (failure to surrender to bail), bail may be refused only if the court is satisfied that there are substantial grounds for believing that if released on bail (whether subject to conditions or not) he or she would fail to surrender to custody, commit an offence whilst on bail, or interfere with witnesses or otherwise obstruct the course of justice.

Offences committed whilst on bail

The existing Bail Act 1976 provision purporting to create an exception to the general right to bail where it appears to a court that the defendant has committed an offence whilst on bail is repealed. It is replaced by a new presumption of law that bail *may not be granted* in such circumstances - unless, that is, the court is satisfied that there is no significant risk of his or her re-offending on bail. Section 14 CJA amends Schedule 1 to the 1976 Act as follows:[3]

> 2A(1) If the defendant falls within this paragraph he *may not be granted bail* unless the court is satisfied that there is no significant risk of his committing an offence (whether subject to conditions or not).
>   (2) The defendant falls within this paragraph if -
>   (a) he is aged 18 or over, and
>   (b) it appears to the court that he was on bail in criminal proceedings on the date of the offence. [Italics supplied]

A court faced with such a situation could, it seems, justifiably refuse bail in any event at its discretion on the basis that there are substantial grounds for believing that the accused person may commit a further offence or offences if allowed bail: but where the court seeks to rely on the new provision set out above this shifts the onus completely onto the defendant. Presumably, the court should, as a matter of good practice if nothing else, inform him or her of this and allow an opportunity for him or her to argue that there is, in fact, 'no significant risk'. Given the closing words of paragraph 2A(1) (above), a court should, seemingly, consider and eliminate (for sound and valid reasons) the possibility of granting conditional bail to the accused person but such a decision will need to be consistent with the court being satisfied that if granted conditional bail and thus released there will be no 'significant risk' of his or her committing an offence.

Absconding whilst on bail

There is also a new presumption that a defendant aged 18 or over who without reasonable cause has failed to surrender to custody *may not be granted* bail, i.e. in

---

[3] The provisions described apply to adults. There are adjusted provisions for juveniles: *Chapter 12.*

this instance unless the court is satisfied there is no significant risk that he or she would fail to surrender if released.[4] There is also an onus on the defendant to surrender as soon as possible after failing to do so. Section 15 CJA 2003 substitutes a new paragraph 6 in Schedule 1 to the Bail Act 1976 which, in its full form, reads as follows:

> 6(1) If the defendant falls within this paragraph, he *may not be granted bail* unless the court is satisfied that there is no significant risk that, if released on bail (whether subject to conditions or not), he would fail to surrender to custody.
>
> (2) Subject to sub-paragraph (3) below, the defendant falls within this paragraph if -
>
> (a) he is aged 18 or over, and
>
> (b) it appears to the court that, having been released on bail in or in connection with the proceedings for the offence, he failed to surrender to custody,
>
> (3) Where it appears to the court that the defendant had reasonable cause for his failure to surrender to custody, he does not fall within this paragraph unless it also appears to the court that he failed to surrender to custody at the appointed place as soon as reasonably practicable after the appointed time.
>
> (4) For the purposes of sub-paragraph (3) above, a failure to give to the defendant a copy of the record of the decision to grant him bail shall not constitute a reasonable cause for his failure to surrender to custody. [Italics supplied]

Other bail-related amendments

The changes outlined above may have the potential to increase greatly the custodial remand population at a time when the Government is seeking to encourage greater use of community sentencing disposals for non-dangerous offenders. Further CJA 2003 amendments dispense with the ordinary six months' time limit for laying an information[5] in relation to offences of absconding on bail contrary to section 6 Bail Act 1976 (see section 15(3) CJA 2003). But where someone has been released on bail in criminal proceedings and this was bail granted by a constable, a magistrates' court will not be able to try that person for an offence under section 6(1) or (2) of the 1976 Act in relation to that bail unless:

- an information is laid within six months from the time of the commission of the relevant offence; or
- if an information is laid for the relevant offence no later than three months from the time of the occurrence of the first events mentioned below to occur after the commission of the relevant offence, i.e.
  —the person surrenders to custody at the appointed place;
  —the person is arrested, or attends at a police station, in connection with the relevant offence or the offence for which he or she was granted bail;
  —the person appears or is brought before a court in connection with the relevant offence or the offence for which he or she was granted bail.

Section 13 CJA 2003 amends section 3(6) Bail Act 1976 so as to allow bail conditions to be imposed for a defendant's own protection and in the same circumstances where he or she might otherwise have been remanded to custody.

---

[4]   Again, there is a variant of this in relation to juveniles: see *Chapter 12*.
[5]   As contained in section 127 Magistrates' Courts Act 1980.

Paragraph 5 of Part 2 of Schedule 1 to the 1976 Act is also amended so that where someone who was charged with and bailed in relation to a *non-imprisonable* offence is re-arrested under section 7 of that Act for absconding, he or she may be refused bail only if the court is satisfied that if released on bail there are substantial grounds for believing that, if released, he or she would fail to surrender to custody, commit an offence, interfere with witnesses or otherwise obstruct the course of justice.

Appeals following bail decisions
Sections 16 to 18 CJA 2003 give effect to recommendations in Lord Justice Auld's *Review of the Criminal Courts* for simplifying bail appeals, including by removing the High Court's bail jurisdiction where this runs concurrently with that of the Crown Court.

Prosecution appeals
The right of the prosecutor to appeal to the Crown Court against a decision by magistrates to grant bail is extended to cover *all* imprisonable offences, and not simply those carrying a maximum penalty of five years or more as under existing law - a quite significant increase in the scope of CPS powers.

Bail and drugs: Restrictions in relation to drugs users
As part of the Government's strategy to target drug use,[6] the CJA 2003 creates a similar presumption to those already noted that bail *will not be granted* to someone aged 18 or over charged with an imprisonable offence who:

- tests positive for a specified Class A drug; or
- refuses to undergo assessment as to his or her dependency or propensity to misuse such drugs; or who
- following an assessment, refuses relevant follow-up action.

In each case this is unless the court is satisfied that there is no significant risk of his or her re-offending while on bail (section 19 CJA 2003 amending section 3 and Schedule 1 to the Bail Act 1976).

ARREST AND CHARGE: A NOTE

Those aspects of the pre-court process that relate to the charging of suspects are dealt with in *Chapter 4*, where they also link on the one hand to the involvement of Crown prosecutors in the process of charging and instituting proceedings and on the other to the new methods of commencing criminal proceedings as created by the CJA 2003.

---

[6]   Concerning which see *Chapters 13* and *14*.

CHAPTER 3

Conditional Cautions

The issuing of cautions - or informal warnings - by the police instead of prosecution has a long history. In the case of juveniles the approach has been formalised in a statutory scheme of reprimands and warnings,[1] but the cautioning of adults has remained a matter of practice rather than legislation. Part 3 CJA 2003 does not create a comprehensive adult cautioning scheme, rather it builds upon the existing (non-statutory) arrangements in this regard. However, where the new scheme of conditional cautions is invoked the whole process becomes a statutory one and the offender subject to what will be clearly defined obligations and liabilities.

Under section 25 CJA 2003 provision is made for the creation and publication by the Secretary of State of a Code of Practice in relation to conditional cautions. At the time of writing only the draft code had been published and this is described later in the chapter.

THE NEW SCHEME

Instead of prosecution, under section 22 CJA 2003 a conditional caution can be given to someone aged 18 or over provided that each of five requirements set out in section 22(3) CJA 2003 (below) is met (section 22(1)). The conditions must have either or both of the following objects (section 22(2)):

- facilitating the rehabilitation of the offender; and/or
- ensuring that he or she makes reparation for the offence.

Conditional cautions can be given by an 'authorised person', meaning a constable, an investigating officer (within the meaning of section 38 Police Reform Act 2002) or someone authorised by a relevant prosecutor for this purpose (section 22(4)). Relevant prosecutor means the Attorney General, the Director of the Serious Fraud Office, the Director of Public Prosecutions (DPP), a Secretary of State, the Commissioners of Inland Revenue, the Commissioners of Customs and Excise or someone who is specified in an order made by the Secretary of State for the purposes of these provisions (section 27 CJA 2003).

The five requirements
As already indicated, there are 'five requirements' which must be met before a conditional caution can be given. These are set out in section 23 CJA 2003 as follows:

- the authorised person must have evidence that the offender has committed an offence;

---

[1] The scheme for juveniles introduced by the Crime and Disorder Act 1998 is unaffected by the CJA 2003. For an outline, see *Child Law*, (go to: www. watersidepress.co.uk)

- a relevant prosecutor must decide that there is sufficient evidence to charge the offender with the offence; and that a conditional caution should be given to the offender in respect of the offence (i.e. a single requirement with two limbs);
- the offender must admit to the authorised person that he or she committed the offence;
- the authorised person must explain the effect of the conditional caution to the offender and warn him or her that failure to comply with any of the conditions attached to the caution may result in his or her being prosecuted for the offence; and
- the offender must sign a document containing
  —details of the offence;
  —an admission by him or her that he or she committed the offence;
  —his or her consent to a conditional caution; and
  —the conditions attached to the caution.

It can be seen that there are various rearrangements of functions and responsibilities. The prosecutor, normally the CPS (but, it also seems, other public prosecutors as appropriate) will decide both whether there is sufficient evidence and, critically, whether a conditional caution should be issued. In the normal course of events it will then be for the police to carry this out (although it can be any 'authorised person' above) and to ensure that the remaining requirements are complied with.

Failure to comply with the conditions of a conditional caution

Perhaps the most significant alteration occurs at the enforcement stage if the offender fails to comply with the conditions attached to the caution. Under the existing (non-conditional) arrangements a simple caution becomes something that is noted on an offender's record. It may (depending on the vagaries of record keeping) surface alongside previous convictions or other antecedent data and be presented to a court at the sentencing stage. Even then, it is uncertain what a court is actually supposed to make of this (see the short commentary at the end of this chapter).

Under section 25 CJA 2003, where a suspect fails 'without reasonable excuse' to comply with any conditions attached to a caution under the new scheme, he or she becomes liable to prosecution for the underlying offence.[2] At that stage, again by way of a fresh departure, the admission document that the offender is obliged to sign before a conditional caution is given under section 24 (above) becomes admissible in such proceedings. At the same time, the conditional caution ceases to have effect. It should perhaps be emphasised that criminal proceedings are discretionary, not required - so that it will still be for the prosecutor to assess the situation post-failure to comply to see whether prosecution is appropriate.

The implications are when someone agrees to a conditional caution they in effect restrict their ability to argue later, when prosecuted, that they were 'not guilty'. Clearly, the intention is to ensure that a guilty plea must automatically follow and in this regard the ground can be seen as moving away from the

---

[2]   Subject to any legal time limit for commencing summary proceedings.

courtroom and into the hands of police and prosecutors. It remains to be seen what ingenious arguments may emerge at the court stage, and whether the provisions hold good in terms of the European Convention On Human Rights.

Involvement of other people

Amendments to the Criminal Justice and Court Services Act 2000 will enable advice to be taken and assistance given to an authorised person (above) in determining whether a caution should be given and what conditions should be attached, including matters relevant to supervision and rehabilitation.

CODE OF PRACTICE

Section 25 CJA 2003 provides for the creation and publication by the Secretary of State of a Code of Practice concerning conditional cautions. It may, in particular, include provision as to:

- the circumstances in which conditional cautions may be given
- the procedure to be followed
- the conditions that may be attached and the time for which they have effect
- the category of constable or investigating officer by whom conditional cautions may be given
- the persons who may be authorised by a relevant prosecutor to issue a conditional caution
- the form which cautions are to take and the manner in which they may be given and recorded
- the places where such cautions can be given; and
- the monitoring of compliance with conditions attached to cautions.

Draft code

A draft of the code must be published and the Secretary of State must consider any representations and he or she may not publish the final version or amend the draft without the consent of the Attorney General. The code must then be laid before Parliament, after which the Secretary of State can bring the code into force by order. The code may similarly be revised from time to time, subject to the same procedures all of which are set out in section 25 CJA 2003.

A draft code published in 2003[3] describes the original development of 'simple cautioning' and emphasises that this will continue so that 'in cases where the [conditional cautioning] criteria are satisfied, a conditional caution will be available as another alternative (alongside a simple caution) to charging the suspect' and that for certain classes of offence there is the alternative of a fixed penalty notice. The code also confirms that a conditional caution 'may only be given with the approval of the CPS, even in cases where it would have been open to the police to *charge* without a reference'[4] (emphasis in original: *Chapter 4*) and anticipates a liaison process between the two agencies.

---

[3] Available from the Criminal Procedure and Evidence Unit, Home Office, Room 356, 50 Queen Anne's Gate, London SW1H 9AT.

[4] See *Chapter 4* concerning when the police can bring certain charges without reference to the CPS.

With regard to decisions whether and when a conditional caution may be appropriate, the draft code states:

3.1 Guidance about existing cautions advises the police that, in considering whether an offender should be charged or cautioned, they should have regard to the seriousness of the offence and to the offender's criminal record. The same considerations will apply to conditional cautions, and the 'gravity factors' devised by [the Association of Chief Police Officers] and issued in [1995] will therefore be relevant in deciding whether an offence may be suitable for a conditional caution.

3.2 What may suggest that a conditional caution would be appropriate is that there is some action or course of conduct which would be conducive to reparation or rehabilitation, which the offender appears able and willing to carry out. Where the performance of this condition (coupled with a caution) would be a preferable outcome to prosecuting the offender, a conditional caution will be appropriate.

3.3 It is not intended to establish a hierarchy between simple and conditional cautions. The latter will not necessarily be used for more serious offences than the former, nor should a conditional caution be regarded as the logical next step for an offender who has already received a simple caution. In general, a suspect who has been cautioned in recent years ought not to be given another caution, be it simple or conditional, for a similar offence.

Concerning adherence to the requirements set out in the CJA 2003 and described earlier in this chapter, the draft code states:

4.1 A conditional caution is a statutory disposal and may be cited in any subsequent court proceedings. The following requirements must be complied with:

(i) The authorised person has evidence that the offender has committed an offence. This will be the evidence on the basis of which the suspect would otherwise fall to be charged, which will include an admission made under caution in interview and any witness statements.

(ii) The prosecutor decides -
(a) that there is sufficient evidence to charge the offender with the offence, and
(b) that a conditional caution should be given to the offender in respect of that offence.

The prosecutor will apply the evidential test in the usual way – i.e. that there would be a realistic prospect of conviction if the offender were to be prosecuted. The prosecutor must also conclude that the public interest would be served by the offender receiving a conditional caution, if he accepts it and subject to his performing the agreed conditions. Since the fall-back is that the offender will be prosecuted if he either does not accept or fails to perform the conditions, the prosecutor must also be satisfied that prosecution would be in the public interest in those contingencies.

(iii) The offender admits to the authorised person that he committed the offence.
A clear and reliable admission to all the elements of the offence is needed. The offender will already have made an admission in interview, but he may not be given a conditional caution unless he maintains his admission at the time when the caution is offered to him.

(iv) The authorised person explains the effect of the conditional caution to the offender and warns him that failure to comply with any of the conditions attached to the caution is likely to result in his being prosecuted for the original offence. The implications of the caution should be explained, including that there are circumstances in which it may be disclosed (such as to certain potential employers, and to a court in any future criminal proceedings) and, where the offence is listed in Schedule 1 to the Sex Offenders Act 1997, that accepting a caution will result in the offender being required to notify the police of their name and address and certain other details.

It should be made clear in explaining the consequences of non-compliance that the conditions are to be performed within the agreed time. It must be explained clearly that failure to comply would result in him being prosecuted for the original offence.

(v) The offender signs a document which contains -
(a) details of the offence
(b) an admission by him that he committed the offence
(c) his consent to being given the conditional caution, and
(d) an agreement to comply with the conditions attached to the caution, which must be set out on the face of the document.

After the offender has admitted to the offence and, having heard the explanation referred to above, has agreed to the conditions, he must sign a pro-forma to this effect. A standard form is attached to this Code and must be used by all forces. This document, which will contain details of the offence; the offender's admission and the conditions and timescale for completing them to which he has agreed, will be admissible as evidence if the offender is subsequently prosecuted for the original offence in the event of non-compliance.

Concerning the 'types of condition' which might be added to a caution, the code explains:

5.1 Conditions attached to a caution must be -

- *Proportionate* to the offence. The offender is unlikely to agree to a condition that is more onerous than the punishment he would be likely to receive if the case were taken to court.
- *Achievable*: the conditions must be ones that the offender could be expected to achieve within the time set, or the only result will be a delayed prosecution (or, in summary cases, the inability to bring a prosecution for lapse of time: see 'Time limits' below).
- *Appropriate:* the conditions should be relevant to the offence or the offender.

5.2 The Act requires that conditions should fall into one or both of two categories: rehabilitation and reparation.

- **Rehabilitation**: this might include mediation, taking part in treatment for drug or alcohol dependency (e.g. self-help groups such as Alcoholics Anonymous), anger management courses, or driving rectification classes and the like. The offender may be expected to pay reasonable costs, if there are any. The fact that provision of some sorts of course may be subject to resource implications (and possibly a waiting list) will need to be taken into account, bearing in mind that completion of any conditions should be swift and achievable within a reasonable time.

• **Reparation**: this might include repairing or otherwise making good any damage caused to property (e.g. by cleaning graffiti), restoring stolen goods, or paying modest financial compensation. Compensation may be paid to an individual or to the community in the form of an appropriate charity.

5.3 The police and CPS should take steps at [Local Criminal Justice Board) level to identify agencies, groups or organisations, voluntary or statutory, which provide such courses etc, and which it may be appropriate to consult when deciding whether a case is suitable for a conditional caution. There may be a role for the National Probation Service in determining whether certain offenders are suitable for a conditional caution

And as to time limits for prosecution:

6.1 For most summary offences there is a time limit for prosecution, and this should be borne in mind when setting the timescale within which conditions are to be completed so that, in the event of non-compliance, there is enough time for a prosecution to proceed.

6.2 Where the condition is for an offender to go on a course of treatment or behaviour/substance abuse, which may take longer than six months to deliver, the [officer in charge] will need to consider whether this is appropriate, depending on the attitude of the offender and the likelihood of compliance. There is no reason why undertaking a course of longer duration should not be a condition, provided that the offender is only required under the terms of the conditional caution (to satisfy the reasonableness test) to attend for part of it. For example, a drugs rehabilitation course may last 12 months to achieve best results. In such a case, the offender might agree under the conditions of his caution, to attend for 4 months, and thereafter it will be up to him to continue the treatment for his own benefit, rather than under any legal compulsion.

Concerning the involvement of victims in what is fundamentally intended to be a restorative aspect of the criminal process the draft code states:

7.1 In the course of interviewing the victim about the offence, it would be useful to ascertain whether any resulting loss, damage or injury is such that it could readily be made good; what the victim's attitude would be towards an offer of reparation from the offender, should one be made; and whether they would be happy for such reparation to be made the condition of the caution. Where a caution (simple or conditional) is at that stage regarded as a possibility, the fact may be mentioned to the victim, but it is vital not to give the impression that the victim's views (if any) will be conclusive as to the outcome, which (it should be explained) is at the discretion of the CPS.

7.2 The Victim Personal Statement (VPS) scheme, which was introduced in October 2001, provides victims with the opportunity to describe the effects of the crime and to have these effects taken into account as the case progresses through the criminal justice system. The scheme is entirely voluntary and there is no obligation on the victim to complete a VPS, but where he or she wishes to do so it is taken by the police immediately after taking a witness statement. Once given, the statement becomes part of the case papers and can be seen by anyone involved in the case including the defence and the offender. If it is subsequently proposed to approach the victim for an interview specifically about conditional cautioning, the contents of the VPS (if he or she has made one) should be considered beforehand.

7.3 Further information and guidance on the VPS scheme can be found . . . at: http://www.homeoffice.gov.uk/justice/victims/personal/index.html

And on restorative justice itself:

8.1 Restorative justice processes bring victims and offenders into direct or indirect contact, where they want this, to discuss the crime and its effects. The restorative processes lead towards outcome agreements in which the parties agree what the offender will do as a response to the crime. Such outcomes might include compensation, reparation, rehabilitative activities or a formal apology. Evidence suggests that restorative justice (RJ) can both reduce re-offending and improve victim satisfaction with the criminal justice system. Conditional cautioning offers a potential way of delivering RJ by making the offender's participation a condition of the caution.

8.2 A key consideration in relation to such restorative processes is whether the victim wants to be involved.

8.3 Training in restorative justice is essential if, with a view to an RJ disposal, victims are to be asked their views on the impact of the crime, about reparative options, or whether they want any kind of contact with the offender (whether direct or indirect).

8.4 Where a police force area, or individual officers, are trained in restorative justice practice, they should, in every case where there is an identifiable personal victim, contact that victim to ask for their views on reparation as a condition of the caution, or whether they would like to be involved in a direct or indirect restorative justice process. Restorative justice processes may also be appropriate for crimes with a corporate victim, or crimes where the community as a whole has suffered. In these cases, or in cases where a personal victim has chosen to have no involvement, officers may still wish to deliver the caution, and decide any conditions of the caution, in a restorative manner. In such cases, community groups might also be consulted as to reparative work offenders could do as the condition of their caution.

8.5 RJ processes can be used as a condition of the caution (where the contact with the victim, direct or indirect, is the condition). Alternatively, they can be used as the decision-making process whereby conditions are decided by the victim and offender. It should be noted that in this second case, the 'outcome agreement' with a victim becomes breachable. Depending on the views of the victim, and any other conditions attached to the caution, the CPS and police will need to take a view as to which use of restorative justice is appropriate in a particular case.

Guidance is also given on determining the place where a caution should be given:

9.1 Conditional cautions will usually be given at the local police station, but there is the option of selecting a location appropriate to the offence; e.g. there may be value in giving it at the place where vandalism has occurred. It is not suitable for conditional cautions to be delivered on the street, or in the offender's home. Where restorative justice forms part of the conditional caution, it may be that the local community centre would be more accessible and less threatening for the victim and others attending a restorative conference than the police station.

Other provisions of the code deal with monitoring and compliance and the processes preceding 'breach' (as well as recording[5]):

10.1 It is essential that there should be robust monitoring of compliance with the conditions of a caution. In some cases it may be appropriate to require the offender to show that the condition has been met (e.g. where he has agreed to attend a course, by producing a letter from the organiser confirming the fact); in others, depending on the nature of the condition, to interview the offender, or even to view the activity being carried out. If the offender attends the police station and can show that the conditions are satisfactorily completed, he may be asked to countersign the conditional caution form.

10.2 Failure to comply with any of the conditions means that the offender may be prosecuted for the original offence. It is for the CPS to decide whether to prosecute, but to enable this to be done the police must first investigate the reason for the offender's non-compliance and whether it amounts to a reasonable excuse, and report to the CPS accordingly. It is for the offender to show why he has not been able to fulfil his obligations.

10.3 Where the CPS are satisfied that there is a reasonable excuse for the offender's failure to meet the conditions, they will have to decide whether the case should be regarded as closed, or whether it would be appropriate to set revised conditions and time limits for their completion. Where this is done, the revised conditions should be recorded and the offender must sign the revised conditional caution form acquiescing in the changes. It would not be appropriate to revise conditions more than once.

10.4 Where conditions have been partially completed, it is for the prosecutor to decide whether to charge the offender or whether the extent of the part-compliance is sufficient to justify regarding the case as closed (in which case the conditional caution would remain on the record).

10.5 In general, however, unless there is a reasonable excuse for the offender's failure to complete the conditions, the expectation is that he will be prosecuted for the original offence. The CPS will inform the police of the decision. The charge may be brought at the police station, or by way of summons (or written charge, when the relevant provision of the Criminal Justice Act 2003 has been implemented; the latter may be done by the CPS). At the same time the conditional caution should be formally terminated, the offender so informed, and relevant police records (PNC and any locally stored) amended accordingly. Court proceedings will then go ahead in the usual way.

ISSUES FOR THE COURTS

The existence of conditional cautioning raises a number of issues for courts if and when it comes to sentencing, at a later stage, for an offence in respect of which

---

[5] The draft on recording of conditional cautions and associated matters was incomplete at the time of going to press.

such a caution was originally given. The initial caution will have been given administratively and as part of what can be described as 'sentencing without judicial process'. It is thus questionable about the extent to which a court can be fixed with the views, implicit or otherwise, of the person responsible for the decision to caution and the extent of any obligations in relation to the caution, whether already performed in part or not. Yet it may be unfair for a defendant to be 'punished again'. In other words, where does the court start, and should it make any allowances for what has gone before. Similar powers to those possessed in relation to conditional cautioning may not be available to a court (or not readily), and the picture is further distorted for this reason. If someone declines to accept a caution with conditions there is no guarantee that the court will take the same view of the facts, and similarly if someone is prosecuted following a breach. There is also the residual problem of what the true legal position is if someone denies the offence despite the fact and existence of his or her earlier signed and now admissible admission, i.e. whether it is conclusive evidence of guilt, which seems unlikely. In any event, an admission does not settle the facts and circumstances of the offence or allow, e.g. for the court's - as opposed to the cautioner's - assessment of any available mitigation. Short of a pragmatic approach, there is ample scope for defence lawyers to emphasise mismatch, conflict and sow confusion.

CHAPTER 4

Charging, Disclosure, Allocation and Sending

Parts 4 to 6 CJA 2003 deal with a range of matters affecting the arrest, charging and bailing of suspects as well as pre-trial matters such as disclosure of evidence, the provision of details of witnesses and exhibits and the allocation of either way cases as between the magistrates' court and Crown Court for trial. They also deal with the 'sending' of cases to the Crown Court for trial or sentence *at the outset* of a case. In this last respect, the CJA 2003 also dispenses with existing law on committal to the Crown Court for sentence *following* summary trial. In tandem with the new charging arrangements, the Act introduces a fresh way of 'instituting' criminal proceedings whenever a public prosecutor is involved.

ARREST AND CHARGE

Changes to the procedures for the immediate *detention* of a suspect for questioning and related bail issues have already been noted in *Chapter 2*. Beyond that stage, new and additional arrangements concerning the *charging* of suspects are set out in Schedule 2 to the CJA 2003 (as invoked by section 28 CJA 2003). Under these the CPS rather than the police will normally determine what charge should be brought, especially where this is not wholly clear at the outset. Overall, the new arrangements are intended to bring about enhanced decision-making during the early stages of a case and to ensure close scrutiny of the implications of bringing a charge *vis-à-vis* later proceedings in court. The police and CPS now work together in local Criminal Justice Units (and in some cases specialist units to deal with particular types of offences) with similar objectives in mind.

Decisions about whether someone should be charged or bailed
Schedule 2 CJA 2003 amends section 37 of PACE by inserting new sections 37A to D of PACE. New section 37A allows the DPP to issue guidance that police custody officers will need to have regard to when deciding whether, in cases where they consider there is enough evidence to charge a suspect, they should release that suspect without charge (with or without bail) or charge him or her. In practice this will be inseparable from questions of when the police must refer a case to the CPS under the new arrangements described below. It can be expected that the police themselves will be able to bring charges in minor cases (including with regard to many purely summary offences), cases where there is an unequivocal acceptance of guilt at the outset and they would probably be disposed of by a magistrates' court, and those where there is a need to bring the suspect to court in order to seek a remand in custody. Clearly, this last mechanism is necessary for high risk offenders as already intimated in *Chapter 1*.

Referring cases to the CPS
Where the police release the suspect without charge but on bail while the case is referred to and considered by the CPS, the new section 37B of PACE provides

that, it is for the CPS to determine whether the suspect should be charged, and, if so, with what offence. The CPS will first have to conclude that the evidence is sufficient, or they may decide that the suspect will be offered a caution - including pursuant to the new scheme for conditional cautions (*Chapter 3*). Accordingly, the suspect will then be charged, cautioned or informed in writing that he or she is not to be prosecuted.

Breach of conditions attached to police bail
The new section 37C of PACE makes provision for dealing with breaches by the suspect of any conditions attached to police bail granted pending a decision by the CPS concerning matters outlined above. An amended section 46A of PACE confers a police power of arrest on reasonable suspicion that bail conditions have been broken. A new section 47(1A) of PACE enables conditions to be imposed where someone is released on bail pending consultations with the CPS.[1]

NEW METHOD OF INSTITUTING PROCEEDINGS

In conjunction with the changes described under the last heading, section 29 CJA 2003 introduces a new method of instituting court proceedings in criminal cases. The method applies to all *public* (but not to *private*) prosecutions.

Charges and requisitions
Under the new arrangements, a public prosecutor may institute criminal proceedings by issuing a document - a 'written charge' - charging someone with an offence (section 29(1)). Where the prosecutor does so, he or she must at the same time issue a further document - called a 'requisition' - requiring the person concerned to appear before a magistrates' court at a given time and place in answer to the charge (section 29(2)).[2] These procedures replace the existing ones for commencing proceedings - under which a prosecutor applies to a court by 'laying an information' (which a public prosecutor is in future barred from doing: section 29(4)) - and for a summons to be issued. In other words, the court is removed from this part of the criminal process altogether. The charge and requisition are required to be served on the person concerned, and copies on the court named in the requisition. Section 29(4) prohibits public prosecutors from laying an information for the purposes of seeking a summons, thereby obliging them to use the new and more streamlined method. But such prosecutors will be able to lay an information for the purposes of obtaining a warrant (section 30(4) CJA 2003).[3] Neither do the new procedures prevent someone already in custody being charged under existing procedures (section 30(4)).

Meaning of 'public prosecutor'
'Public prosecutor' is defined in section 29(4) CJA 2003 as any of the following (or people authorised by them to institute criminal proceedings):

---

[1] Contrast the position in relation to 'street bail', as described in *Chapter 2*.
[2] There will be a need for the courts and police to have workable understandings concerning court hearing/listing arrangements matters if such cases are to be satisfactorily scheduled.
[3] But this need no longer be substantiated on oath for that purpose: see later in the chapter.

- a police force (within the meaning of the Prosecution of Offences Act 1985);
- the Director of the Serious Fraud Office;
- the DPP (which in day-to-day practice will include all Crown prosecutors);
- the Attorney General;
- a Secretary of State;
- the Commissioners of Inland Revenue;
- the Commissioners of Customs and Excise; or
- anyone specified in an order made by the Secretary of State to this end.

Prosecutions brought by 'non-listed' prosecutors

The existing procedure in section 1 Magistrates' Courts Act 1980 (MCA 1980) continues regarding any prosecutor not named in the CJA 2003 list (section 30(4) CJA 2003). The right of a private individual to lay an information etc. is similarly unaffected (subject to standard exceptions, e.g. where the right to start proceedings is limited, in all cases, to the Attorney General or DPP). Where a public prosecutor takes over a 'non-listed' prosecutor's case - as, e.g. he or she may do as a matter of discretion - that public prosecutor will be able to rely on a valid information already laid by the non-listed prosecutor.

Form, content etc. of charges and requisitions

Section 30 CJA 2003 makes further provision concerning the new method, including so that rules under the MCA 1980 can regulate 'the form, content, recording, authentication and service' of charges and requisitions and make 'such other provisions' as appear to the Lord Chancellor/Secretary of State for Constitutional Affairs to be necessary or expedient. References in existing provisions to informations and summonses will normally be construed, in future, as referring also to written charges and requisitions.

OATHS

Under section 31 CJA 2003, the requirements of section 1(3) MCA 1980 (warrants 'in the first instance') and section 13(3) (warrants following non-appearance by the defendant at court) whereby a warrant may not be issued unless the underlying information is substantiated on oath are abolished. These changes do not necessarily mean that magistrates cannot ask for supporting information or even, where appropriate, evidence on oath - as a matter of inherent discretion and good practice - before deciding whether they are satisfied that a warrant is appropriate. There are certain other minor or associated amendments.[4]

DISCLOSURE

Part 5 of the CJA 2003 amends various provisions of the Criminal Procedure and Investigations Act 1996 concerned with the pre-trial disclosure of evidence by the prosecution and the defence. In the latter case the changes are significant, in that they substantially extend the information that will be available to prosecutors.

---

[4] But evidence on oath is necessary for certain warrants: see *Chapter 13*.

Unused material
Section 3 of the 1996 Act is amended so as to create a fresh, single and objective test concerning when unused prosecution material (in effect material that is surplus to prosecution requirements or tactics) must be disclosed to the defence.[5] The new test will require the prosecutor to disclose:

> . . . any prosecution material which has not previously been disclosed to the accused and which might reasonably be considered capable of undermining the case for the prosecution against the accused, or of assisting the case for the accused.

A new section 7A of the 1996 Act imposes a continuing duty on prosecutors to disclose unused material. Section 7A provides that the section applies *at all times* after the prosecutor has provided initial prosecution disclosure under section 3, or has purported to do so. This duty continues until the accused is acquitted, convicted or the prosecutor decides not to continue with the case. The prosecutor must keep under review the question of whether there is any material that meets the new 'undermining or assisting' disclosure test already described. If there is, he or she must disclose the relevant material to the accused as soon as is reasonably practicable or within any time limit specified in regulations made under section 12 of the 1996 Act.

When complying with the requirement to review the unused prosecution material the prosecutor must take account of the state of affairs *as it stands at the time, including the prosecution case* (new section 7(4) of the 1996 Act). Where the prosecutor receives a defence statement[6] and as a result of that statement is required to make further disclosure in accordance with section 7A, he or she must do so within the relevant period specified in regulations made under section 12 of the 1996 Act or where applicable give a written statement that no disclosure is required.

Meaning of 'prosecution material'
Prosecution material is defined as material in the prosecutor's possession, or which he or she has been allowed to inspect pursuant to a Code of Practice under the Criminal Procedure and Investigations Act 1996 (section 7A(6)); and the prosecutor should disclose unused material as he or she does so when carrying out ordinary, initial prosecution disclosure under the Act (see below). Material must not be disclosed if the court, on application by the prosecutor, concludes that it is not in the public interest to disclose it, and has so ordered (section 7(7)); and material must not be disclosed to the accused under this section if disclosure is prohibited under the Regulation of Investigatory Powers Act 2000.

Application by the defence for disclosure of unused material
Section 8 of the Criminal Procedure and Investigations Act 1996 is amended by section 38 CJA 2003 so as to enable the accused person to apply to the court for further disclosure of unused prosecution material in certain circumstances. The conditions are that the defence has given a defence statement under the defence disclosure provisions described later in this chapter and the prosecutor has

---

[5] The new test replaces the existing two-stage test that applies to primary and secondary disclosure.
[6] Served under any of the provisions described in the next part of this chapter.

complied with his or her continuing duty to disclose, or has purported to comply with that duty, or failed to comply with it. The accused can then apply to the court for an order that the prosecutor disclose material, to the accused, provided that he or she has reasonable cause to believe that there is prosecution material which should have been - but has not been - disclosed pursuant to the prosecutor's continuing duty in that regard.

Defence disclosure

Section 33 CJA 2003 amends section 5 of the Criminal Procedure and Investigations Act 1996 so as to provide for the 'cross-service' of defence statements following an order of the court. The court may make such an order of its own motion or on the application of any party to the proceedings.

A new section 6A of the 1996 Act prescribes the content of a defence statement (replacing existing provisions in 5(6) to (9) of the 1996 Act). Under existing law, an accused person is required to set out - in general terms - the nature of his or her defence. The effect of the new provision is to require him or her to provide a more detailed statement. Certain existing requirements are replicated, including provisions requiring the accused to give details of any alibi on which he or she seeks to rely (in future the details must include the date of birth of alibi witnesses). This apart, the main changes are that the accused will need to set out the nature of his or her defence, including any particular defences on which he or she intends to rely. He or she must also indicate any points of law that will be taken.

Contents of a defence statement

A new section 6A of the 1996 Act defines 'defence statement' and lists its contents. The accused will be required to provide a written statement:

- setting out the nature of his or her defence, including any particular defences on which he or she intends to rely;
- indicating the matters of fact on which he or she takes issue with the prosecution and in each case why; and
- indicating any point of law he or she wishes to take, including as to the admissibility of evidence or abuse of process, and any authority on which he or she intends to rely for that purpose.

Alibi

Similarly, under new section 6A(2), where the defence statement discloses an alibi, the accused must give particulars, including:

- the name, address and date of birth of any witnesses he or she believes are able to give evidence in support of the alibi, or as many of these details as are known to him or her, when the defence statement is given; and
- if he or she does not have this information, any information in his or her possession that might be of 'material assistance' in identifying or finding any such witness where their details are not known to the accused at the time of the defence statement (when they would thus need to be disclosed under the first of these points).

'Evidence in support of an alibi' means

> . . . evidence tending to show that by reason of the presence of the accused at a particular place or in a particular area at a particular time, he was not, or was unlikely to have been, at the place where the offence is alleged to have been committed at the time of its alleged commission.[7]

The Secretary of State is given power to prescribe in regulations further details that are to be contained in defence statements and such regulations will be subject to the affirmative resolution procedure.

Updating a defence statement

A new section 6B(3) of the Criminal Procedure and Investigations Act 1996 imposes a continuing duty under which the accused person must provide an updated defence statement within a period specified by regulations made under section 12. If he or she has nothing further to add, they may instead give a written statement to that effect. Updated statements must comply with the same requirements applicable to those defence statements given initially (see above).

New sections 6B(5) and (6) provide for the 'cross-service' of updated statements following an order of the court (made of its own motion or on the application of a party). These mirror the provisions for the initial statement.

Notification of intention to call defence witnesses

An accused person will not be required to provide advance notice that he or she personally intends, or does not intend, to give evidence at his or her trial. However, a new section 6C of the 1996 Act imposes a requirement to serve, before his or her trial, a notice setting out the details of any witnesses he or she intends to call to give evidence. The witnesses' names, addresses and dates of birth must be provided to the court and prosecutor within a time limit in regulations made under section 12 of the 1996 Act. As with alibi witnesses, if the address is not known, the accused must provide any information that might assist in identifying or finding the witness. However, new section 6C(2) provides that if details of any alibi witnesses have already been provided as part of the defence statement in accordance with new section 6A(2), further details do not have to given under this provision.

New section 6C(4) requires the accused to give an amended notice if he or she later decides to call a witness not named in the notice, or if he or she decides not to call someone on the list, or where he or she discovers information concerning the whereabouts of a witness.

Expert witnesses who have been 'consulted'

A new section 6D to the 1996 Act imposes a novel requirement on the accused to serve, before the trial, a notice giving details of the name and address of any expert witness *consulted*. Notice is required in respect of each such expert. If details of the expert have already been provided under the basic requirement to

---

[7] This reproduces the definition in section 11(8) Criminal Justice Act 1967 under which defence notice of alibi was necessary on committal to trial in the Crown Court.

notify an intention to call defence witnesses (as already outlined above), a notice under section 6D is not required. The point is that the court must be given notice where the expert has been consulted but there is no intention to call him or her, perhaps because the expert's opinion runs counter to the accused person's case. Here, it seems, the prosecution will be able to approach and possibly call that expert to give evidence.[8]

Other provisions concerning defence disclosure

A new section 6E inserted into the 1996 Act provides that a defence statement served on behalf of an accused, by his or her solicitor, is deemed to have been given on the authority of the accused person, unless the contrary is proved. It is also provided that where it appears to the judge at a pre-trial hearing (as defined in Part 4 of the 1996 Act) that the accused person has not fully complied with the requirements described above, the judge must warn him or her that there is the possibility of comment being made or inferences being drawn from that fact. New sections 6E(4) to (6) apply where there is a trial before judge and jury in the Crown Court. They allow the judge, of his or her own motion or on the application of a party, to give to the jury a copy of the defence statement. If the judge does so, he or she may direct that it be edited to exclude inadmissible material. The defence statement that will be given to the jury is the updated statement as opposed to the initial statement where both have been provided. Otherwise it is the initial defence statement.

Faults in disclosure by the defence

Section 39 CJA 2003 substitutes a new section 11 Criminal Procedure and Investigations Act 1996 extending the existing list of defence failures to disclose and removing the requirement that the leave of the court be obtained before making comment in respect of some of these. The new section 11 provides that a court or jury may draw inferences from certain faults (set out in that section) in relation to disclosure by the accused in deciding whether he or she is guilty. However, the accused person cannot be convicted solely on the basis of such an inference.

Code of practice for police interviews of witnesses notified by accused

Section 40 CJA 2003 inserts a new section 21A of the 1996 Act so as to provide for a code of practice - to be prepared by the Secretary of State - which will apply whenever police, or non-police investigators, interview someone (i.e. a witness or expert) whose details have been disclosed under the disclosure requirements described above. Failure to have regard to the code cannot, in itself, render the person responsible for the failure liable to criminal or civil proceedings (section 21A(11)), but the code will be admissible in evidence in all criminal and civil proceedings and courts are required to take its provisions, or a failure to have regard to them, into account where the code or the failure appears to be relevant to a question before them (section 21A(12)).

---

[8]   Under general principle, there is 'no property' in a witness.

'ALLOCATION AND SENDING'

Section 41 CJA 2003 invokes Schedule 3 CJA 2003, Part 1 of which amends various existing statutes concerning decisions by magistrates' courts on whether cases which are triable either way should be tried in the magistrates' court (i.e. summarily) or the Crown Court (on indictment). The schedule also provides for 'sending' to the Crown Court of those either way cases that need to go there. Part 2 of Schedule 3 also contains minor and consequential amendments to various statutes.

The Magistrates' Courts Act 1980 (MCA 1980)
Schedule 3 clarifies that the preliminary stages of an either way case, including plea before venue[9] and allocation procedures - as outlined in this part of this chapter - may take place before a single magistrate. However, a single lay magistrate may not conduct a contested trial or impose sentence,[10] but can accept a plea of guilty. Paragraph 3 also limits the sentence that may be imposed where someone pleads guilty to a 'low-value offence'.[11]

Paragraph 5 of Schedule 3 substitutes a new section 19 MCA 1980 setting out the procedure to be followed by the magistrate in determining whether an either way offence to which the defendant has not so far indicated a guilty plea should be tried summarily or on indictment. The new procedure, known as 'allocation', differs from the existing one, in particular in that:

- the prosecutor must be given an opportunity to inform the magistrates' court of the accused's previous convictions (if any). Under the CJA 2003 these are generally aggravating factors which serve to increase the seriousness of the present offence (but see further in *Chapter 7*), and hence the potential sentence and suitable venue for trial or sentence; and
- the court must have regard to any allocation guidelines issued as 'definitive guidelines' by the Sentencing Guidelines Council under section 170 CJA 2003 (see *Chapter 7*).

The new section 19 MCA 1980 reads as follows:

(1) The court shall decide whether the offence appears to it more suitable for summary trial or for trial on indictment.
(2) Before making a decision under this section, the court -
    (a) shall give the prosecution an opportunity to inform the court of the accused's previous convictions (if any); and
    (b) shall give the prosecution and the accused an opportunity to make representations as to whether summary trial or trial on indictment would be more suitable.
(3) In making a decision under this section, the court shall consider -

---

[9] I.e. the situation where an accused person can indicate his or her plea to the court before it comes to determine the appropriate venue for trial.
[10] In contrast to a district judge (magistrates' courts), who is, when sitting alone, empowered to conduct a summary trial or to sentence people.
[11] i.e. Criminal Damage of a value below £2,000.

(a) whether the sentence which a magistrates' court would have power to impose for the offence would be adequate; and

(b) any representations made by the prosecution or the accused under subsection (2)(b) above,

and shall have regard to any allocation guidelines (or revised allocation guidelines) issued as definitive guidelines under section 170 of the Criminal Justice Act 2003.

(4) Where -

(a) the accused is charged with two or more offences; and

(b) it appears to the court that the charges for the offences could be joined in the same indictment or that the offences arise out of the same or connected circumstances,

subsection (3)(a) above shall have effect as if references to the sentence which a magistrates' court would have power to impose for the offence were a reference to the maximum aggregate sentence which a magistrates' court would have power to impose for all of the offences taken together.

(5) In this section any reference to a previous conviction is a reference to -

(a) a previous conviction by a court in the United Kingdom; or

(b) a previous finding of guilt in -

(i) any proceedings under the Army Act 1955, the Air Force Act 1955 or the Naval Discipline Act 1957 (whether before a court-martial or any other court or person authorised under any of those Acts to award a punishment in respect of any offence); or

(ii) any proceedings before a Standing Civilian Court.

(6) If, in respect of the offence, the court receives a notice under section 51B or 51C of the Crime and Disorder Act 1998 (which relate to serious or complex fraud cases and to certain cases involving children respectively), the preceding provisions of this section and sections 20, 20A and 21 below shall not apply, and the court shall proceed in relation to the offence in accordance with section 51(1) of that Act.

New procedures in relation to either way offences

Paragraph 6 of Schedule 3 substitutes a new section 20 MCA 1980 setting out the procedures to be followed by a magistrates' court where it decides that a case *is* suitable for summary trial. As under existing law, the magistrates' court's overriding consideration will be the adequacy of its own sentencing powers viewed in relation to the seriousness of the offence or offences charged. Here it should be noted that magistrates' maximum powers and also the maximum penalty where an either way offence is tried summarily are each raised to 12 months under the (independent provisions of) the CJA 2003 (see *Chapter 7*). Similarly, as under the existing law, defendants must be told that they can either consent to be tried summarily or, if they so choose ('elect' is the term commonly used), they can be tried by a jury in the Crown Court. As already explained in *Chapter 1*, this longstanding right to elect trial by jury[12] continues without alteration. A defendant who does exercise that right risks the higher maximum penalties available in the Crown Court if convicted, of course.

Once a magistrates' court *has* assumed jurisdiction within the terms of the new allocation processes it will generally no longer be possible for it to commit

---

[12] Or 'trial by peers', so-called, said by some people to be a right derived from Magna Carta - but in modern times the result of offences being define by statute as 'triable either way'. Generally speaking, trial in the Crown Court will be before a jury, but subject in future to the arrangements for 'judge-alone' trials described in *Chapter 5*.

the individual concerned to the Crown Court for sentence. Under existing law it can do so *following trial and conviction,* but this will normally no longer be possible in such circumstances and the offender will not be able to receive a sentence beyond 12 months (or an aggregate term of 15 months: *Chapter 7*). But this lack of a 'reserve' power to commit for sentence will not apply at earlier, preliminary stages, following the indication of sentence procedures described below, nor where committal is with a view to an extended sentence or sentence for public protection being passed by the Crown Court (*Chapter 10*).

Indication of sentence
In a further new departure, a defendant will have the opportunity of requesting an indication from a magistrates' court concerning whether - if he or she pleads guilty before magistrates - the sentence would be a custodial one or not. The magistrates' court will have a discretion whether to give such an indication, and where one *is* given, the accused person will also have the opportunity to reconsider any indication concerning plea. If he or she still decides to plead guilty, the magistrates' court will proceed to sentence.

Following these procedures, a custodial sentence will only be available if that likelihood was originally indicated, and the option of committal to the Crown Court for sentence (in section 3 Powers of Criminal Courts (Sentencing) Act 2000) will not be available where the court proceeds to deal with the case.[13] Otherwise (i.e. if the defendant declines to reconsider his or her indication of plea, or where no sentence indication was given) he or she will have a choice between accepting summary trial or electing trial in the Crown Court (as under existing procedures).

Where an indication of sentence is given and the defendant does not choose to plead guilty on the basis of it, the sentence indication is not binding on either magistrates who later try the case summarily or on the Crown Court.

Sections 20 and 20A in their new form
Given the central nature of sections 20 and 20A MCA 1980 it seems useful to set out those provisions in their full (but edited) form which also serves to emphasise the points made under the last two headings. New section 20 reads:

(1) If the court decides under section 19 [MCA 1980: see above] that the offence appears to it more suitable for summary trial, the following provisions of this section shall apply (unless they are excluded by section 23 below).
(2) The court shall explain to the accused in ordinary language -
   (a) that it appears to the court more suitable for him to be tried summarily for the offence;
   (b) that he can either consent to be so tried or, if he wishes, be tried on indictment; and
   (c) in the case of a specified offence (within the meaning of section 224 of the Criminal Justice Act 2003 [see *Chapter 10*]), that if he is tried summarily and is convicted by the court, he may be committed for sentence to the Crown Court

---

[13] Although committal for sentence under section 3A Powers of Criminal Courts (Sentencing) Act 2000 will be available where the criteria for an extended sentence or a sentence for public protection appear to be met: see, generally, *Chapter 10*.

under section 3A of the Powers of Criminal Courts (Sentencing) Act 2000 if the committing court is of such opinion as is mentioned in subsection (2) of that section.

(3) The accused may then request an indication ('an indication of sentence') of whether a custodial sentence or non-custodial sentence would be more likely to be imposed if he were to be tried summarily for the offence and to plead guilty.

(4) If the accused requests an indication of sentence, the court may, but need not, give such an indication.

(5) If the accused requests and the court gives an indication of sentence, the court shall ask the accused whether he wishes, on the basis of the indication, to reconsider the indication of plea which was given, or is taken to have been given, under section 17A or 17B above.

(6) If the accused indicates that he wishes to reconsider the indication under section 17A or 17B above, the court shall ask the accused whether (if the offence were to proceed to trial) he would plead guilty or not guilty.

(7) If the accused indicates that he would plead guilty the court shall proceed as if -
  (a) the proceedings constituted from that time the summary trial of the information; and
  (b) section 9(1) above were complied with and he pleaded guilty under it.

(8) Subsection (9) below applies where -
  (a) the court does not give an indication of sentence (whether because the accused does not request one or because the court does not agree to give one);
  (b) the accused either -
    (i) does not indicate, in accordance with subsection (5) above, that he wishes; or
    (ii) indicates, in accordance with subsection (5) above, that he does not wish, to reconsider the indication of plea under section 17A or 17B above; or
  (c) the accused does not indicate, in accordance with subsection (6) above, that he would plead guilty.

(9) The court shall ask the accused whether he consents to be tried summarily or wishes to be tried on indictment and -
  (a) if he consents to be tried summarily, shall proceed to the summary trial of the information; and
  (b) if he does not so consent, shall proceed in relation to the offence in accordance with section 51(1) of the Crime and Disorder Act 1998.

New section 20A then sets out supplementary provisions in relation to the position where summary trial appears more suitable:

(1) Where the case is dealt with in accordance with section 20(7) above, no court (whether a magistrates' court or not) may impose a custodial sentence for the offence unless such a sentence was indicated in the indication of sentence referred to in section 20 above.

(2) Subsection (1) above is subject to sections 3A(4), 4(8) and 5(3) of the Powers of Criminal Courts (Sentencing) Act 2000.

(3) Except as provided in subsection (1) above -
  (a) an indication of sentence shall not be binding on any court (whether a magistrates' court or not); and
  (b) no sentence may be challenged or be the subject of appeal in any court on the ground that it is not consistent with an indication of sentence.

(4) Subject to section 20(7) above, the following shall not for any purpose be taken to constitute the taking of a plea -
  (a) asking the accused under section 20 above whether (if the offence were to proceed to trial) he would plead guilty or not guilty; or

(b) an indication by the accused under that section of how he would plead.

(5) Where the court gives an indication of sentence under section 20 above, it shall cause each such indication to be entered in the register.

(6) In this section and in section 20 above, references to a custodial sentence are to a custodial sentence within the meaning of section 76 of the Powers of Criminal Courts (Sentencing) Act 2000, and references to a non-custodial sentence shall be construed accordingly.

Sending to the Crown Court

Under a substituted section 21 MCA 1980, where the court decides that trial in the Crown Court appears more suitable, it will proceed to 'send' the case to the Crown Court. The new provision is as follows:

> If the court decides under section 19 [MCA 1980] that the offence appears to it more suitable for trial on indictment, the court shall tell the accused that the court has decided that it is more suitable for him to be tried on indictment, and shall proceed in relation to the offence in accordance with section 51(1) of the Crime and Disorder Act 1998.

The case will thus, in future, proceed to the Crown Court in the way that indictable only cases do under existing law.

Plea before venue in case of offenders under the age of 18

Paragraph 10 of Schedule 3 CJA 2003 adds new sections 24A to 24D to the MCA 1980. These introduce a procedure similar to that in sections 17A to 17C of the 1980 Act (i.e. 'plea before venue') to cases involving defendants who are under 18. These will apply in certain cases where magistrates have to decide whether a juvenile[14] defendant should be sent to the Crown Court for trial: in his or her own right, or for trial alongside an adult defendant.

Abolition of the power to switch between procedures

Paragraph 11 of Schedule 3 to the 2003 Act amends section 25 MCA 1980. The existing power to 'switch' between summary trial and committal proceedings is abolished in favour of a new right being given to the prosecutor to apply for a case that has been allocated for summary trial to be tried on indictment instead. That application must be made to the court before summary trial begins and must be heard before any other application or issue relating to summary trial.

Order of procedure etc.

Paragraphs 15 to 20 of Schedule 3 CJA 2003 amend the Crime and Disorder Act 1998 so as to:

- establish the order in which a magistrates' court is to apply various procedures in respect of either way offences (para. 17 which inserts the new section 50A of the 1998 Act set out below);
- substitute a new section 51 Crime and Disorder Act 1998 so that it applies not only (as under existing law) to indictable-only offences (and cases related to these), but also if an either way case involving an adult is allocated for trial on indictment. The provisions for sending to the Crown

---

[14] Other revised committal procedures for juveniles are noted in *Chapter 12*.

Court related cases against the same defendant or another defendant (including a juvenile) are thereby continued (para. 18);

- insert into the Crime and Disorder Act 1998 a new section 51A, which replaces the existing provisions for transferring cases - where the principal defendant is a juvenile - to the Crown Court for trial; and new sections 51B and 51C, which subsume the transfer provisions in section 4 Criminal Justice Act 1987 (which applies to serious fraud cases) and section 53 of the Criminal Justice Act 1991 (child witness cases). The procedure in sections 51B and 51C will continue to be initiated, as under existing law, by the issue of a notice by the prosecutor. (All para. 18.)

The newly inserted section 50A Crime and Disorder Act 1998 provides:

(1) Where an adult appears or is brought before a magistrates' court charged with an either-way offence (the 'relevant offence'), the court shall proceed in the manner described in this section.

(2) If notice is given in respect of the relevant offence under section 51B or 51C below [transfer proceedings], the court shall deal with the offence as provided in section 51 below.

(3) Otherwise -
- (a) if the adult (or another adult with whom the adult is charged jointly with the relevant offence) is or has been sent to the Crown Court for trial for an offence under section 51(2)(a) or 51(2)(c) below -
  - (i) the court shall first consider the relevant offence under subsection (3), (4), (5) or, as the case may be, (6) of section 51 below and, where applicable, deal with it under that subsection;
  - (ii) if the adult is not sent to the Crown Court for trial for the relevant offence by virtue of sub-paragraph (i) above, the court shall then proceed to deal with the relevant offence in accordance with sections 17A to 23 of the 1980 Act;
- (b) in all other cases -
  - (i) the court shall first consider the relevant offence under sections 17A to 20 (excluding subsections (8) and (9) of section 20) of the 1980 Act;
  - (ii) if, by virtue of sub-paragraph (i) above, the court would be required to proceed in relation to the offence as mentioned in section 17A(6), 17B(2)(c) or 20(7) of that Act (indication of guilty plea), it shall proceed as so required (and, accordingly, shall not consider the offence under section 51 or 51A below);
  - (iii) if sub-paragraph (ii) above does not apply-
    (a) the court shall consider the relevant offence under sections 51 and 51A below and, where applicable, deal with it under the relevant section;
    (b) if the adult is not sent to the Crown Court for trial for the relevant offence by virtue of paragraph (a) of this sub-paragraph, the court shall then proceed to deal with the relevant offence as contemplated by section 20(9) or, as the case may be, section 21 of the 1980 Act.

(4) Subsection (3) above is subject to any requirement to proceed as mentioned in subsections (2) or (6)(a) of section 22 of the 1980 Act (certain offences where value involved is small).

(5) Nothing in this section shall prevent the court from committing the adult to the Crown Court for sentence pursuant to any enactment, if he is convicted of the relevant offence [where such power still exists].

Reporting restrictions

Paragraphs 21 to 28 of Schedule 3 CJA 2003 amend the Powers of Criminal Courts (Sentencing) Act 2000 in various respects. The most significant of these changes concerns the committal to the Crown Court for sentence of either way offences. This power will no longer be available in cases where the magistrates' court has dealt with the case having accepted jurisdiction (whether as a contested case or a guilty plea) but will be limited to cases where a guilty plea has been indicated at plea before venue.

Where the defendant is charged with several either way matters

If a defendant is charged with a number of related either way offences, pleads guilty to one of them at the plea before venue stage and is sent to the Crown Court to be tried for the remainder, the existing power in section 4 of the Powers of Criminal Courts (Sentencing) Act 2000 to 'scoop up' other matters and to send offences to which he or she has pleaded guilty to the Crown Court for sentence is retained.

Mode of trial for certain firearms offences pending 'allocation and sending'

Section 42 CJA 2003 makes transitional arrangements so as to allow defendants under the age of 18 to be sent to the Crown Court for trial where they have committed certain firearms offences (and were aged 16 or over at that time). These interim arrangements are scheduled to be replaced by permanent ones when the new allocation and sending procedure is introduced.

CHAPTER 5

Juries, 'Live Links' and Evidence

A much heralded aspect of the CJA 2003 has been the tightening of the criteria in relation to people who, under the existing provisions, 'escape' jury service. The relevant changes are contained in section 321 CJA 2003, which invokes Schedule 33.[1] Paragraph 1 of that schedule amends the Juries Act 1974 by inserting a new section 1 of the 1974 Act. This provides:

> (1) Subject to the provisions of this Act, every person shall be qualified to serve as a juror in the Crown Court, the High Court and county court and be liable accordingly to attend for jury service when summoned under this Act if -
>> (a) he is for the time being registered as a parliamentary or local government elector and is not less than 18 nor more than seventy years of age;
>> (b) he has been ordinarily resident in the United Kingdom, the Channel Islands or the Isle of Man for any period of at least five years since attaining the age of 13;
>> (c) he is not a mentally disordered person; and
>> (d) he is not disqualified for jury service.

Other provisions of Schedule 33 abolish (except in the case of mentally disordered people) the categories of *ineligibility* for, and *excusal* from jury service as of right. The effect is that certain groups of people who currently *cannot*, or *need not*, do jury service will be required to perform jury service unless they can put forward a satisfactory reason as to why they should not. The schedule also amends the list of categories of people who are *disqualified* from jury service.

Ineligibility for and excusal from jury service
The new provisions will remove the existing status of 'ineligibility' for jury service and of entitlement to be 'excused as of right' from a number of people who - in future - will thus become potential jurors. Under existing law, members of the judiciary, other people concerned with the administration of justice and the clergy are ineligible. This will no longer be the case. Other people, including those above 65 years of age, MPs, doctors, followers of certain religions and (in certain circumstances) members of the armed forces, are under existing law entitled to refuse to serve on a jury - but this entitlement will disappear once the relevant provisions of the CJA 2003 are in force.

All such people will need to apply putting forward their 'good reasons' to be excused from jury service (or where applicable for this to be deferred) - under section 9 (or 9A) of the 1974 Act. Further provisions make corresponding changes to the jury summoning offence provisions in section 20 Juries Act 1974.

Disqualification from jury service
Schedule 33 to the CJA 2003 also substitutes fresh categories of people who are disqualified altogether from jury service. These are people who are on bail or who have served, or are serving, custodial sentences or community orders of

---

[1] Paragraph references in this part of *Chapter 5* are to those in Schedule 33 unless otherwise stated.

various types and the list has been updated to reflect changes in sentencing legislation, including those introduced by the CJA 2003 itself. The new list is contained in a fresh Schedule 1 to the Juries Act 1974 (as inserted by para. 15 of Schedule 33 to the CJA 2003). In summary, people are disqualified if they:

- are on bail (within the meaning of the Bail Act 1976);
- have at any time been sentenced in the UK, Channel Islands or Isle of Man to imprisonment for life, detention for life or custody for life, detention during Her Majesty's pleasure or that of the Secretary of State, imprisonment or detention for public protection, an extended sentence[2] or to a term of imprisonment or detention of five years or more;
- have at any time in the last ten years in the UK, Channel Islands or Isle of Man served any part of a sentence of imprisonment or detention, or received a suspended sentence of imprisonment or suspended detention;
- have at any time in England and Wales had made in respect of them a community order under section 177 Criminal Justice Act 2003 (see *Chapter 8*), a community rehabilitation order, a community punishment order, a community punishment and rehabilitation order, a drug treatment and testing order or a drug abstinence order (including under court martial, or corresponding orders in other UK jurisdictions).

Armed forces personnel

With the abolition of 'excusal as of right', service personnel who wish to avoid jury service will, like other people, need to apply showing 'good reason' why they should not serve. However, a commanding officer's certificate will be regarded as conclusive evidence of good reason for the purposes of these provisions, at least in so far as that, on its production, a jury service summons will be deferred. If there has already been a deferral or the commanding officer certifies that absence would be prejudicial for a given period of time, then service personnel will be excused altogether from the obligation. This is without prejudice to their being summoned for jury service in future.

The Jury Central Summoning Bureau

Where someone has been summoned for jury service, he or she may be excused (on showing 'good reason') or his or her jury service deferred. This discretion currently rests with the Jury Central Summoning Bureau (part of the Department of Constitutional Affairs), which administers jury summoning on behalf of the Crown Court as 'the appropriate officer' under the Juries Act 1974. The Lord Chancellor/Secretary of State for Constitutional Affairs is required to issue guidance as to the manner in which the functions of the appropriate officer are exercised and for such guidance to be laid before Parliament and to be published (paragraph 12 of Schedule 33, inserting a new section 9AA of the 1974 Act).

Jurors' allowances

Further changes allow jurors to be paid their statutory allowances (by the Court Service which administers this aspect) 'otherwise than by means of cash'. Some court facilities enable staff to obtain refreshments by non-cash means, such as a

---

[2]   Under sections 227, 228 CJA 2003 or 210A Criminal Procedure (Scotland) Act 1995: see *Chapter 10*.

voucher system or 'swipe cards'. The new provisions will enable the Crown Court to extend such methods to jurors.

TRIAL WITHOUT A JURY: 'JUDGE-ALONE' TRIALS

Amongst the more controversial of the provisions in the CJA 2003 are those concerning trial without a jury, or 'judge-alone' trials. The provisions are narrower than originally proposed. A proposal to allow defendants to apply for such trials was abandoned at the eleventh hour as part and parcel of a number of late adjustments in the House of Lords which allowed the CJA 2003 onto the Statute Book. The surviving provisions - contained in Part 7 CJA 2003 - allow trials without a jury, i.e. what have been dubbed 'judge-only' or 'judge-alone' trials, where:

- the prosecutor applies for this in relation to certain fraud charges (section 43 CJA 2003); or
- the prosecutor applies for this where there is a danger of jury tampering (section 44 CJA 2003); or
- a trial has collapsed because of jury tampering and the jury has had to be discharged, e.g. due to intimidation or bribery (section 46 CJA 2003).

Application by the prosecutor in relation to certain fraud cases

Section 43 CJA 2003 applies where one or more defendants are tried on indictment and notice is given by the prosecutor under section 51B Crime and Disorder Act 1998 (which relates to notices in serious and complex fraud cases) in respect of that Act or those offences. The prosecutor may apply to a judge of the Crown Court for the trial to be conducted without a jury. Provided that the judge is satisfied that:

> . . . the complexity of the trial or the length of the trial (or both) is likely to make the trial so burdensome to the members of a jury hearing the trial that the interests of justice require that serious consideration should be given to the question whether the trial should be conducted without a jury

(i.e. the precondition contained in section 43(5) CJA 2003), he or she may make an order that the trial be conducted without a jury; and if not so satisfied must refuse the application (section 43(3)). It is important to note, in relation to this particular limb, that the judge can order trial without a jury. But he or she may not make such an order without the approval of the Lord Chief Justice or a judge nominated by him or her (section 43(4)). In exercising the discretion, the trial judge must have regard to any steps that might reasonably be taken to reduce the complexity or length of the trial. A step is 'not to be regarded as reasonable if it would significantly disadvantage the prosecution' (section 43(6), (7)).

Application by the prosecutor in relation to jury tampering

Similarly, the prosecutor may, under section 44 CJA 2003, make similar application where jury tampering is anticipated. In this situation there are two conditions concerning which the judge must be satisfied, as follows:

. . . the first condition is that there is evidence of a real and present danger that jury tampering would take place. (section 44(4))

Section 44(6) provides examples of cases where there may be evidence of such a real and present danger', i.e. a case where the trial is a retrial and the jury in the previous trial was discharged due to jury tampering; a case where tampering has occurred in previous criminal proceedings involving the same defendant or defendants; or one where there has been intimidation, or attempts at intimidation, of a witness in the trial. The second condition is that:

. . . notwithstanding any steps (including the provision of police protection) which might reasonably be taken to prevent jury tampering, the likelihood that it would take place would be so substantial as to make it necessary in the interests of justice for the trial to be conducted without a jury. (section 44(5))

Further, special procedures are laid down in relation to applications under sections 43 and 44 above, whereby the relevant application must be dealt with at a preparatory hearing and reporting restrictions are invoked.

Discharge of a jury where there is jury tampering

Section 46 CJA 2003 contemplates a quite different situation to those already outlined above: where there is a trial by jury but tampering actually happens during it. The position is then that where a judge is minded to discharge the jury 'and he or she is so minded because jury tampering has taken place', certain set procedures must be followed. The judge must inform the parties that he or she is so minded and of the grounds for this - and allow representations (section 46(2)). Where, after considering any such representations, he or she discharges the jury, the judge may make an order that the trial is to continue without a jury 'if, but only if' he or she is satisfied that jury tampering has taken place and that to continue the trial without a jury would be fair to the defendant or defendants (section 46(3)). All this is subject to the overriding consideration that if the judge considers it necessary in the interests of justice for the trial to be terminated, then he or she *must* terminate it (section 46(4)).

When terminating a trial, the judge may make an order that any new trial be conducted without a jury if satisfied that both of the conditions in section 44 (above) are fulfilled (section 46(5)) and nothing in section 46 affects an application by the prosecutor being made under either section 43 or 44 (both above) in relation to any new trial that takes place following termination of a trial - or any other powers the judge may have to terminate a trial.

Appeals and reasons for decisions

The CJA 2003 provides a right of appeal to the Court of Appeal for both prosecution and defence against a determination to continue a trial in the absence of a jury, or to order a retrial without a jury because of jury tampering (section 47 CJA). Where a trial is conducted or continued without a jury, and a defendant is convicted, the judge is required to give his or her reasons for that conviction (section 48).

In the latter case, the court must be satisfied that the level and duration of the police protection that would be necessary for the members of a jury hearing the trial would be excessively burdensome to a typical juror. Alternatively (or additionally), a court must be satisfied that the risk of jury tampering would remain sufficiently high notwithstanding any steps (including police protection) that could reasonably be taken to prevent it, to make it necessary in the interests of justice for the trial to be conducted without a jury.

'LIVE LINKS'

The use of a live link between two locations by means of a television camera, screens and a secure line for transmission has become increasingly commonplace since first employed to enable child witnesses of physical or sexual abuse to give their evidence out of sight of the accused person. It has also been increasingly used for remand purposes when the 'live link' has been between the prison and the courtroom. Part 8 CJA 2003 makes more general provision in relation to witnesses. Section 51 provides that a witness - *other than the defendant* - may, if the court so directs, give evidence through a live link in certain criminal proceedings listed in that section. These are:

- a summary trial;
- an appeal to the Crown Court arising out of such a trial;
- a trial on indictment;
- an appeal to the criminal division of the Court of Appeal;
- the hearing of an Attorney General's reference under sections 9 or 11 Criminal Appeal Act 1995;
- a hearing before a magistrates' court or the Crown Court which is held after the defendant has entered a guilty plea; or
- a hearing before the Court of Appeal under section 80 CJA 2003 (which deals with the quashing of acquittals: see *Chapter 6*).

The direction mentioned above may be given on application by a party or of the court's own motion (section 51(3)) but cannot be given unless the court is satisfied that it is in the interests of the efficient or effective administration of justice for the person concerned to give evidence via a live link; and the court has been notified by the Secretary of State that suitable facilities exist and that such notice has not been withdrawn (section 51(4), (5)).

In considering whether to direct use of a live link, the court must consider all the circumstances of the cases, including in particular:

- the availability of witnesses;
- the need for a witness to attend in person;
- the importance of the witnesses' evidence to the proceedings;
- the views of the witness;
- the suitability of the facilities at the place where the witness would give evidence via a live link; and
- whether a direction might tend to inhibit any party to the proceedings from effectively testing the witness's evidence (section 51(7)).

The court must state in open court its reasons for refusing an application for a direction to use a live link and, if a magistrates' court, cause them to be entered in the court register (section 51(8)). Certain supplementary provisions (including for rescission of a direction) are set out in section 52 CJA 2003.

EVIDENCE

The CJA 2003 makes fundamental changes in relation to the rules of evidence, primarily in relation to the situations in which evidence of bad character or hearsay evidence can be introduced in a criminal trial - in each case by abolishing and replacing the existing law. There are also important new provisions concerning the use of video recordings and of documents by witnesses to refresh memory. It should be noted that previous convictions also remain relevant in other contexts, i.e. in relation to 'allocation' (*Chapter 4*) and sentencing (*Chapter 7*).

'BAD CHARACTER'

One of the more controversial aspects of the CJA 2003 is its extension of the scope for admissibility of an accused person's bad character as part of the case against him or her. Traditionally, the situations in which such evidence has been admissible at all have been closely restricted. It has been accepted that there are dangers that inappropriate inferences and conclusions are likely to be drawn from such evidence,[3] so that the provisions described below have been universally criticised by civil liberties groups and defence lawyers alike who see them as open to abuse and miscarriages of justice. The Government's response has been along the lines that 'We must learn to trust juries and magistrates'.[4] The issue is perhaps not so much one of trust, but of the fallibility of human nature.

Under section 99(1) CJA 2003 'The common law rules governing the admissibility of evidence of bad character in criminal proceedings are abolished'. Section 99(2) provides that this is subject to section 118(1) CJA 2003 in so far as it preserves the rule under which in criminal proceedings a person's *reputation* is admissible for the purposes of proving his or her bad character. In turn, section 118 preserves 'Any rule of law under which in criminal proceedings evidence of a person's reputation is admissible for the purpose of proving good or bad character' (a note to section 118 makes it clear that this rule is preserved only so far as 'it allows a court to treat such evidence as proving the matter concerned').

'Bad character' is defined by section 98 CJA 2003 as meaning evidence of, or of a disposition towards, misconduct on his or her part, other than evidence that '(a) has to do with the alleged facts of the offence with which the defendant is charged, or (b) is evidence of misconduct in connection with the investigation or prosecution of that offence'.

---

[3] Summed up in the adage 'Give a dog a bad name and hang him'.
[4] A response that has also been used to justify the removal of the existing bar on magistrates sitting to hear a case after they have heard about an accused person's previous convictions during an earlier bail application (for this change see *Chapter 13*).

Non-defendants

Section 100(1) CJA 2003 deals with evidence of bad character in relation to 'persons other than the defendant', in other words usually witnesses for the prosecution or possibly a co-accused (see later in the chapter). It provides that:

> (1) In criminal proceedings evidence of the bad character of a person other than the defendant is admissible if and only if -
> (a) it is important explanatory evidence,
> (b) it has substantial probative value in relation to a matter which -
> (i) is a matter in issue in the proceedings, and
> (ii) is of substantial importance in the context of the case as a whole, or
> (c) all parties to the proceedings agree to the evidence being admissible.

For the purposes of the above, evidence is 'important explanatory evidence' if (a) without it, the court or jury would find it impossible or difficult properly to understand other evidence in the case, and (b) its value for understanding the case as a whole is substantial. In assessing 'probative value' the court must have regard to the following statutory factors (and any others it considers relevant):

- the nature and number of the events, or other things, to which the evidence relates;
- when those events or things are alleged to have happened or existed;
- where
  —the evidence is evidence of a person's misconduct, and
  —it is suggested that the evidence has probative value by reason of similarity between that misconduct and other alleged misconduct,
  the nature and extent of the similarities and the dissimilarities between each of the alleged instances of misconduct; and
- where
  — the evidence is evidence of a person's misconduct,
  — it is suggested that that person is also responsible for the misconduct charged, and
  — the identity of the person responsible for the misconduct charged is disputed,
  the extent to which the evidence shows or tends to show that the same person was responsible each time.

Except as above, evidence of the bad character of someone other than the defendant must not be given without leave of the court.

The defendant's own bad character

Under section 101(1) CJA 2003, in criminal proceedings evidence of the defendant's bad character is admissible if, but only if:

(a) all parties to the proceedings agree to the evidence being admissible,
(b) the evidence is adduced by the defendant himself or is given in answer to a question asked by him in cross-examination and intended to elicit it,
(c) it is important explanatory evidence,
(d) it is relevant to an important matter in issue between the defendant and the prosecution,

(e) it has substantial probative value in relation to an important matter in issue between the defendant and a co-defendant,

(f) it is evidence to correct a false impression given by the defendant, or

(g) the defendant has made an attack on another person's character.

Section 101(2) CJA 2003 directs the court to sections 102 to 106 of that Act which contain provisions to supplement this. Further, under sections 101(3) and (4):

(3) The court must not admit evidence under subsection (1)(d) or (g) if, on an application by the defendant to exclude it, it appears to the court that the admission of the evidence would have such an adverse effect on the fairness of the proceedings that the court ought not to admit it.

(4) On an application to exclude evidence under subsection (3) the court must have regard, in particular, to the length of time between the matters to which that evidence relates and the matters which form the subject of the offence charged.

'Important explanatory evidence' has the same meaning as in relation to non-defendants (see section 102 CJA 2003). 'Matters in issue between the defendant and the prosecution' are expressly stated to include the questions whether:

- the defendant has a propensity to commit offences of the kind with which he is charged, except where his having such a propensity makes it no more likely that he is guilty of the offence;
- the defendant has a propensity to be untruthful, except where it is not suggested that the defendant's case is untruthful in any respect.

Also, where a defendant's propensity to commit offences of the kind with which he is charged is in issue this may (without prejudice to any other way of doing so) be established by evidence that he has been convicted of:

- an offence of the same description as the one with which he is charged; or
- an offence of the same category as the one with which he is charged.

However, this does not apply in the case of a particular defendant if the court is satisfied, by reason of the length of time since the conviction or for any other reason, that it would be unjust for it to apply in his or her case. Two offences are of the same *description* as each other if the statement of the offence in a written charge or indictment would, in each case, be in the same terms; and two offences are of the *same category* as each other if they belong to the same category of offences prescribed for the purposes of these provisions of the CJA 2003 by the Secretary of State. Only prosecution evidence is admissible under section 101(1)(d) above.

Matters in issue between the defendant and a co-defendant

Under section 104(1) CJA 2003, evidence which is relevant to the question whether the defendant has a propensity to be untruthful is admissible on that basis under section 101(1)(e) only if the nature or conduct of his or her defence is such as to undermine the co-defendant's defence; and under section 104(2) only evidence: (a) which is to be (or has been) adduced by the co-defendant, or (b) which a witness is to be invited to give (or has given) in cross-examination by the co-defendant, is admissible under section 101(1)(e).

'Evidence to correct a false impression'
For the purposes of section 101(1)(f):

(a) the defendant gives a false impression if he is responsible for the making of an express or implied assertion which is apt to give the court or jury a false or misleading impression about the defendant;
(b) evidence to correct such an impression is evidence which has probative value in correcting it.

Under section 105(2) CJA 2003, a defendant is treated as being responsible for the making of an assertion if -

(a) the assertion is made by the defendant in the proceedings (whether or not in evidence given by him),
(b) the assertion was made by the defendant-
(i) on being questioned under caution, before charge, about the offence with which he is charged, or
(ii) on being charged with the offence or officially informed that he might be prosecuted for it,
and evidence of the assertion is given in the proceedings,
(c) the assertion is made by a witness called by the defendant,
(d) the assertion is made by any witness in cross-examination in response to a question asked by the defendant that is intended to elicit it, or is likely to do so, or
(e) the assertion was made by any person out of court, and the defendant adduces evidence of it in the proceedings.

Under section 105(3) CJA 2003, defendants who would otherwise be treated as responsible for the making of an assertion shall not be so treated if, or to the extent that, they withdraw it or disassociate themselves from it. Under section 105(4), where it appears to the court that a defendant, by means of his or her conduct (other than the giving of evidence) in the proceedings, is seeking to give the court or jury an impression about himself or herself that is false or misleading, the court may if it appears just to do so treat the defendant as being responsible for the making of an assertion which is apt to give that impression. Section 105(5) provides that 'conduct' includes appearance or dress.
Evidence is admissible under section 101(1)(f) only if it goes no further than is necessary to correct the false impression and only prosecution evidence is admissible under that provision.

Attacking another person's character
Under section 106(1) CJA 2003, a defendant makes an attack on another person's character (for the purposes of section 101(1)(g)) if:

(a) he adduces evidence attacking the other person's character,
(b) he (or any legal representative appointed under section 38(4) of the Youth Justice and Criminal Evidence Act 1999 (c. 23) to cross-examine a witness in his interests)

asks questions in cross-examination that are intended to elicit such evidence, or are likely to do so, or

(c) evidence is given of an imputation about the other person made by the defendant -
(i) on being questioned under caution, before charge, about the offence with which he is charged, or
(ii) on being charged with the offence or officially informed that he might be prosecuted for it.

And also:

In subsection (1) 'evidence attacking the other person's character' means evidence to the effect that the other person -
(a) has committed an offence (whether a different offence from the one with which the defendant is charged or the same one), or
(b) has behaved, or is disposed to behave, in a reprehensible way;
and 'imputation about the other person' means an assertion to that effect.

Under section 106(3) CJA 2003, only prosecution evidence is admissible under section 101(1)(g).

Contaminated evidence: Stopping the case

Under section 107(1) CJA 2003 if, on a defendant's trial before a judge and jury for an offence:

(a) evidence of his bad character has been admitted under any of paragraphs (c) to (g) of section 101(1), and
(b) the court is satisfied at any time after the close of the case for the prosecution that -
(i) the evidence is contaminated, and
(ii) the contamination is such that, considering the importance of the evidence to the case against the defendant, his conviction of the offence would be unsafe,
the court must either direct the jury to acquit the defendant of the offence or, if it considers that there ought to be a retrial, discharge the jury.

Under section 107(2) CJA 2003, where (a) a jury is directed under subsection (1) to acquit a defendant, and (b) the circumstances are such that, apart from this subsection, the defendant could if acquitted of that offence be found guilty of another offence, the defendant may not be found guilty of that other offence if the court is satisfied as mentioned in section 107(1)(b) in respect of it.

Under section 107(3) CJA 2003, if (a) a jury is required to determine under section 4A(2) of the Criminal Procedure (Insanity) Act 1964 (c. 84) whether a person charged on an indictment with an offence did the act or made the omission charged, (b) evidence of the person's bad character has been admitted under any of paragraphs (c) to (g) of section 101(1), and (c) the court is satisfied at any time after the close of the case for the prosecution that: (i) the evidence is contaminated, and (ii) the contamination is such that, considering the importance of the evidence to the case against the person, a finding that he did the act or made the omission would be unsafe, the court must either direct the jury to acquit the defendant of the offence or, if it considers that there ought to be a rehearing, discharge the jury.

The provisions do not prejudice any other power a court may have to direct a jury to acquit a person of an offence or to discharge a jury.

Under section 107(5), for the purposes of this section a person's evidence is contaminated where: (a) as a result of an agreement or understanding between the person and one or more others, or (b) as a result of the person being aware of anything alleged by one or more others whose evidence may be, or has been, given in the proceedings, the evidence is false or misleading in any respect, or is different from what it would otherwise have been.

Offences committed by the defendant when a child
Under section 108 (1) CJA 2003, section 16(2) and (3) of the Children and Young Persons Act 1963 (offences committed by a person under 14 disregarded for purposes of evidence relating to previous convictions) cease to have effect. But under section 108(2), in proceedings for an offence committed or alleged to have been committed by a defendant when aged 21 or over, evidence of his or her conviction for an offence when under the age of 14 is not admissible unless (a) both offences are indictable only, and (b) the court is satisfied that the interests of justice require the evidence to be admissible.

Section 108(3) CJA 2003 expressly states that subsection (2) applies in addition to section 101 (general provisions relating to a defendant's character).

Assumption of truth in assessment of relevance or probative value
Section 109(1) states that a reference to the relevance or probative value of evidence is 'on the assumption that it is true'. But this is subject to section 109(2), which allows this assumption to be displaced (albeit setting a high standard):

> In assessing the relevance or probative value of an item of evidence for any purpose of [these provisions], a court need not assume that the evidence is true if it appears, on the basis of any material before the court (including any evidence it decides to hear on the matter), that no court or jury could reasonably find it to be true.

The court's duty to give reasons for rulings
Under section 110 CJA 2003, where the court makes a relevant ruling (a) it must state in open court (but in the absence of the jury, if there is one) its reasons for the ruling; (b) if it is a magistrates' court, it must cause the ruling and the reasons for it to be entered in the register of the court's proceedings. 'Relevant ruling' means one (a) whether an item of evidence is evidence of a person's bad character; (b) whether an item of such evidence is admissible under section 100 or 101 (including rulings under section 101(3)); (c) under section 107 (contaminated evidence).

Rules of court
Section 111(1) CJA 2003 enables rules of court to be made for the purposes of the CJA 2003. Section 111(2) states that the rules may, and, where the party in question is the prosecution, must, contain provision requiring a party who: (a) proposes to adduce evidence of a defendant's bad character, or (b) proposes to cross-examine a witness with a view to eliciting such evidence, to serve on the defendant such notice, and such particulars of or relating to the evidence, as may be prescribed. Further, the rules may provide that the court or defendant may, in such circumstances as may be prescribed, dispense with a requirement imposed by virtue of subsection (2). In considering the exercise of its powers with respect

to costs, the court may take into account any failure by a party to comply with a requirement imposed by virtue of subsection (2) and not dispensed with by virtue of subsection (3).

Under section 111 (5), the rules may: (a) limit the application of any provision of the rules to prescribed circumstances; (b) subject any provision of the rules to prescribed exceptions; (c) make different provision for different cases or circumstances.

Under section 111(6) 'nothing in this section prejudices the generality of any enactment conferring power to make rules of court'; and no particular provision of this section prejudices any general provision of it.

HEARSAY

Historically, there has been reluctance to allow hearsay (or 'second-hand') evidence to be given in criminal trials, principally on the basis of the inherent unreliability of statements or assertions which are not first-hand and which cannot be directly tested in cross-examination by the other party. It takes just a moment's reflection to realise that if, e.g. someone repeats what another person has said there is no real way of knowing what changes of emphasis or intended meaning may have occurred, not to say that the person repeating a remark etc. in question may comprehend it in a quite different way from the person who made it. Given the serious consequences that flow from a criminal conviction, only certain carefully justified and strictly confined exceptions to the rule against hearsay have emerged in several centuries of criminal trials. The position is otherwise in civil matters where hearsay has been widely admissible from at least the 1960s onwards.

It is important to remember that even where hearsay *is* admitted as evidence in a criminal case a higher standard of proof applies than in a civil case, 'beyond reasonable doubt', and that the evidence remains to be weighed by the court which will, e.g. take account of its actual provenance and any risks of inaccuracy or mistake inherent in the 're-telling'. Certain hearsay items, however, may be as sound as an original, first-hand statement, as where evidence of the contents of a document is made admissible and that document was compiled by a person with first-hand knowledge. There may still be difficulties in testing such evidence, nonetheless and it is always for the court to decide what effect any piece of evidence may have in the overall context of a trial.

Admissibility of hearsay: The general position post-CJA 2003

The CJA 2003 abolishes the existing, common law hearsay rule and (subject to certain items that are expressly preserved) the exceptions to it and creates a new statutory code under which hearsay evidence may be admissible under given heads reflecting - but not reproducing - certain of those exceptions. A key provision is section 114(1) to (3) CJA 2003 which sets out the circumstances in which a statement that is not given in oral evidence from the witness box during criminal proceedings, i.e. by the person with first-hand knowledge (and sometimes called an 'out-of-court' statement) can be used as evidence of the facts stated within it. The overall intention can be gleaned from the Home Office guidance notes to the Act which explain the situation as follows:

If B was charged with robbery of a jewellers, the prosecution might want A to testify that B told her that he was 'outside the jewellers at midday on Monday' in order to prove that B was outside the jewellers at the relevant time. As [the provisions of the CJA 2003] remove the common law rule against the admission of such hearsay evidence, this out-of court statement will be admissible in A's testimony, *provided* it comes under one of the following heads:

- It is admissible under a statutory provision;
- It is admissible under a common law rule preserved by [Part 11 of the CJA 2003];
- The parties agree that it can go in; or
- The court gives leave to admit the statement.

Before a court can grant leave to admit such a statement (i.e. under the fourth head above (as per section 114(1)(d) CJA 2003), it must be satisfied that it is in the interests of justice to admit the evidence. The intention is thus that a criminal court should be able to admit out-of-court statements that do not fall within any of the three preceding categories of admissibility, provided that it is cogent and reliable. Section 114(2) sets out certain factors (but not necessarily all the factors) that the court must consider when deciding whether to grant under section 114(1)(d). These include:

- the degree of relevance of the statement in proving a matter in issue in the trial (always assuming the statement to be true: see later);
- the circumstances in which it was made (if, of course, it was in fact made);
- the extent to which it supplies evidence that would not otherwise be available;
- the creditworthiness of the maker of the statement;
- the reason why oral evidence cannot be given;
- the extent to which the other party can challenge the statement; and
- the risk of unfairness.

It can be seen that the list focuses on whether the circumstances surrounding the making of the out-of-court statement indicate that it can be viewed as reliable enough to be admitted in evidence, despite the fact that the original maker of that statement will not be subject to cross-examination. Nonetheless, section 114(3) CJA 2003 provides that any out-of-court statement may still be excluded, e.g. a confession statement which does not satisfy the further requirements of sections 76 and 78 PACE.

Statements covered by the new provisions

Section 115 sets out the kind of statements covered by the provisions. One purpose is to overturn the effect of *R. v. Kearley* [1992] 2 AC 228 that 'implied assertions' are covered by the hearsay rule and therefore *prima facie* inadmissible. Under section 115(3), a statement will be one to which the new provisions apply if it is the purpose of the person making the statement to:

- cause the hearer to believe that the matter stated is true or to act on the basis that it is true; or
- cause a machine to operate on the basis that the matter is as stated.

Thus, section 115 alters the common law position so that such implied assertions are not prevented from being admissible. Equally, where the assertion relates to a failure to record an event (sometimes called 'negative hearsay'), it will not be covered by the provisions if it was not the purpose of the person who failed to record the event to cause anyone to believe that the event did not occur. Section 115(2) then preserves the rule whereby statements not based on human input fall outside the ambit of the hearsay rule. Tapes, films or photographs which directly record the commission of an offence and documents produced by machines which automatically record a process or event or perform calculations will not therefore be covered.

Cases in which a witness is 'unavailable'

Section 116 lists various categories under which first-hand hearsay evidence, whether oral or documentary, will be admissible, provided that the witness is unavailable to testify for a statutory reason. A statement will be admissible (subject to the further conditions outlined below) if the person who made it is:

- dead;
- ill;
- absent abroad;
- disappeared; or
- in fear.

Section 116(2)(e) and (4) CJA 2003 provides for the admissibility, with the *leave* of the court, of statements of witnesses who are too frightened to testify (or continue testifying) provided that the interests of justice do not decree otherwise. In considering the interests of justice, the court should have regard to the contents of the statement; any risk of unfairness to other parties in a case; the fact that 'special measures' directions[5] may be made in relation to a witness under the Youth Justice and Criminal Evidence Act 1999; and any other relevant circumstances; and 'fear' is to be widely construed.

Various other conditions apply to the admissibility of evidence under section 116. Thus a statement can only be adduced in evidence to show the *truth* of any matter stated if:

- the witness's oral evidence would have been admissible itself; and
- the person who made the statement is identified to the court's satisfaction (thereby allowing the opposing party to challenge the absent witness's credibility under section 124 CJA 2003: see later).

In addition, even if all the relevant conditions noted above are satisfied, the evidence will not be allowed if a party, or someone acting on his or her behalf, causes the unavailability of the original maker of the statement (section 116(5)).

Business documents and the like

Section 117 provides for the admissibility of statements in documentary records provided that certain conditions are met. These conditions are that:

---

[5] Whereby a child witness can give evidence other than face-to-face with the accused in court.

- the document was created or received by someone in the course of a trade, business, profession or as the holder of a paid or unpaid office; and
- the person who supplied the information in the statement had or may reasonably be supposed to have had personal knowledge of the matters dealt with in the statement; and
- each person through whom the information was supplied received the information in the course of a trade, business, profession or other occupation or as the holder of a paid or unpaid office.

This reflects existing law relating to business and other documents (i.e. in section 24 Criminal Justice Act 1988: to be repealed). However, in the case of documents prepared for the purpose of criminal investigations or proceedings, the statement will only be admissible if the supplier of the information is unavailable or cannot reasonably be expected to recall any of the matters dealt with in the statement. Even where a statement in a documentary record meets the conditions in section 117, evidence will be excluded if considered unreliable. Section 117(6) and (7) allow the court to direct that a statement shall not be admissible if there is reason to doubt its reliability on the basis of its contents, source of information, mode of supply, or circumstances of creation or reception.

Preservation of common law categories of admissibility
Section 118 CJA 2003 preserves certain common law exceptions to the existing hearsay rule so that, in specified circumstances, an out-of-court statement will be admissible as evidence of any statements contained in it. These are:

- **public information:** including published works, public documents, records of certain courts, treaties, Crown grants, pardons and commissions, and evidence relating to a person's age or date of birth;
- **reputation as to character:** which will be admissible as evidence either of good or bad character;
- **reputation or family tradition:** which will be admissible as evidence to prove or disprove pedigree, the existence of marriage, a public or general right, or the identity of a person or thing;
- *res gestae:* explained separately below;
- **confessions:** provided that they satisfy sections 76 and 78 of PACE;
- **admissions by agents:** which will be admissible against an accused person as evidence of any fact stated in them;
- **'common enterprise':** whereby a statement made by any party to a common enterprise is admissible against another party to that enterprise as evidence of any matter stated; and
- **expert evidence:** the rule permitting an expert to give evidence of any relevant matter forming part of his or her professional expertise - even though not acquired from personal experience - and to draw upon technical information widely used by members of his or her profession.

The *res gestae* exception
The CJA 2003 preserves (in statutory form) the rule whereby reported words that are very closely connected to a relevant event - such as the instant, unthinking and natural reactions or comments of a bystander - are deemed to be capable of

forming reliable accounts in certain circumstances. Evidence of these may be admitted if any one of the following pre-conditions is met:

- the statement is made by a person who was so emotionally overpowered by an event that the possibility that he or she was lying can be disregarded;
- the statement accompanied an act which can properly be evaluated as evidence only if considered together with the statement (e.g. if the act does not make sense without the statement); or
- the statement relates to a physical sensation or mental state, such as an intention or emotion.

Inconsistent statements

Section 119 CJA 2003 clarifies the relationship between hearsay evidence and previous inconsistent statements and thereby looks to settle a problem of evidence that began in the late nineteenth century. The section provides that if a witness admits that he or she has made a previous inconsistent statement (or it has been proved that he or she made such a statement) this is not only evidence which undermines his or her 'credibility' but also evidence that can, subject to consideration by the court, establish the truth of its contents. The Home Office explanatory notes envisage the following type of situation:

> A makes a statement to the police that she saw B 'outside the jewellers' at mid-day on Monday'. A does not testify at the trial but her statement is admitted under Section 116 [above] . . . section 124 [CJA 2003: see later] provides that evidence can be admitted in this type of situation in relation to the credibility of A . . . to prove that A had made another statement inconsistent with this statement (for example, A had said earlier that she did not see B on Monday at all). Section 119(2) provides that if there is such an inconsistent statement, it not only goes to the credibility of A, but it is also admissible as to the truth of its contents (that A did not see B on Monday).

Other previous statements by witnesses

Section 120 CJA 2003 makes other previous statements admissible as evidence of the truth of their contents (not merely, e.g. to bolster the credibility of a witness's testimony in court) as follows:

- to statements to rebut a suggestion that a witness's oral evidence is untrue;
- in the situation where a witness is 'refreshing his or her memory' from a written document. If he or she is cross-examined on the document and it is received in evidence, it will be evidence of anything contained in it;
- a previous statement will be admissible as evidence of the facts contained in it provided the witness states that he or she made the statement and believes it to be *true and* one of the following conditions is met:
  — it describes or identifies a person, place or thing (including, e.g. objects like a vehicle registration number); or
  — it was made when the incident was fresh in the witness's memory and he or she cannot reasonably be expected to remember the matters stated. The intention here being that where a witness has to rely on someone else, or a document, or both to complete details which he or she can no longer remember, this should affect the weight of the evidence, but not its inadmissibility; or

—it consists of a complaint by a victim of the alleged offence made as soon as could reasonably be expected after the conduct in question, and the witness gives oral evidence in relation to the matter. Here, there is a further requirement for such a statement to be admissible, i.e. the complaint must not stem from a threat or a promise.

Multiple hearsay: Extra requirements in the interests of caution

Section 121 CJA 2003 sets out the approach that criminal courts should take to multiple hearsay, i.e. where information has passed via more than one person before being recorded or relayed. Under section 121 a hearsay statement is admissible to prove the fact that another statement was made in three instances:

- where either of the statements is admissible under sections 117 (business documents), 119 (inconsistent statements) or 120 (other previous statement of a witness);
- all parties to the proceedings agree; or
- the court in its discretion determines to admit the statement.

The test for the court in such circumstances is whether it is satisfied that the value of the evidence under consideration, taking into account how reliable the statement appears to be, is so high that the interests of justice require the later statement to be admissible for that purpose. This residual discretion would seem to be intended for exceptional circumstances where multiple hearsay does not fall within a specified category of admissibility but should nevertheless be admitted in the interests of justice.

Documents produced as exhibits

Section 122 CJA 2003 provides that if a statement previously made by a witness is admitted in evidence and produced as an exhibit (under sections 119 or 120 CJA 2003 (above)), a jury should not take it with them when they retire to their room unless the court considers this appropriate or all the parties agree to this.

Capability to make statement

Section 123 CJA 2003 states that an out-of-court statement cannot be admitted under sections 116, 119 or 120 (above) if the maker of the statement did not have the 'required capability' to make a statement at the time when it was made. A statement may thus not be admitted if anyone who supplied or received the information or created or received the document did not have that capability, or, where that person cannot be identified, cannot reasonably be assumed to have had that capability. Under section 123(2) a person is deemed to have capability for the purposes of this provision if he or she can understand questions put to him or her and give answers which can be understood.[6]

Credibility

Section 124 CJA 2003 makes provision for challenges to the credibility of the maker of a hearsay statement who does not give testimony in the proceedings. If

---

[6] This reflects the test for witness competence contained in section 53 Youth Justice and Criminal Evidence Act 1999.

such a statement is admitted as evidence of a matter stated in it, there are certain rights for the person against whom that evidence has been admitted to produce, in specified circumstances, evidence to discredit the maker of the statement or to show that he or she has contradicted himself or herself.[7]

Stopping the case where evidence is unconvincing

Section 125(1) CJA 2003 places a duty on the Crown Court to stop a case and either direct the jury to acquit the defendant, or discharge the jury, if the case against him or her is based wholly or partly on an out-of-court statement that is so unconvincing that, considering its importance to the case, a conviction would be unsafe. This only arises in relation to jury trials (or by virtue of paragraph 4 of Schedule 7 to 'service courts'). In the magistrates' court it seems to have been assumed that the magistrates themselves - as the tribunal of both law and fact - will be duty bound to dismiss the case at the end of the prosecution case (and even if no submission was made) under the general law.

Similarly, section 125(2) imposes a corresponding duty on a judge to direct the jury to acquit of any other offence not charged, of which they could convict by way of an alternative to the offence charged, if satisfied that a conviction would be unsafe - and section 125(3) extends that duty to cases under the Criminal Procedure (Insanity) Act 1964 where the jury is required to determine whether a defendant, who is deemed unfit to plead, did the act (or made the omission) charged.

The court's general discretion to exclude evidence

Section 126 gives the court a discretion to exclude what in effect would be 'superfluous' out-of-court evidence if it is satisfied that the value of the evidence is substantially outweighed by the undue waste of time which its admission would entail. The provision preserves both the existing common law power for the court to exclude evidence where its prejudicial effect is out of proportion to its probative value and the discretion in section 78 of PACE in relation to the admission of unfair evidence.

Preparatory work by experts

Section 127 seeks to address the problem that arises where information relied upon by an expert witness is outside his or her personal experience (such as work carried out by an assistant) and which cannot be proved by other admissible evidence. Seemingly, the Government intends that the rules about advance notice of expert evidence will be amended so as to require advance notice of the name of any person who has prepared information on which the expert has relied. It is also envisaged that any other party to the proceedings will be able to apply for a direction that any such person must give evidence in person - but a direction will only be given if the court is satisfied this is in the interests of justice. In cases where no such application is made in respect of any assistant in the list of witnesses, or an application is made but refused, section 127 will allow the expert witness to base his or her evidence on any information

---

[7] Replacing a corresponding provision: section 28(2) and paragraph 1 of Schedule 2 to the CJA 1988.

supplied by that assistant on matters of which that assistant had personal knowledge. The provision applies if:

- the statement was prepared for the purpose of criminal proceedings;
- the assistant had or might reasonably be supposed to have had personal knowledge of the matters stated; and
- a notice has been given under the advance notice rules (*Chapter 4*) of the name of a person who has prepared a statement on which it is proposed the expert should base any opinion or inference, and the nature of matters stated.

The expert may then base an opinion or inference on the statement and any information so relied upon will be admissible as evidence of its truth. Further provisions of section 127 allow a party to the proceedings to apply for an order that the exception should not apply in the interests of justice.

Confession evidence
Section 128 CJA 2003 inserts a new section 76A into PACE. The existing position is that whilst the prosecutor cannot not make use of a confession which was obtained in breach of PACE, a co-defendant could do so to undermine another co-defendant's account or to strengthen his or her own case. The new section 76A applies the same rules to confessions adduced by a co-defendant to those adduced by the prosecutor under PACE, i.e. the confession will not be allowed if obtained by oppression or it is rendered unreliable.[8]

Unlike the requirements for the prosecutor, under section 76A, the co-accused would only need to satisfy the court on the balance of probabilities that the confession was not obtained by oppression or in circumstances likely to render it unreliable. The rule is maintained that the exclusion of a confession does not affect the admissibility of facts discovered as a result of that confession.

Representations other than by a human being
Section 129 states that if a statement generated by a machine is based on information implanted into it by a human, its output will only be admissible if it is proved that the information was accurate. The common law presumption is preserved that a mechanical device has been properly set or calibrated.

Depositions
Section 130 repeals those provisions of the Crime and Disorder Act 1998 which provided that a judge could overrule an objection to a deposition (in effect an earlier statement made by a witness) being read as evidence if he or she considered this to be in the interests of justice.

Evidence at a retrial
In addition to the provisions concerning retrials and 'double jeopardy' described in the *Chapter 6*, section 131 CJA 2003 provides that if a retrial is ordered by the Court of Appeal, evidence must be given orally if it was given that way at the

---

[8] 'Oppression' is defined in identical terms to the same term in section 76(8) of PACE.

original trial except in certain defined situations, in which case a transcript of the earlier evidence may be used, i.e. where:

- all parties agree to the evidence being admitted;
- a witness is unavailable in accordance with section 116 (above); or
- a witness is unavailable for a reason other than those in section 116 and his or her evidence is admitted under the residual discretion afforded by section 114 (above).

Rules of court

Section 132 CJA 2003 confers a power to make rules of court about the provisions in the CJA 2003. The intention is that rules of court will govern both the notice and leave procedures. It is further provided that the court or jury can, with leave, draw an adverse inference from the failure of a party to comply with prescribed requirements.

Proof of statements in documents

Section 133 CJA 2003 corresponds to section 27 Criminal Justice Act 1988, whereby a statement in a document can be proved by producing either the original document or an authenticated copy. This is intended to cover all forms of copying including the use of modern imaging technology.

EVIDENCE BY WAY OF VIDEO RECORDINGS

Section 137 CJA 2003 allows a video recording of an interview with a witness (other than the accused person), or a part of such a recording, to be admitted as the evidence-in-chief of the witness in a wider range of circumstances than under existing law. Section 137(1) provides that a criminal court can authorise such a video recording to replace evidence-in-chief provided that:

- the person claims to be a witness to the offence (or part of it) or to events closely connected to the offence;
- the video recording of the statement was made at a time when events were fresh in the witness's memory; and
- the alleged offence can only be tried in the Crown Court or is an either way offence prescribed by order of the Secretary of State.

If it satisfies these requirements, the court may admit the recording provided that:

- the witness's recollection of events is likely to be significantly better at the time he or she gave the recorded account than by the time of the trial; and
- it is in the interests of justice to admit the recording, having regard to whether the recording is an early and reliable account from the witness, whether the quality is adequate, and any views which the witness may have about using the recording for this purpose.

Further, evidence given by way of a video recording is to be treated as if given orally in court, provided that the witness asserts its truth by giving evidence of this. Where the recording (or part of one) is admitted under section 137, section 138(1) states that the recording should be the final statement of any matters dealt with adequately within the recording for the purpose of the witness's evidence-in-chief. Section 138(2) allows video recordings to be edited where the interests of justice so require. In determining whether to allow only an edited recording to be used, the court will have to consider whether the parts sought to be excluded are so prejudicial as to outweigh the desirability of using the whole recording.

REFRESHING MEMORY

Section 139 CJA 2003 creates a presumption in favour of a witness in criminal proceedings refreshing his or her memory from a document whilst giving evidence provided that:

- he or she indicates that the document represents his or her recollection at the time he or she made it; and
- his or her recollection was likely to be significantly better at the time the document was made (or verified).

The fact that the witness has read the statement before giving his or her testimony does not affect this presumption. In view of the practical difficulties associated with memory refreshing in the witness box from an audio or video recording, section 139 also makes provision for a witness to refresh his or her memory from a transcript of such a recording. These provisions dispense with common law rules restricting the purposes for which such evidence was capable of being used and whereby, among other things, a witness had to demonstrate that such a statement was made 'contemporaneously' with the events to which it related as required following cases such as *R. v. Benjamin* (1913) 2 Cr App Rep 146 which concerned a police officer's notebook.

CHAPTER 6

Prosecution Appeals and the Retrial of Serious Allegations (Exceptions to 'Double Jeopardy')

The CJA 2003 introduces extra prosecution rights of appeal and also provides for the retrial of certain offences by way of exception to the historic principle that someone cannot be twice tried for the same offence, sometimes called *autrefois acquit* - but perhaps best known in common parlance as the rule against 'double jeopardy'. The new law is contained in Parts 9 (appeals) and 10 CJA 2003 (double jeopardy). Section 18 CJA 2003 also extends certain appeal rights of the prosecutor in relation to bail decisions (see *Chapter 2*).

PROSECUTION APPEALS

Part 9 CJA 2003 introduces a range of measures conferring new rights of appeal on the prosecutor in respect of certain rulings made during the proceedings by a judge. Section 57 CJA 2003 provides that such rights apply 'in relation to a trial on indictment'. Although the prosecutor is to have these rights, they do not extend to a ruling that the jury be discharged or where an appeal lies to the Court of Appeal under some other enactment, e.g. from a ruling at a preparatory hearing about the admissibility of evidence or on a point of law. Leave to appeal must be obtained from the judge concerned or the Court of Appeal.

General right of appeal in respect of rulings

Section 58 CJA 2003 applies where the judge makes a ruling 'at an applicable time'[1] and this relates to one or more offences included in the indictment. Thereafter, that ruling has no effect whilst the prosecutor is able to take the steps to challenge it described in section 58(4), under which an appeal is possible if:

    (a) following the making of the ruling, the prosecution
        (i) informs the court that it intends to appeal, or
        (ii) requests an adjournment to consider whether to appeal, and
    (b) if such an adjournment is granted, it informs the court following the adjournment that it intends to appeal.

These rights will cover the situation where a judge rules that there is no case to answer or when some other ruling 'terminates' a trial, whether made at a pre-trial hearing or later. Two types of ruling appear to be in mind, i.e. those that are:

- *terminating in themselves*, i.e. when a judge withdraws a case from the jury; or
- so fatal to the prosecution case that *the prosecutor proposes to treat them as terminating* by offering no further evidence at that stage.[2]

---

[1] Meaning at 'any time (whether before or after the commencement of the trial) before the start of the judge's summing-up to the jury: see section 58(13) CJA 2003. The new appeal is thus interlouctory in nature. Thereafter existing appeal etc. arrangements come into play.

[2] But without prejudice to the right to do so if an appeal is successful: see later in the text.

Depending on the circumstances, the judge will decide[3] whether the appeal should follow an expedited route (when the trial is simply adjourned pending the outcome of the appeal) or a non-expedited route (when any existing jury may be discharged). In either case, the termination and acquittal are 'placed on hold' and the ruling and any consequences are of no effect while the prosecutor considers - subject to an adjournment which the judge may allow for this purpose - whether to appeal and until any appeal is concluded or abandoned. The prosecutor must agree to an acquittal if it should turn out that leave to appeal is not granted or the appeal is abandoned (see section 58(8) to (11)).

The Court of Appeal can confirm, reverse[4] or vary the judge's ruling. If it confirms the ruling, it must order the acquittal of the defendant for the offence to which the appeal relates - and it has a discretion to do so in other circumstances. It may only order that proceedings in the Crown Court should continue or that a fresh trial should be held, if this is necessary in the interests of justice. Both the prosecutor and defendant have a further right of appeal to the House of Lords on a point of law of general public importance.

Section 58(6) and (7) applies where there are two or more offences or 'multiple rulings' are involved (ordinarily only one ruling can be appealed at a time):

(6) Where the ruling relates to two or more offences -
  (a) any one or more of those offences may be the subject of the appeal, and
  (b) if the prosecution informs the court in accordance with subsection (4) [above] that it intends to appeal, it must at the same time inform the court of the offence or offences which are the subject of the appeal.
(7) Where -
  (a) the ruling is a ruling that there is no case to answer, and
  (b) the prosecution, at the same time that it informs the court . . . that it intends to appeal, nominates one or more other rulings which have been made by a judge in relation to the trial on indictment at an applicable time and which relate to the offence or offences which are the subject of the appeal,
the other ruling, or those other rulings are to be treated as the subject of the appeal.

Expedited and non-expedited appeals
Section 59 CJA 2003 provides that where the prosecutor informs the court in accordance that he or she intends to appeal, the judge must decide whether or not the appeal should be expedited (see the basic explanation above). If he or she decides that it should be, he or she may order an adjournment. If the judge decides that the appeal should not be expedited, he or she may either: order an adjournment; or discharge the jury (if already sworn in). The judge or Court of Appeal has power to reverse a decision to expedite an appeal, thus transferring the case to the slower route. If a decision is reversed, the jury may be discharged.

Proceedings for offences not affected by rulings
Section 60 CJA 2003 also applies where the prosecutor informs the court in accordance that he or she intends to appeal a ruling so that proceedings may be

---

[3] It seems likely that this and other areas of judicial discretion will be exercised in accordance with rules of court (made under section 73 CJA 2003 or otherwise) and other appropriate guidance.
[4] But only within the terms of section 67 (see later).

continued in respect of any offence which is not the subject of the appeal. Whether they are allowed to is likely to depend on general principles of fairness.

Determination of the appeal by the Court of Appeal

Under section 61 CJA 2003, the Court of Appeal may confirm, reverse[5] or vary any ruling to which the prosecutor's appeal relates as follows:

(3) Where the Court of Appeal confirms the ruling, it must, in respect of the offence or each offence which is the subject of the appeal, order that the defendant in relation to that offence be acquitted of that offence.

(4) Where the Court of Appeal reverses or varies the ruling, it must, in respect of the offence or each offence which is the subject of the appeal, do any of the following -
   (a) order that proceedings for that offence may be resumed in the Crown Court,
   (b) order that a fresh trial may take place in the Crown Court for that offence,
   (c) order that the defendant in relation to that offence be acquitted of that offence.

(5) But the Court of Appeal may not make an order under subsection (4)(a) or (b) . . . unless it considers it necessary in the interests of justice to do so.

Sections 59(7), (8) apply if the appeal concerns a ruling of no case to answer and one or more other rulings are dealt with at the same time (see above):

(7) Where the Court of Appeal confirms the ruling that there is no case to answer, it must, in respect of the offence or each offence which is the subject of the appeal, order that the defendant in relation to that offence be acquitted of that offence.

(8) Where the Court of Appeal reverses or varies the ruling that there is no case to answer, it must in respect of the offence or each offence which is the subject of the appeal, make any of the orders mentioned in subsection (4)(a) to (c) [see above] (but subject to subsection (5)).

Right of appeal in respect of an evidentiary ruling

Under section 62 CJA 2003, the prosecutor may appeal in respect of a single qualifying evidentiary ruling;[6] or two or more qualifying evidentiary rulings. 'Qualifying evidentiary ruling' means 'an evidentiary ruling of a judge in relation to a trial on indictment which is made at any time (whether before or after the commencement of the trial) before the opening of the case for the defence'.[7]

The prosecutor may not appeal in respect of a single qualifying evidentiary ruling unless that ruling relates to one or more qualifying offences[8] (whether or not it relates to any other offence). Nor may he or she appeal in respect of two or more qualifying evidentiary rulings unless each ruling relates to one or more qualifying offences (whether or not it relates to any other offence). If the prosecutor intends to appeal under section 62, he or she must, before the opening

---

[5] Subject to section 67 CJA 2003: see later in the chapter.

[6] Evidentiary ruling means a ruling relating to the admissibility or exclusion of any prosecution evidence: see section 62(9) CJA 2003.

[7] Section 62(2) CJA 2003. Contrast the general right of appeal under section 58 above, which is normally confined to individual rulings (and available until start of the summing-up to the jury).

[8] 'Qualifying offence' means an offence listed in Schedule 4, Part 1 CJA 2003: section 62(9) CJA 2003. These offences range from murder, manslaughter and kidnapping to rape and a range of other sexual offences, certain drug offences, robbery with a weapon, arson with intent to endanger life, certain war crimes, hostage-taking, hijacking and conspiracy. The Secretary of State may amend Part 1 of that schedule by order to add, remove or modify a description of offence.

of the case for the defence, inform the court of the intention to do so; and of the ruling or rulings to which the appeal relates.

Under section 62(6), in respect of the ruling, or each ruling, to which the appeal relates: the qualifying offence, or at least one of the qualifying offences, to which the ruling relates must be the subject of the appeal; and any other offence to which the ruling relates may, but need not, be the subject of the appeal. The prosecutor must, at the same time that he or she informs the court of the intention to appeal, inform it of the offence or offences that are the subject of the appeal.

Pursuant to section 62(8), the defence case opens when - after the conclusion of the prosecution case - the earliest of the following events happens:

- evidence begins to be adduced by or on behalf of a defendant;
- it is indicated to the court that no evidence will be adduced by or on behalf of a defendant; or
- the defence case is opened, as permitted by section 2 Criminal Procedure Act 1865.

It is expressly provided that nothing in section 62 affects the right of the prosecutor to appeal in respect of an evidentiary ruling under section 58 CJA 2003 (which provides for a more general right of appeal) as outlined above.

Condition that an evidentiary ruling significantly weakens prosecution case

Under section 63 CJA 2003, leave to appeal may not be given in relation to an appeal under section 62 unless the judge or Court of Appeal is satisfied that the relevant condition is fulfilled. Further, in relation to an appeal in respect of a single evidentiary ruling, the relevant condition is that the ruling significantly weakens the prosecution case in relation to the offence or offences that are the subject of the appeal. With two or more evidentiary rulings, the condition is that the rulings *taken together* significantly weaken that case.

Expedited and non-expedited appeals

As with the more general appeals described above, under section 64 CJA 2003, once a prosecutor informs the court of his or her intention to appeal in accordance with section 62 (above), the judge must decide whether or not the appeal should be expedited. The obligations, rights, procedures and effects are then similar to those for general rulings as noted above.

Continuation of proceedings for offences not affected by rulings

Similarly again, section 65 CJA 2003 provides that other proceedings may be continued in respect of any offence which is not the subject of the appeal.

Powers of the Court of Appeal

On an appeal under section 62, the Court of Appeal may, in accordance with section 66 CJA 2003, confirm, reverse[9] or vary any evidentiary ruling to which the appeal relates. In addition, it must, in respect of the offence or each offence that is the subject of the appeal, order one of the following (section 66(2)):

---

[9] Subject to section 67 CJA 2003: see under next heading.

(a) that proceedings for that offence be resumed in the Crown Court,

(b) that a fresh trial may take place in the Crown Court for that offence,

(c) that the defendant in relation to that offence be acquitted of that offence.

These provisions are designed to ensure that the Court of Appeal will always make clear what is to happen next. By virtue of Section 66(3), the Court of Appeal may only order an acquittal (i.e. under head (c) above) if the prosecution has indicated that it does not intend to continue with the prosecution of that offence. This appears to be designed to cater for the situation where the prosecutor anticipates that the effect of a given ruling on the prosecution would be so damaging that he or she does not wish to proceed with the prosecution.

Reversal of rulings

Under section 67 CJA 2003, the Court of Appeal may not reverse a ruling on an appeal under Part 9 CJA 2003 - whether in relation to the general right of appeal against a judge's ruling or in respect of an evidentiary ruling - unless it is satisfied that it: was wrong in law; or involved an error of law or principle; or was one that it was not reasonable for the judge to have made.

Effect on time limits in relation to preliminary stages

Section 22 Prosecution of Offences Act 1985 (which deals with the power of the Secretary of State to set time limits in relation to the preliminary stages of criminal proceedings) is amended by the insertion of a new section 22(6)(B) which provides that:

> Any period during which proceedings for an offence are adjourned pending the determination of an appeal under Part 9 of the Criminal Justice Act 2003 shall be disregarded, so far as the offence is concerned, for the purposes of the overall time limit and the custody time limit which applies to the stage which the proceedings have reached when they are adjourned.

RESTRICTIONS ON REPORTING

Section 71 CJA 2003 forbids publication of reports of appeals occurring under the various provisions of Part 9 CJA 2003 as described above. This overall prohibition is mitigated by section 71(7) and (8) which confirms that the restriction ends with the conclusion of the relevant trial. Neither does it apply to the usual purely formal details, including the court venue, the nature of the offences, or the names of the accused person, witnesses and legal representatives. Under section 71(2) to (4) the judge, Court of Appeal or the House of Lords can order a reporting restriction to be lifted, either in its entirety or to a specified extent. If one or more defendants objects to this, such an order can only be made if it would be in the interests of justice (section 75(5) and (6)). Other powers or restrictions affecting reporting of criminal cases are preserved (section 71(10)).

Offences in connection with reporting

Section 72 CJA 2003 applies where a publication includes a report in contravention of section 71. Where the publication is by way of a newspaper or periodical, any proprietor, editor or publisher commits the offence. In relation to a 'relevant programme' (essentially including television and radio programmes) any body corporate[10] engaged in providing the programme service in which that programme is included together with any person having functions in relation to the programme corresponding to those of an editor of a newspaper. In other situations, any person publishing the report commits an offence; and where an offence is proved to have been committed by a body corporate but with the consent or connivance of, or neglect on the part of, one of its officers, that officer (as well as the body corporate) is also guilty of the offence.

The maximum penalty on summary conviction is a fine not exceeding level 5 (£5,000). Proceedings may only be instituted in England and Wales by or with the consent of the Attorney General.[11]

Some further definitions and limitations

For the purposes of Part 9 CJA 2003, section 71 provides a number of further definitions and limitations: thus 'ruling' includes a decision, determination, direction, finding, notice, order, refusal, rejection or requirement; and any reference to a judge is normally a reference to a judge of the Crown Court. There is no right of appeal under Part 9 in respect of a ruling in relation to which the prosecutor has previously informed the court of his or her intention to appeal under either section 58(4) or 62(5). Where a ruling relates to two or more offences but not all of those offences are the subject of an appeal under Part 9, nothing in Part 9 is to be regarded as affecting the ruling so far as it relates to any offences which are not the subject of the appeal. Also, where two or more defendants are charged jointly with the same offence, the provisions apply as if the offence, so far as relating to each defendant, were a separate offence (so that, e.g. any reference to a ruling that relates to one or more offences includes a ruling which relates to one or more of those separate offences).

EXCEPTIONS TO THE 'DOUBLE JEOPARDY' RULE

The double jeopardy rule has a long and opaque history. It is a simple thing to say that 'a man or woman shall not be twice tried for the same offence' - a rule possibly traceable to Magna Carta - but quite another to determine what this means in practice, since there are many offences that, for legal purposes, are similar to one another - where the same legal or basic factual ingredients are involved, or where the facts that establish one offence necessarily embrace those of another - so that once someone has been acquitted of one offence it would be wrong to try him or her for some other matter. A considerable body of law has built up around such matters. Whatever the changes described below, it should be noted that this underlying body of law will remain applicable - in the background - to cases covered by the new law but more obviously in relation to cases not covered by it.[12]

---

[10] Or Scottish partnership.

[11] Special provisions apply to Northern Ireland.

[12] It does not seem necessary to outline these existing principles here, merely to allude to their existence. In recent times and in popular culture, the 'double jeopardy' rule has been linked with the Stephen Lawrence case in which four defendants were acquitted of an allegedly racist murder

The existing rule against a second trial is often said to be grounded in finality of proceedings, a further argument being that if an investigator or prosecutor knows that he or she may have a second 'bite at the cherry' he or she may prepare less thoroughly (and thus less fairly) at the outset. But with advances in technology including DNA testing and the ability to examine documents and materials more closely it has become possible to re-open old files many years on and long after the events in question. There are thus cases where it can now be shown unequivocally that someone who was once acquitted must have been guilty (and of course vice versa: and the miscarriage of justice cases).

Retrial of certain serious offences

Section 75 CJA 2003 deals with cases that may be retried. The provisions come into play where someone has been tried for and acquitted of a qualifying offence on indictment in England and Wales (i.e. in the Crown Court); or on appeal against a conviction, sentence or finding on indictment; or on appeal from such a decision. Qualifying offences are listed in Schedule 5 CJA 2003[13] to include:

- murder, attempted murder and manslaughter;
- kidnapping;
- a range of offences under the Sexual Offences Acts (SOA) 1956 or 2003 (as applicable), i.e. rape, attempted rape, sexual intercourse with a girl below the age of 13, incest by a man with a girl under 13, assault by penetration, causing someone to engage in sexual activity without consent (provided within section 4(4)(a) to (d) of the SOA 2003), rape of a child under 13, attempted rape of child under 13, assault of a child under 13 by penetration, causing a child under 13 to engage in sexual activity (provided within section 8(2)(a) to (d) SOA 2003), sexual activity with a person with a mental disorder impeding choice (provided within section 30(3)(a) to (d) SOA 2003), and causing a person with a mental disorder impeding choice to engage in sexual activity (provided with section 31(3)(a) to (d) SOA 2003);
- a range of drugs offences all relating to Class A drugs, i.e. unlawful importation, unlawful exportation, fraudulent evasion in respect of such a drug, and producing or being concerned in its production;
- criminal damage by fire ('arson') endangering life or property;
- causing an explosion likely to endanger life or property;
- intent or conspiracy to cause an explosion likely to endanger life or property;
- genocide, crimes against humanity and war crimes;
- grave breaches of Geneva Conventions;
- directing a terrorist organization;
- hostage-taking; and
- conspiracy to commit any of the above offences.[14]

---

and the subsequent MacPherson Report that was critical of the Metropolitan Police Service. A campaign grew for at least some of the accused to be tried again after 'better' evidence came to light. The changes are in fact based on a report of the Law Commission which was already working on the issue and to which the government referred matters following MacPherson. However, the CJA 2003 encompasses a wider range of offences than the commission envisaged.

[13] Full statutory references for listed offences can be found in the Schedule. The list given here only contains such references where there is a special limitation.

[14] A broadly comparable list for Northern Ireland is contained in Part 2 of Schedule 5 to the CJA 2003.

Offences of aiding, abetting, counselling or procuring such offences are also included by virtue of Part 3 of Schedule 5 to the CJA 2003 as are offences under relevant enactments 'as amended from time to time'.

Someone who has been thus acquitted is also treated as having been acquitted of any qualifying offence of which he or she could have been convicted in those proceedings and the new law also applies where there has been a finding of 'not guilty by reason of insanity' or where the accused was found to be under a disability for the purposes of section 4 Criminal Procedure (Insanity) Act 1964 (section 75(2)). There are inter-jurisdictional arrangements within the UK (see section 75(4)) and certain other foreign jurisdictions (section 75(5)).

The provisions apply whether the acquittal was before or after the passing of the CJA 2003. However, it will be interesting to see whether this provision is compatible with Article 6 of the European Convention On Human Rights[15] pursuant to which there can be no punishment without law, no retrospective criminal legislation.

Application to bring proceedings for a retrial

A prosecutor is not given *carte blanche* to commence proceedings. Under section 76 CJA 2003, he or she may apply to the Court of Appeal for an order:

- quashing someone's acquittal; and
- ordering him or her to be retried for the particular qualifying offence.

Similarly, where an acquittal took place in another part of the UK, the prosecutor can apply for the Court of Appeal's ruling as to whether it is a bar to proceedings and if it is not then an order for a retrial (section 76(2)). The consent of the DPP is required to such an application and the DPP can only give that consent if satisfied that:

- there is evidence as respects which the requirements of section 78 CJA 2003 are met;
- it is in the public interest[16] for the application to proceed; and
- any trial pursuant to such an order would not be inconsistent with obligations of the UK under Article 31 or 34 of the Treaty on European Union relating to the principle of *ne bis in idem.*[17]

Once an application has been made the Court of Appeal must make the order applied for or otherwise dismiss the application dependent on whether the criteria in relation to 'new and compelling evidence' and the 'interests of justice' are met (section 77(1)). Similarly, where it decides that the acquittal *is* a bar to

---

[15] The whole Act is certified as being so compatible, of course.
[16] The terms 'public interest' or 'interests of justice' figure as criteria at several points in the CJA 2003 both in relation to the courts and the Secretary of State. It is difficult to view such terms as affording other than a broad discretion to act fairly and responsibly in the circumstances, balancing community interests with those of accused people, victims and others. Seemingly, such terms (however impressive they may sound) confer considerable authority on individuals to decide 'what is right' in a given situation, restrained by few, if any rules. Further, they may carry different meanings at different times and from different perspectives, e.g. judicial, political or administrative.
[17] Which regulates the prosecution of offenders as between member states.

proceedings, it must either make the order applied for if the 'new and compelling evidence' and the 'interests of justice' tests are satisfied, or otherwise make a declaration that the acquittal is a bar to the person in question being tried for the offence (section 77(3)). If it determines that the acquittal is not a bar to retrial, it must make a declaration to that effect (section 77(4)).

'New' and 'compelling' evidence
'New evidence' is defined as evidence not adduced in the proceedings in which the person was acquitted (nor, if those were appeal proceedings, in earlier proceedings to which the appeal related). It is 'compelling' if it is reliable, substantial and in the context of the outstanding issues, it appears highly probative of the case against the acquitted person (section 78(2) and (3) summarised).

'Outstanding issues' are issues in dispute in the proceedings in which the person was acquitted and, if they were appeal proceedings, any other issues remaining in dispute from earlier proceedings to which the appeal related; and it is irrelevant whether any evidence would have been admissible in earlier proceedings against the acquitted person (sections 78(4) and (5)).

The 'interests of justice' test
Under section 79 CJA 2003 the requirements of the interests of justice test are met if 'in all the circumstances it is in the interests of justice to make the order' applied for by the prosecutor, something to be determined having regard, in particular (i.e. but not exclusively) to:

- whether existing circumstances make a fair trial unlikely;
- the length of time since the offence was allegedly committed;
- whether it is likely that the new evidence would have been adduced in the earlier proceedings but for the failure by an officer or a prosecutor to act with due diligence or expedition; and
- whether since the earlier proceedings, or, if later, since the commencement of the Part 10 CJA 2003, any officer or prosecutor has failed to act with due diligence or expedition.

Procedure, evidence and appeals
Section 80 contains the procedural arrangements where a prosecutor wishes to make an application and/or charge a suspect, including a power in the Court of Appeal to extend the limits for the latter. There are rights to be heard and represented. At any one hearing the Court of Appeal can consider more than one application (whether or not relating to the same person), but only if the offences concerned could be tried on the same indictment. Further provisions of section 80 amend the Criminal Appeal Act 1968 giving an appeal to the House of Lords on an order for a retrial or ruling on whether proceedings are barred by a previous acquittal.

Reporting restrictions
Section 82 CJA 2003 introduces reporting restrictions designed to preserve the interests of justice whilst a retrial is pending and section 83 provides for the penalties where the restriction is breached. Where it appears to the Court of

Appeal that the inclusion of any matter in a publication would give rise to a substantial risk of prejudice to the administration of justice in a retrial, it may order that the matter is not to be included in any publication while the order has effect. This it can only do if it appears necessary in the interests of justice. Under section 83, offences of failing to comply with such an order attract a maximum penalty of a Level 5 fine and are tried summarily. Proceedings can only be brought by or with the consent of the Attorney General.[18]

The retrial itself and procedures leading to it
Sections 84 to 91 deal with the retrial itself and other procedures leading to it ranging from the authorisation of the investigation to arrest, charge and bail. Sections 92 to 97 deal with the functions of the DPP, rules of court, and a number of other supplementary matters including the applicability of the new law to the Armed Forces, its interpretation and appeals.

---

[18] There are special provisions within section 83 CJA 2003 in relation to Northern Ireland.

Type of sentence	Use/availability etc. under the CJA 2003	Other key points
Life imprisonment (Mandatory)	Existing law deals with mandatory life sentences for murderers (and certain other mandatory lifers).	Crown Court only. Special release provisions (*Chapter 11*). Key emphasis on risk assessment.
Life imprisonment (Discretionary) and **Public protection** (*Chapter 10*)	Offenders convicted of a 'serious offence' where there is a risk of 'serious harm' to the public that attracts a discretionary life sentence or at least 10 years imprisonment must normally receive an indeterminate sentence - either **life imprisonment** or a sentence for **public protection**.	Crown Court only. Special release provisions (*Chapter 11*). Key emphasis on risk assessment. With sentences for public protection from dangerous offenders the court sets the part of the sentence to be served for the purposes of punishment and deterrence.
Extended sentence (*Chapter 10*)	Sexual and violent offenders (other than those covered by the above sentences) convicted of a 'specified offence' must normally be given an **extended sentence**, i.e. one with an 'appropriate custodial term' of at least 12 months reflecting the seriousness of the offence plus an 'extension period' set by the court and usually involving long-term supervision in the community on release to protect the public from 'serious harm'.	Dangerous offenders: Crown Court only. No need for a 'serious offence': contrast last category above. CJA 2003 provisions replace existing law on extended sentences. Extended supervision can be for up to five years for violent offenders and eight years for sexual offenders during which they can be recalled to prison for breach of licence. Key emphasis on risk assessment.
Discretionary sentence: 12 months or more (See note at start of *Chapter 10*) Revised 'so serious' threshold. Must be the *shortest* sentence commensurate with the seriousness of the offence. Alternatively, failure to express 'willingness' to a community order that requires this. One new basis: failure to comply with a pre-sentence drug test.	Where the seriousness of an offence merits it, an 'ordinary' discretionary sentence of **12 months or over** can be passed unless excluded by the above categories. Courts can recommend but not impose licence conditions. No special provision in the CJA 2003 but general changes apply, e.g. statutory purposes of sentencing, threshold criteria, aggregate powers etc.	Only the Crown Court can pass a sentence above 12 months. No committal for sentence once magistrates have assumed jurisdiction re an either way offence but they can sentence up to 12 months (65 weeks in aggregate). Correct allocation by them at the outset critical (*Chapter 4*). NB No 'protection of the public' criterion within the 'ordinary' bases for custody (as there was under the CJA 1991).
'Under 12 months' (*Chapter 9*) Revised 'so serious' threshold. Must be the *shortest* sentence commensurate with the seriousness of the offence. Alternatively, failure to express 'willingness' to a community order that requires this. One new basis: failure to comply with a pre-sentence drug test.	All sentences **below 12 months** must be one of the new-style shorter sentences of **custody plus, intermittent custody** or a **suspended sentence**. In each case the minimum overall term is 28 weeks and the maximum 51 weeks (65 weeks in aggregate for magistrates). There are special rules for custodial and licence periods depending on the type of sentence and with a minimum of two weeks/14 days to be served in custody. Courts set licence conditions. Suspended sentences are reviewable by the court.	Depending on which sentence is used, requirements are **added by the court** and form the basis of community obligations during the term of the sentence or when the offender is on licence at the end of or during it. See *Chapters 8, 9* concerning how and when individual requirements can be used in relation to a given sentence. No power to commit for sentence once magistrates have assumed jurisdiction re an either way offence. Correct allocation by them at the outset critical (*Chapter 4*).
Community sentence (*Chapter 8*) Revised 'serious enough' threshold test. Requirements must be the most suitable for the offender and restriction of liberty must be commensurate with the seriousness of the offence.	A single **generic order** comprising requirements selected from a statutory 'menu' (see panel at end of chapter) replaces existing range of individual community orders. Can be used for a persistent offender instead of a fine in certain circumstances (see *Chapter 7*).	The generic order is the 'most onerous' sentencing option where the seriousness of an offence does not merit at least 28 weeks imprisonment. Emphasis on sanctions via 'incremental' breach provisions. Secretary of State can make community sentences reviewable.
Fine (*Chapter 7*) Fines must 'reflect' the seriousness of the offence.	Broadly speaking law is unchanged but a community sentence can sometimes be used instead of a fine (above). Two revised enforcement mechanisms: unpaid work/driving disqualification.	In practice there is a new emphasis on the enforcement and collection of fines.
Discharge	Absolute and conditional discharges continue as per existing law.	

Statutory 'general purposes' of sentencing affect all decisions*

(*but some sentences, including for certain lifers and for 'dangerous offenders' (*Chapter 10*) are obligatory.

Reasons and explanations must be given for most sentence decisions: see *Appendix*

CHAPTER 7

The New Sentencing Framework

For many people, the changes to sentencing law in the CJA 2003 - contained principally in Part 12 of the Act and associated provisions[1] - will be a central feature of the new law. Part 12 is substantial. It comprises nine separate 'chapters': some directly concerned with the structure of the sentencing framework, others given over to particular aspects of sentencing ranging from life sentences to deferment of sentence, drug treatment and testing and firearms offences. The CJA 2003 - which builds on certain aspects of existing law but otherwise makes novel provision - contains:

- a range of **general provisions** about sentencing by criminal courts including new, statutory purposes of sentencing;
- **thresholds** for community sentences and custody;
- **criteria** and accompanying provisions for each of those types of sentence;
- special custodial provisions relating to **dangerous offenders**, including **violent** and **sexual offenders**;
- extensive provisions about **release** from custody and **post-custody supervision;**
- **breach** and **enforcement provisions** and others concerning **recall** to prison; and
- various **ancillary provisions** relating to sentencing.

In addition - and a key feature of the new law - the Act creates a Sentencing Guidelines Council (SGC) under the chairmanship of the Lord Chief Justice. The work of the SGC is described later in this chapter. The new framework is intended to be clearer and more flexible than before.[2] A further intention of Government is that courts will be equipped to provide every offender with a sentence that best meets the needs of his or her particular case, and at whatever level of seriousness. Sentences, it is claimed, will be 'more effectively managed'. In this context, the new arrangements are occurring at the same time as a potentially fundamental 'reconstruction' of HM Prison Service and the National Probation Service to create a National Offender Management Service (NOMS) following proposals in *Managing Offenders, Reducing Crime* ('the Carter Report') (see further in *Chapter 14*).

How the CJA 2003 affects the existing framework

To assist later, more detailed explanation, the following points summarise some of the things that the CJA 2003 'does and does not do':

- the **seriousness** of an offence remains the key factor in sentencing in ordinary circumstances, i.e. any special considerations apart, it is the seriousness of the offence that usually determines the appropriate level of

---

[1] Much of the detail is consigned to various schedules to the Act.
[2] There are obvious risks in such 'flexibility' including of 'ratcheting-up' sentences, lack of any coherent structure, inconsistency and vague reasoning in support of sentence decisions.

sentence and the length or amount of sentence. However, this is subject to certain provisions allowing or confirming that courts have a degree of flexibility in relation to levels of sentence[3] and special measures in relation to public protection from dangerous offenders including extended sentences for violent and sexual offenders;

- the existing **threshold tests** for:
  — community sentences (the 'serious enough' test); and
  — custodial sentences (the 'so serious' test)
  are retained but re-enacted in modified terms or with renewed emphasis;
- in a novel departure, the court is statutorily obliged to have regard to prescribed **purposes** of sentencing;
- **discharges** (whether absolute discharges or conditional discharges) remain untouched by the Act and can still be used whenever appropriate;[4]
- the provisions relating to **fines** and their enforcement are, broadly speaking, re-enacted without major alteration (the position is summarised later in this chapter)
- the existing range of community orders is dispensed with in favour of a new **'generic community order'**. The generic order - explained in detail in *Chapter 8* - is constructed by the court from a 'menu' of statutory requirements. These reflect either existing community sentences or requirements of the kind that can be added to an existing community rehabilitation order. However, it is important to stress that this same menu (or certain 'choices' from it) will also be available where requirements are added in relation to suspended sentences or licences during release from custody. In this sense the menu does not 'belong' to the generic community order or to any particular level, or stage of sentence. It exists in a free-standing form for use in the various situations noted in *Chapters 8 to 11*.
- **custodial sentences** of less than 12 months are replaced by an entirely new regime comprising:
  — **'custody plus'** - immediate imprisonment followed by a period of at least 26 weeks post-release supervision in the community (the 'plus' element being this supervision together with any added requirements);
  — **'intermittent custody'** - known informally as 'weekend gaol' or 'part-time gaol' - again with supervision and the prospect of added requirements in relation to licence periods during the sentence and at the end of it; and
  — a new-style **suspended sentence** - sometimes called 'custody minus': where the 'minus' element is represented by the fact that the offender will not normally serve an actual term of imprisonment provided that he or she complies with added requirements and does not commit further offences whilst his or her suspended sentence is still running.[5]

---

[3] E.g. they can move upwards from a fine to a community sentence in the case of a persistent offender (section 151 CJA 2003); and can always mitigate downwards (section 166).

[4] Principally where punishment is inexpedient or inapropriate. Discharges are excluded from further consideration here, but see, e.g. *The Sentence of the Court*,(go to www.watersidepress.co.uk)

[5] Representing a major advance on the existing situation where the offender will not have any such obligations: although he or she may now be fined in addition, which the court must consider.

These 'less than 12 months' sentences are further described in *Chapter 9*.

- in relation to offenders from whom the public needs to be protected, the CJA 2003 contains a range of **dangerous offender** provisions (*Chapter 10*). Depending on the type of offence and its maximum penalty, these either *require* or *allow* sentences designed to ensure that such people are kept in custody for substantial periods of time and/or remain under post-custody supervision for significant periods. The dangerous offender provisions are addressed to three distinct categories of offenders:
  - **lifers**
  - certain other **long-term prisoners** who will receive sentences for public protection; and
  - other, possibly lesser - though still 'dangerous' - **violent** and **sexual offenders** for whom the Act creates **extended sentences.** The 'extended part' of such a sentence involves supervision in the community on release (often for a substantial period as set by the court), once an 'appropriate custodial term' commensurate with 'seriousness' has been served.[6]
- There is an emphasis on:
  - **drug-testing** and rehabilitation, both before and as part of a sentence
  - **electronic monitoring** both in relation to the generic community order and when an offender is released into the community following or during a custodial sentence;[7]
- there is, overall, greater flexibility for courts to 'move between' different sentences and different levels of sentence;
- certain aspects of the generic community sentence and of the suspended sentence will be reviewable by the court as well as a stricter enforcement code (both these aspects representing an upwards and 'incremental' shift in sentencing powers); and
- courts must have regard to definitive sentencing and allocation guidelines issued by the Sentencing Guidelines Council.

Beyond the sentencing framework

The framework also needs to be understood in the context of the simultaneous changes of jurisdiction as between Crown Courts and magistrates' courts and it is integral to all 'allocation and sending decisions' as outlined in *Chapter 4*. These are themselves bound up with changes to magistrates' maximum custodial sentencing powers, the fact that magistrates will be unable, post-CJA 2003, to commit to the Crown Court for sentence *once they have assumed jurisdiction* in relation to an either way offence (see later in the chapter) and - in terms of practical operation - the prospect of new, common rules of procedure that will apply to both level of court (*Chapter 1*).

Beyond the basic framework, there are extensively revised provisions concerning release from custody and post-custody supervision. However, it can be noted at this stage that - in a novel departure and in relation to sentences of

---

[6] Subject, normally, to release at the half-way point of the custodial term, and except if the offender is returned to prison during the 'extension period' as described in *Chapters 10* and *11*.

[7] Including on home detention curfew (HDC), although not specifically dealt with by the CJA 2003.

below 12 months - post-custody supervision under 'licence conditions' is generally provided for by the court at the time of passing sentence (or in the case of a suspended sentence when it is 'activated': *Chapter 9*) - both in terms of duration and content. The arrangements in relation to longer sentences or where an offender is recalled to prison are described in *Chapter 11*.

GENERAL PROVISIONS

The new sentencing provisions stem from recommendations contained in *Making Punishments Work: Report of a Review of the Sentencing Framework for England and Wales* (Home Office, 2001) ('The Halliday report') which looked comprehensively at sentencing in its existing and historical contexts, ranging from underlying principles to the costs and benefits of particular outcomes. That report recommended, among other things, that any new sentencing framework should do more to support crime reduction and reparation while at the same time meeting the needs of punishment.

Aims and purposes of sentencing
For the first time in relation to adults, statutory purposes of sentencing that 'any court dealing with an offender . . . must have regard to' in arriving at its decision are listed, in section 142(1) CJA 2003. These are:

(a) **punishment** of offenders;
(b) **reduction of crime** (including through deterrence);
(c) **reform and rehabilitation of offenders;**
(d) **protecting the public**; and
(e) **reparation** by offenders to people affected by their offences.

These prescribed purposes suggest that courts will need to give yet greater and more careful attention to giving of reasons (see, generally, the *Appendix*). But they do not apply: to someone under 18 at the time of *conviction*;[8] where the sentence is mandatory, fixed or required by law; where other provisions set minimum or required custodial sentences (including in relation to certain 'dangerous offenders' or the Firearms Act 1968); or in relation to hospital orders or similar disposals under the Mental Health Act 1983 (section 142(2)).

Meaning of 'sentence'
In relation to the general sentencing provisions of the CJA 2003, 'sentence' includes 'any order made . . . when dealing with an offender for his or her offence' (section 142(3)), and thus e.g. not simply sentences proper but ancillary orders such as compensation or disqualification rank as sentences in relation to the statutory purposes and associated provisions.

---

[8] When the youth justice purposes in the Crime and Disorder Act 1998 apply (alongside the 'welfare principle' and in combination with the new sentencing thresholds of the CJA 2003): see *Chapter 12*.

Statutory and 'other' purposes

Whether all five of the general purposes of sentencing will always be achievable or compatible in a given case seems doubtful, and ultimately choices may need to be made and aims prioritised through a process of balanced (but possibly weighted) decision-making. The new statutory purpose of reparation emphasises the Government's wish to 'rebalance' the system more in favour of victims whilst remaining fair to offenders - and its commitment more generally to forms of restorative justice.

It is unclear whether the new statutory purposes of sentencing prevent a court from having regard to further relevant aims in so far as these are not inconsistent with or intrinsically part of those purposes to which the court 'must have regard', e.g. what have traditionally been called 'general objects' of sentencing. These included retribution (although this would probably, in future, be seen as an aspect of punishment) and reflecting public concern (omitted from the CJA 2003 list, albeit the Government has been keen to encourage the agencies to create greater confidence in the criminal justice system).

Seriousness

Conventionally, the seriousness of an offence has always been the central factor in determining a starting point for punishment, to which aggravating or mitigating factors are then applied to arrive at a proportionate final outcome. Aggravating factors are those things that may, depending on the particular offence and overall circumstances, make an offence more serious than the norm or sentence 'starting point' for a given type of offence, such as planning, preparation, breach of trust or the fact that the offender selected a vulnerable victim; mitigating factors have the opposite effect, such as provocation, purely impulsive actions, accidental oversight or acting out of genuine fear.[9] The dangerous offender provisions described in *Chapter 10* apart, this will continue to be the case post-CJA 2003. However, section 143 CJA 2003 sets out various matters that a sentencer *must* consider in determining the seriousness of an offence, and which demand a modified perspective:

- the offender's **culpability** in committing the offence; and
- any **harm** caused by the offence, intended by it, or which 'might foreseeably' have been caused.

And there four situations where a court is required to treat an offence as more serious than it would have done and thus, in practice (and other things being equal) to impose a more severe penalty:

- **previous convictions:** if an offender has one or more previous convictions, the court must treat *each* of these as an aggravating factor if it considers that 'it can reasonably be so treated' having regard in particular to:
  —the nature of the offence to which the previous conviction relates and its relevance to the current offence; and
  —the time that has elapsed since the conviction.
  Whilst such previous conviction(s) must have happened in the UK (or have been a finding of guilt in service disciplinary proceedings (defined in

---

[9] For a less simplistic guide see *The Sentence of the Court* (go to www.watersidepress.co.uk).

section 305(1) CJA 2003) the court is 'not prevented' from treating a foreign conviction as an aggravating factor where appropriate (section 143(4) and (5) CJA 2003);

- **offences committed on bail:** where the offender was on bail at the time of committing an offence this must - as under existing law - be treated as an aggravating factor (section 143(3) CJA 2003);

- **racial or religious aggravation:** where the offence is racially or religiously aggravated[10] this must - as under existing law - be treated as an aggravating factor (section 145 CJA 2003). But section 145 is not engaged when the offence is itself defined as so aggravated under the Crime and Disorder Act 1998 (which provides for certain aggravated forms of assault, criminal damage, public order offences and harassment and correspondingly higher maximum sentences), i.e. there is, in other words, no 'double weighting';

- **hositility based on sexual orientation or disability:** where the offence involves either of these kinds of hostility towards a victim this must be treated as an aggravating factor (section 146 CJA 2003). The hostility may be actual or presumed and it is immaterial whether it is also based, to any extent, on any other factor. The hostility demonstrated towards the victim for this purpose may be at the time of the offence or immediately before or after it. Disability is defined as 'any physical or mental impairment'.

Timely plea of guilty

There is also a general requirement (reflecting existing law) leading to a reduction in sentence for a timely plea of guilty. Section 144 CJA 2003 provides that where an offender pleads guilty, the court must 'take into account' the stage in the proceedings when his or her intention to do so was indicated and the circumstances of that indication. There is even a special rule in relation to required custodial sentences pursuant to section 110(2) or 111 Powers of Criminal Courts (Sentencing) Act 2000: the court is 'not prevented' from making a reduction to reflect a guilty plea provided that the sentence imposed is not less than 80 per cent of the required sentence. The principle of allowing a discount on the basis that an offender has saved time, expense, resources and not put the victim or witnesses to the ordeal of appearing in court is well-established and in practice, depending on its timing, a guilty plea has normally attracted a sentence discount of 'up to about one third'. But given the scope for variation, such discounts may be an appropriate matter for the attention of the Sentencing Guidelines Council (below).

NEW APPROACHES AND SHIFTS OF EMPHASIS

Some of the revised requirements described above will seem familiar to judges, magistrates and other practitioners, if not now expressed in the precise terms

---

[10] As defined in section 28 Crime and Disorder Act 1998. Broadly speaking, where an offence is accompanied by hostility based on the victim's membership (or presumed membership) of a racial or religious group, or where the offence is motivated by such hostility. There may be a need for caution or even an explanation where a specific aggravated version of an offence exists which could have been charged but was not.

that they once were. Seemingly, attention will need to be paid in particular to items such as:

- 'culpability': what precisely does the duty to consider the offender's culpability (as required by section 143 above) mean or add to existing approaches? To an extent, the offender's 'blameworthiness', 'fault' or 'guilt' (terms that figure in dictionary definitions of culpability) have always been central to a court's reasoning when assessing the seriousness of an offence, but this becomes quite explicit under the CJA 2003;
- 'foreseeable of harm': questions may also arise in relation to that aspect of section 143 (again relevant to assessments of seriousness) requiring a court to consider foreseeable harm, i.e. whether the test here is subjective or objective; and
- there are also question marks concerning the potential relevance, comparability and availability of reliable information about a foreign conviction - and the effect that such a conviction ought properly to have on sentence now, in England and Wales.

In contrast, considerations such as the timeliness of a guilty plea or the fact that an offence was committed on bail or in circumstances of religious, racial or other specified aggravation represent familiar territory, even if existing approaches will need to be applied with newly spelt out overall purposes of sentencing in mind. Provisions concerning hostility based upon sexual orientation or disability will no doubt be dealt with by analogy. It may well be that the potential for 'choice' and 'prioritising' of factors in a given case should be viewed as part of the idea that sentencing should be more flexible and responsive to individual needs: but such thinking needs to be balanced by great caution if the criteria overall (taken also alongside the flexibility to move between levels of sentence) are not to render the entire process meaningless.

Previous convictions

The extent to which previous convictions can properly affect seriousness has always been a difficult area of sentencing law. The position was never satisfactorily resolved in relation to what became section 151(1) Powers of Criminal Courts Act 2000, although the CJA 2003 does now avoid and dispense with one existing difficulty whereby previous responses to sentences can, theoretically, have a similar effect - even if few, if any, lawyers ever understood how and why that provision, now abandoned by the CJA 2003, was supposed to operate. The original version of the CJA 1991 sought to restrict heavily the extent to which previous convictions might be taken into account when assessing the seriousness of the present offence, but that approach contributed to the infamous 1993 political U-turn on certain provisions of the 1991 Act. The niceties of finality in sentencing and arguments that taking previous convictions into account meant that someone was being punished again for past behaviour never seem to have appealed widely to sentencers, or the media.

The new approach in the CJA 2003 under which *each* previous conviction *must* be treated as an aggravating factor represents a radical departure - and debate is now likely to shift to questions of when a court can 'reasonably so treat' a previous conviction as a mandatory aggravating factor (and it will inevitably prolong the sentencing process and bring increased demands in relation to reasons for decisions). The Home Office, in its guidance notes to the Act, asserts that 'Any previous convictions that are recent and relevant should be regarded as an aggravating factor which should increase the severity of the sentence'[11] - and indeed other arguments are likely to prove equally pragmatic. They may reduce perhaps to no more than assertions such as 'The offender has had his or her chance', or been warned (impliedly from the existence of an earlier conviction, perhaps, or even expressly by a previous court), but has continued to offend ('That must make it more serious, mustn't it? - and if the Act says that each conviction *must* be treated as an aggravating factor that's an end of the matter'). It is, in fact, hard to progress beyond rationalisation and noticeable that, in contrast to many key outcomes under the CJA 2003, the court is not expressly required to explain itself in these circumstances.[12]

The requirement to take *each* previous conviction into account applies however serious or trivial those convictions are; and even where they do not in fact serve to aggravate seriousness they may result in a community sentence rather than a fine for a persistent offender (see below). As already explained in *Chapter 4*, previous convictions are relevant at the time of an 'allocation and sending' decision by magistrates (which also imports that courts will have a proper understanding of when and how they increase the seriousness of the offence) so that the issue should perhaps be one which the new Sentencing Guidelines Council should address as a priority. As explained in *Chapter 5*, previous convictions can, under the CJA 2003, also be used to establish guilt.

Deterrence
Predictably, perhaps, 'deterrence' (included under the purpose of reduction of crime) may cause debate given the voluminous literature and comment pointing to the tenuous nature of the link between a given sentence and the future behaviour, either of the offender or other people (i.e. 'general deterrence').[13]

THRESHOLD CRITERIA: 'GENERAL RESTRICTIONS'

The CJA 2003 introduces what it terms 'general restrictions' on sentencing, including in relation to community sentences and custody. These represent a mix of what have been termed 'thresholds' together - as part of the 'flexibility' introduced by the Act - with added provisions allowing a given level of sentence to be used without direct regard to the threshold under consideration. Thus, although the main indicator for sentencing will still be its link to the seriousness of an offence, the sentencing outcome may depart from this on occasion.

Community sentences: The 'serious enough' test
In substance and broad effect, the CJA 2003 re-enacts the existing 'serious enough' threshold for a community sentence but with a revised emphasis and

---

[11] The Home Office also asserts that the provisions are a strengthening of section 151 CJA 1991 (*sic*).

[12] Although reasons and explanations are always required in the more generals sense: see *Appendix*.

[13] The key ruling under existing law is that of Lord Taylor in *R. v Cunningham* (1993) 14 Cr App. R. (S.) 386. Lord Taylor stated that 'custodial sentences in particular are meant to punish and deter' (both now statutory purposes under the CJA 2003 for all sentences not just custodial ones).

without the need for an imprisonable offence (as there is for certain existing community orders) and provided that the offence itself is serious enough. It deals quite separately with the menu of ingredients mentioned earlier in this chapter from which the single, generic community sentence can be constructed by the court. These matters are dealt with in *Chapter 8*. The threshold criteria as newly laid down are to be found in section 148 CJA 2003, which stresses what a court *must not* do, something which in itself would seem to demand of courts that they be guarded yet ultimately quite positive in their decisions, opinions and supporting reasons:

(1) A court must not pass a community sentence on an offender unless it is of the opinion that the offence, or the combination of the offence and one or more offences associated with it, was serious enough to warrant such a sentence.

(2) Where a court passes a community sentence which consists of or includes a community order -

(a) a particular requirement or requirements forming part of the community order must be such as, in the opinion of the court, is, or taken together are, the most suitable for the offender, and

(b) the restrictions on liberty imposed by the order must be such as in the opinion of the court are commensurate with the seriousness of the offence, or the combination of the offence and one or more offences associated with it.[14]

Unless the threshold in section 148(1) is met the court is effectively restricted to a fine or an absolute or conditional discharge (except where section 151 applies: see next heading). References to decisions being based on the offence and one or more associated offences (in effect meaning offences for which the offender is being sentenced at the same time) and the requirement to ensure that the restriction on liberty involved is commensurate with the seriousness of such offences are retained and re-enacted. What is new is the practical task of matching this principle to the generic sentence, with all the opportunities that the menu of requirements presents for 'fanciful' outcomes. A wish to achieve some perceived end via a generic sentence carries with it consequent risk of exceeding the appropriate level of restriction of liberty, or raising the offender up the sentencing tariff (which will also have implications if he or she is convicted of something else on a future occasion). It also risks placing excessive or unrealistic expectations on an offender, with a correspondingly increased risk of non-compliance. The new-style breach provisions in Schedule 8 to the CJA 2003 - which among other things allow custody to be used for a non-imprisonable offence - are then more punitive and represent a further upwards and 'incremental' shift in sentencing. The result is that punishment may easily become disproportionate.[15]

The shift to a style of drafting whereby the court 'must not' pass a custodial sentence is significant, the emphasis now being far more on the threshold as a mandatory restriction or barrier. Neither, it seems, should it be taken - when that threshold is actually reached - that a court 'must' conversely pass a community sentence, this remaining a matter for the court's discretion. A

---

[14] Comparable threshold criteria also apply to youth community orders subject to certain subtleties reflecting the fact that the generic sentence does not apply to juveniles: see *Chapter 12*.

[15] See further in *Chapter 8*.

number of provisions of the CJA specifically allow the court to move downwards within the sentencing framework.

Community sentences for persistent offenders instead of a fine

Notwithstanding what is said in the last paragraph above, there is an additional need to rethink existing approaches due to section 151 CJA 2003. This provision allows a court to use a community sentence *instead of a fine* (i.e. an upwards move) for a persistent offender who has been previously fined - thus by-passing the 'serious enough' test altogether. As already indicated, previous convictions can aggravate the seriousness of an offence (section 143). Alternatively - or even, in theory, where they do not have that effect - they will be capable, under section 151 of leading to a community sentence rather than a fine. The provisions allow community orders to be passed on persistent offenders aged 16 or over who have been previously fined by a UK court (or in service disciplinary proceedings). It is interesting to reflect on whether, in the light of the new statutory purposes of sentencing, the driving purpose ought to be punishment, rehabilitation, crime prevention or all three.

The criteria state that where on three or more occasions such an offender has after attaining the age of 16 had passed on him or her a sentence consisting only of a fine (disregarding compensation: section 151(5); and other 'non-fine' sentences: section 151(5)) but the threshold criteria for a community sentence would - despite the fact that previous convictions must normally be taken into account - not otherwise be reached, the court can use a community order instead of a fine. The court must consider that 'having regard to all the circumstances ... it would be in the interests of justice to make such an order'. Those circumstances include the nature of the previous matters, their relevance and the time since the offender's conviction for them (section 151(3)).

Other matters affecting community sentences

Community sentences cannot be passed where a different sentence is fixed or required by law (section 150 CJA 2003).[16] Where the offender has been remanded in custody, the court may have regard to time so spent in relation to the offence in question or any other founded on the same facts or evidence (section 149),[17] in effect when deciding on the 'amount' of restriction of liberty that should be involved. Seemingly, there will be an onus on courts to produce a workable and consistent approach to such reductions. Again, this may well be a suitable matter for consideration by the Sentencing Guidelines Council (below).

Discretionary custodial sentences: the 'so serious' test

Similarly, in relation to discretionary custodial sentences - whether for under 12 months or for 12 months and above - the existing 'so serious' threshold test for

---

[16] i.e. sentences fixed by law or under sections 225 to 228 CJA 2003 (dangerous offenders), sections 110 or 111 Powers of Criminal Courts (Sentencing) Act 2000 or section 51A Firearms Act 1968. The corollary is that an offender can receive a community sentence whenever imprisonment remains discretionary (including in relation to violent and sexual offenders) - always assuming that such a disposal is appropriate. See also the comments later in this chapter concerning such offences.

[17] This may mean that courts will need to resort to looking at 'old' cases about when an offence can be said to be so based, including perhaps in relation to pre-CJA 2003 double jeopardy rulings. There is a similar rule where the defendant gets a custodial sentence (see section 240 CJA 2003).

custody is retained subject to certain modifications and, again, a new emphasis on what a court *must not* do. This test will thus apply to the short new-style sentences described in *Chapter 9* as well as to longer sentences provided that they are not fixed or required by law, as are certain of the dangerous offender provisions described in *Chapter 10*. The same revised underlying criteria and rules described earlier in this chapter for determining how serious an offence is apply to custody as they do to a community sentence, including the effect of any previous convictions, offending on bail, racial or other aggravation or the timeliness of a guilty plea - in addition to the multifarious 'plus' and 'minus' factors that may exist in an individual case. Section 152(2) provides:

> The court must not pass a custodial sentence unless it is of the opinion that the offence, or the combination of the offence and one or more offences associated with it, was so serious that *neither a fine alone nor a community sentence can be justified* for the offence. (Emphasis supplied)

The points already made in relation to community sentences concerning a shift of emphasis to 'must not' are equally apposite in relation to custody and in particular one effect, it seems, is that a court will retain a discretion even where the threshold is in fact reached.[18] The italicised words are new. The CJA 1991 required that 'no other sentence can be justified' so that the CJA 2003 provision is more forthright and again it seems that courts will need to be more sure and positive in order to be satisfied that the threshold has been reached. The test is otiose where the sentence is fixed or required by law (section 151(2)).

The existing exception allowing a custodial sentence to be passed where someone refuses a community sentence is also retained (now expressed in terms of 'nothing prevents' this outcome), i.e. nothing prevents a custodial sentence where the offender fails to express a willingness to comply with a requirement proposed by the court and provided that, legally speaking, such a requirement necessitates an expression of willingness[19] (section 152(3)).

A final, existing CJA 1991 basis for custody, i.e. 'to protect the public from serious harm from the offender' (which only applied in the case of violent or sexual offenders) has been sacrificed in favour of the dangerous offender provisions (again see *Chapter 10*), including those for extended sentence.[20]

Failure to comply with a pre-sentence drug test
There is, however, one new addition to the bases for custody. Under section 152(3)(b) CJA 2003 custody can be used where the offender fails to comply with an order for a pre-sentence drug test under section 161(2) CJA 2003 (see *Chapter 13*) (and even though the 'so serious' threshold is not met).[21]

Under section 161 a pre-sentence drug test is available to assist the court in its decision whether or not to pass a community sentence. It enables the court to make an order, in the case of a convicted offender who is at least 14 years of

---

[18] This could well herald a revival of the 'alternative to custody' approach of former times.

[19] Few community sentence orders/requirements do, or will, require 'willingness' or consent.

[20] As will be seen from *Chapter 10* extended sentences involve a decision about the 'appropriate custodial period' (based on the seriousness of the offence) to which is then added the 'extension period' (i.e. usually a long period of supervision in the community).

[21] There are further 'new routes to custody', within the breach provisions for community sentences or following failure to comply with a drug rehabilitation requirement: see *Chapter 8*.

age,[22] to be tested to see whether the offender has any specified Class A drug[23] in his or her body. Failure to provide a sample without reasonable excuse is punishable by a maximum fine on Level 4 (currently £2,500 in the case of an adult) in addition to the sentence imposed for the original offence. There is a pre-condition that the court must have been notified by the Secretary of State that the power to make such orders is exercisable by that particular court and that notice must not have been withdrawn (section 161(6)).

Length of discretionary custody
Under section 153(2) CJA 2003, a custodial sentence:

> . . . must be *for the shortest term* (not exceeding the permitted maximum) that in the opinion of the court is commensurate with the seriousness of the offence, or the combination of the offence and one or more offences associated with it. [Italics supplied]

There is no underlying change,[24] but there is an important modification as per the words in italics whereby an unequivocal duty is placed on sentencers to order *the shortest term* commensurate with the seriousness of an offence. The terms 'commensurate' and 'associated offence' are familiar territory - the former a basis of proportionality since the CJA 1991 and the latter meaning, broadly speaking, an offence for which the offender is being sentenced at the same time. In a sense the provision thus serves to confirm that principles of proportionality or 'just deserts' continue, but in a modified form. To this extent and depending on what guidance may stem from the Sentencing Guidelines Council (see later), the broad import of much sentencing case law will remain relevant.

It is by linking the length of custody directly to the shortest term - but essentially the *term* - that in relation to all sentences below 12 months section 153(2) serves to create a minimum custodial sentence for all courts of 28 weeks.[25] This is the minimum term for custody plus, intermittent custody and the new-style suspended sentence (see *Chapter 9*). It compares with the existing sentence of six months that in practice - rather than as part of the sentence itself - is broken down into time actually served in prison followed by a licence period in the community. Under the CJA 2003 the minimum overall term of 28 weeks is broken down into a minimum 'custodial period' or 'custodial days' of 'two weeks' (custody plus/suspended sentence) or '14 days' (intermittent custody) plus a licence element. Viewed another way, only where the seriousness of the offence merits at least 28 weeks (rather than two weeks or 14 days) will it be possible to use custody in future. This legislative approach contrasts with that in

---

[22] See *Chapter 12* for the extra requirements for juveniles.

[23] Within Part 3 Criminal Justice and Court Services Act 2000: section 161(8) CJA 2003.

[24] But considerations of public protection have been removed to the dangerous offender provisions. Section 153 does not apply in certain situations, in very broad terms those where a custodial sentence is fixed or required by law, including post-CJA 2003 under the Firearms Act 1968.

[25] The minimum term under section 132 MCA 1980 of five days is preserved by the CJA 2003 (see section 154(7)) but will apply only, e.g. to fine default, contempt of court and kindred matters. In effect magistrates' minimum custodial *sentencing* powers will - in terms of relating the seriousness of an offence to the overall sentence of imprisonment - jump from five days to 28 weeks.

relation to the extended sentence where length of sentence is expressly linked to the 'appropriate custodial part' of such a sentence (*Chapter 10*).

It seems that Parliament wished to maximise the use of generic community sentences at lower levels of seriousness - i.e. where 'seriousness' does not merit a custodial sentence of at least 28 weeks. This would also be in line with other provisions of the CJA 2003 whereby 'nothing prevents' any appropriate mitigation (section 166) and powers of imprisonment of less than six months have been abolished in relation to an extensive list of offences (and other sentencing powers correspondingly increased: the Secretary of State, in effect, being given a 'reserve' power to accommodate any further examples that may 'pop up' afterwards: see later). But in certain scenarios, the rationale is less clear, as where offenders refuse a pre-sentence drug test, do not express willingness to comply with certain community requirements or breach community sentences. These are all situations where custody becomes possible and the 'so serious' *threshold* test in section 152(2) CJA 2003 is dispensed with - but not the *length* of custody test in section 153(2), which 'harks back' to the shortest sentence commensurate with the seriousness of the original offence.

Changes to the maximum custodial powers of magistrates

Among other changes to magistrates' court's sentencing powers, the CJA 2003 brings about a general increase in their maximum powers of imprisonment. In a major jurisdictional shift, the upper sentencing limit for an individual offence is increased from six months to 12 months (section 154 CJA 2003). This is subject to there being any lower limit for the offence itself. If there is, that lower limit continues to apply. But 'unless expressly excluded' the 12 month limit applies even if the offence in question is one for which an offender would otherwise be liable on summary conviction to more than 12 months (a rarity in practice). It can, however, be noted that the new-style sentences of 'below 12 months' outlined in *Chapter 9* will be expressed in weeks or days, not months, so that the new overall limits need to applied with 'translation' in mind.

Simultaneously, in relation to either way offences the new maximum sentence on summary conviction becomes 12 months per offence (section 282 CJA 2003 amending section 32 MCA 1980), so that there is a bringing into line of magistrates' maximum powers generally. The Secretary of State is given wide powers to restrict or increase such maxima (section 283). These particular provisions should also now be viewed in the light of the new 'allocation and sending' provisions described in *Chapter 4*, alterations to the rules about committal for sentence to the Crown Court (below) and forthcoming Criminal Procedure Rules common to all criminal courts as mentioned in *Chapter 1*.

None of these changes affects prosecutions for offences committed before the start date for the statutory provision in question.

The power of magistrates to imprison for non-payment of a fine is not restricted by the normal 12 months limit (section 154(4)). 'Fine' includes pecuniary penalties but not forfeitures or compensation: section 154(5).

Consecutive terms of imprisonment in magistrates' courts

Magistrates' courts are given a new maximum period for aggregate custodial sentences. Section 155 CJA 2003 amends section 133 Magistrates' Courts Act

1980 (MCA 1980), with the effect that consecutive sentences must not exceed 65 weeks in aggregate. Where there is more than one either way offence, the limit will also be 65 weeks by virtue of this same provision.

Committal to the Crown Court for sentence

It is when magistrates' powers would not in themselves be sufficient that - in relation to an either way offence - the question of committal to the Crown Court for sentence arises. As intimated in *Chapter 4*, if a case is deemed unsuitable for summary trial then it will be sent straightaway to the Crown Court. Post-CJA 2003, it will also need to be sent to the Crown Court for sentence *before magistrates assume jurisdiction* themselves - since there will no longer be a 'reserve' power to commit for sentence thereafter - i.e. once magistrates have decided that a case is suitable for summary trial and have determined to deal with it summarily within the allocation procedures described in *Chapter 4* (except in relation to dangerous offenders).[26]

The basic idea appears to be to 'force the hand' of the magistrates' court at the allocation and sending stage as to whether its own increased powers (to 12 months per either way offence or 65 weeks in aggregate: above) would suffice if the accused person were to be convicted.

Adjustments to sentencing powers for some individual summary offences

The CJA 2003 contains a wide-ranging revision of magistrates' maximum powers (upwards and downwards) in relation to a range of summary offences. First, section 280(1) CJA 2003 together with schedule 25 removes the punishment of imprisonment for certain summary matters. That schedule lists over 100 different categories of offence ranging from being idle and disorderly under the Vagrancy Act 1824 to various matters under the Town Police Clauses Act 1847, Children and Young Persons Act 1933 (allowing a child to be used for begging) and Wireless Telegraphy Act 1949.[27] Conversely, section 280(2) and Schedule 26 increase the maximum term of imprisonment for certain other summary offences from four months or less to 51 weeks.[28]

Comparable changes appear in section 281 CJA 2003 concerning certain offences punishable with a maximum term of five months imprisonment or less which are not listed in Schedules 25 or 26. Section 281(2) allows the Secretary of State to amend a 'relevant enactment' so as to make such an offence no longer punishable by imprisonment or to raise its maximum sentence to 51 weeks. If an

---

[26] The relevant changes to the MCA 1980 do not apply where magistrates have dealt only with plea before venue, but there can be no committal for sentence once there has been a non-binding indication of sentence within the allocation provisions as outlined in *Chapter 4*: see section 20(7) MCA 1980 as inserted by para. 6 of Schedule 3 to the CJA 2003 and also the new section 3(1)(b) Powers of Criminal Courts (Sentencing) Act 2000 as inserted by para. 22 of Schedule 3.

[27] Other noteworthy instances of the abolition of imprisonment include: betting in streets and public places (Betting, Gaming and Lotteries Act 1963); offences relating to children and public performances (Children and Young Persons Act 1963); taking or destroying fish (Theft Act 1968); wrongful disclosure of information (Transport Act 2000); and making a false statement as to means (under either the MCA 1980 (section 84) or CJA 1991 (section 20A)).

[28] Seemingly, to correspond with the new short forms of custodial sentence of 28 to 51 weeks described in *Chapter 8*. Some 60 categories of offence are involved ranging from trespassing on the railway and being found drunk to certain 'lesser' offences under the Firearms Act 1968, interfering with vehicles, offences relating to processions or assemblies, various drink-driving-related matters and others concerning closure of noisy premises under the Anti-social Behaviour Act 2003.

existing provision attracts a maximum sentence of six months on summary conviction, this is raised to 51 weeks (the effect of sections 281(5) and (6)).

Other changes to penalties
The CJA 2003 increases a range of other penalties, the most significant of which perhaps are certain drug-related offences (section 284 and Schedule 28); aggravated vehicle taking (which will attract a sentence of up to 14 years) and causing death by dangerous driving (14 years) (section 285); and certain penalties under section 174 Road Traffic Act 1988 (section 286) as well as setting minimum penalties for certain firearms offences (section 287: see *Chapter 13*). Certain firearms offences will become indictable only (section 288). Other main sentencing provisions that are superseded by the CJA 2003 are dealt with in section 303; and an extensive list of miscellaneous amendments appears in Schedule 32 (invoked by section 304).[29]

Release on licence and recall to custody
As will be seen from *Chapter 9* which deals with the new forms of sentence the courts themselves will often be responsible for setting periods of release and licence conditions. Where this is not the case, CJA 2003 creates a revised scheme for release on licence and recall to custody (when the Secretary of State may normally take over the setting of conditions afresh in any event). The full scheme and its variants - including the arrangements also for lifers and dangerous offenders - is outlined in *Chapter 11*.

THE 'MENU' OF REQUIREMENTS: A NOTE

One important shift of thinking demanded by the CJA 2003 is 'away from compartmentalised ideas' about sentences. To an extent, this goes hand-in-glove with a unified approach to correctional services, the creation of the National Offender Management Service and the development of accredited programmes that are adaptable to different punishment scenarios. The concept of a 'menu' of requirements from which the new generic community sentence, custody plus, custody minus, intermittent custody and parole or licence conditions can be developed has already been noted - and it is fundamental to further understanding to note the requirements that can be employed. Further details of each and the circumstances when they can be used are given in later chapters.

Twelve basic requirements to select from
As indicated earlier in the chapter, none of the requirements 'belongs' to any particular form of sentence - albeit that historically they have been largely associated with community sentences. The requirements can be used in relation to community orders, various aspects of the new short forms of custodial order or licence arrangements as appropriate - and according to whether or not they appear on the 'menu' in a given situation. Their basic character is set out in a wholly free-standing way within sections 199 to 223 CJA 2003. For clarity, the

---

[29] There are also provisions in relation to endangered species to tie in with European obligations and dealing with maximum sentences for offences to protect wild fauna and flora (see section 307).

approach in this work has been to outline each of the requirements in detail in *Chapter 8* (which deals with the new generic community order) and then to note variations where applicable in *Chapters 9* and *11* (which deal with the new forms of imprisonment and release from custody, respectively). The requirements do not feature directly in relation to the dangerous offender provisions described in *Chapter 10.* In brief, those requirements are:

<table>
<tr><td>

- unpaid work;
- activity;
- programme;
- prohibited activity;
- curfew;
- exclusion;

</td><td>

- residence;
- mental health treatment;
- drug rehabilitation;
- alcohol treatment;
- supervision; and
- attendance centre (to age 25).

</td></tr>
</table>

They can be used in relation to:

- the generic community sentence: any requirement from the above list subject to the court's decision on the appropriate level of restriction of liberty and the suitability of the order for a given offender (*Chapter 8*);
- custody plus: only certain restricted choices (*Chapter 9*);
- intermittent custody: only certain restricted choices (*Chapter 9*);
- the new-style suspended sentence, in two different contexts: at the point of - and as part of - the suspended sentence when any requirements from the list can be added; and as licence components if and when the suspended sentence is later activated, when the same restricted choices apply as for custody plus (*Chapter 9*);
- release on licence: only certain restricted choices (*Chapter 11*).

Electronic monitoring can be added to any of the 12 basic requirements as appropriate, and in relation to certain requirements it normally should be.[30] It should be re-emphasised that, when sentencing, the statutory purposes of sentencing and the threshold for the particular level of sentence (whether a community order or custody as appropriate) must first be met.[31] It is not simply a question of working towards a seemingly desirable (or tempting) outcome, whether for individual, social, community or other reasons.

INFORMATION AND PRE-SENTENCE REPORTS

Before forming certain opinions about the appropriateness or otherwise of custody or a community sentence, the court must 'take into account all such information as is available to it about the circumstances of the offence or (as the case may be) of the offence or offences associated with it, including any aggravating factors or mitigating factors' (section 156(1)). This applies to decisions about:

---

[30] Home detention curfew, which usually nowadays involves electronic monitoring and which is expanding, also operates but independently of the CJA 2003.
[31] Allowing for flexibility to 'move between sentence levels' under the CJA 2003 described earlier.

- the 'serious enough' community sentence threshold and the extent of restriction of liberty created by the requirements of a generic community sentence (i.e. under section 148(1), 2(b) (adults), 3(b) (juveniles);
- the 'so serious' custody threshold (under section 151(2)) or the length of a discretionary custodial sentence (under section 153(2)).

In contrast, there is a discretion under section 156(2) to take any available information into account when deciding upon the suitability of a community sentence for a particular offender (i.e. pursuant to section 148(2)(a) (adults) or 148(3)(a) (juveniles).[32]

Pre-sentence reports (PSRs)
In certain situations the court must 'obtain and consider' a PSR. Broadly speaking, the CJA 2003 reflects existing law, so that (subject to what is said below) a PSR is, by virtue of section 156(3), mandatory before deciding upon:

- the 'so serious' threshold for custody, the length of custody or when considering the risk to the public posed by dangerous offenders pursuant to sections 225(1)(b), 226(1)(b), 227(1)(b), 228(1)(b)(i) CJA 2003;[33] or
- the 'serious enough' test for a community order or the extent of restriction of liberty or the suitability of the offender for a particular requirement or requirements to be imposed by that order.

Again, reflecting existing law the above requirement does not apply where the court deems a PSR to be 'unnecessary' (section 156(4)) or in the case of a juvenile, when at least the most recent of any previous PSRs must be considered or failing that a new one must be obtained (the effect of section 156(5): and see, generally, *Chapter 12*).

No sentence is invalidated by failure to comply with these provisions, but any court on appeal must obtain and consider a PSR unless of the opinion that the court below was justified in dispensing with one or the higher court obtains and considers such a report or itself deems one to be unnecessary (again subject to parallel 'non-dispensing' provisions to those already noted above concerning juveniles (section 156(6), (7) and (8)). Seemingly, there were no legal rulings on the meaning of 'unnecessary' under the CJA 1991, signifying perhaps that this factual concept caused little difficulty under comparable existing provisions.

Definition of PSR
A PSR is defined in section 158(1) as a report which:

(a) with a view to assisting the court in determining the most suitable method of dealing with an offender is made or submitted by an appropriate officer, and
(b) contains information as to such matters, presented in such manner, as may be prescribed by rules made by the Secretary of State.[34]

---

[32] But any failure to consider relevant matters might be in breach of human rights law.
[33] These provisions concern life sentences for public protection, sentences of detention for public protection and extended sentences for certain sexual or violent offences.
[34] Conventionally, since 1991, by way of National Standards whether or not constituting the 'statutory instrument' envisaged by the original version of this requirement.

A key change is the abandonment of the requirement that such a report be *in writing* so that both PSRs and what have become known as specific sentence reports (SSRs: a more targeted form of PSR addressed towards focussed community punishment outcomes) could, post-CJA 2003, be given orally (similarly with medical reports: see later). 'Appropriate officer' means for adults an officer of a local probation board and, for juveniles, such an officer, a social worker or a member of a youth offending team (or YOT) (section 158(2)).

Disclosure of PSRs
The existing disclosure provisions are in effect restated by the CJA 2003 (the apply where a report is not given orally in open court). Under section 159, the court must hand a copy to:

- the offender or his or her counsel (barrister) or solicitor;
- if the offender is under the age of 18, any parent or guardian[35] who is present in court (although there is a savings provision allowing the court, where information appears likely to create a risk of significant harm to the offender, to withhold content from either the offender or his or her parent etc. (section 159(3)); and
- the prosecutor ('the person having conduct of the proceedings'), except where he or she is not of a description prescribed by the Secretary of State when the report need not be given where the court considers that this would be appropriate (section 159(4).

No disclosed information may be used for purposes other than determining whether to make and making representations to the court, e.g. by a prosecutor that a version of events in the report is known to be misleading or incorrect.

Reports other than PSRs
The CJA 2003 widens the extent to which copies of reports must be given to people as described above. Section 160 CJA 2003 covers the situation where a report other than a PSR is made to a court (other than a youth court) with a view to assisting the court in determining the most suitable method of dealing with any person for an offence. This would appear to cover, e.g. the existing community punishment assessment or in future a comparable report concerning an unpaid work requirement (*Chapter 8*) or a report in breach proceedings. There are comparable disclosure provisions to those under section 159 above, but minus a requirement to disclose matters to the prosecutor.

Mental disorder and medical reports
Dedicated provisions come into play where the offender is 'or appears to be' mentally disordered, something that courts have been urged to prioritise generally in recent times. The court must obtain and consider a medical report before passing a custodial sentence other than one fixed by law (section 157).

---

[35] Or, where a local authority has parental authority and the offender is in care or provided with local authority accommodation pursuant to 'social services functions' (see Local Authority Social Services Act 1970), that authority. In the case of juveniles, harm has the meaning ascribed by section 31 Children Act 1989.

There are comparable provisions, considerations, criteria and appeal provisions to those affecting PSRs (above) and concerning dispensing with a medical report. Information that relates to the offender's mental condition must be considered from wherever it derives including 'the likely effect of [a] sentence on [the offender's mental] condition and on any treatment that may be available for it' (section 157(3)).

As under existing law, 'mental disorder' is that falling within the Mental Health Act 1983 and 'medical report' means one submitted orally or in writing by a registered medical practitioner approved for the purposes of section 12 of the 1983 Act as having special experience in diagnosis or treatment.

MITIGATION OF SENTENCE

Quite apart from 'mitigating factors' that affect the serious of an offence itself, sentences of a court may always be mitigated on other grounds relating to the overall circumstances of a particular case or offender.

General power to mitigate

Section 166 CJA 2003 (which re-enacts existing law with certain modifications) contains wide-ranging 'nothing prevents' provisions in relation to mitigation of sentence and for dealing appropriately with mentally disordered offenders. Thus 'Nothing . . . prevents a court from mitigating an offender's sentence by taking into account any such matters as, in the opinion of the court, are relevant in mitigation of sentence'. This provision, section 166(1), applies regardless of the threshold criteria for discretionary custody, a generic community sentence or fine (or the pre-sentence report requirements). It is specifically reinforced by section 166(2) which states (in effect) that if - after concluding that the 'so serious' test for custody described earlier in this chapter is met, by ruling out a fine or community sentence as not being justified (under section 152(2) CJA 2003) - the court then considers that there is mitigation pointing towards a lesser punishment, it can still impose a community sentence or fine even though it had earlier ruled both of these out.

The totality principle

Similarly, section 166(3) CJA 2003 re-affirms what is generally described as the 'totality principle' under which a court may consider the 'total punitive weight' of a sentence by taking into account 'any other penalty included in that sentence' (e.g. so as to give priority to compensation over a fine, or perhaps to shorten a prison sentence to acknowledge enforced seizure of assets or reparation).

Mental disorder

Section 166(5) makes it clear that nothing in the new sentencing provisions of the CJA 2003 is to be taken as requiring a court to pass a custodial sentence, or any particular form of custodial sentence, on a mentally disordered offender within the meaning of the Mental Health Act 1983, as restricting any power under the 1983 Act to deal with such an offender as the court considers appropriate. See also section 294 CJA 2003 concerning the duration of directions by the Secretary of State concerning prisoners who are transferred to hospital whilst serving a prison term; and the 'access to the Parole Board' provisions in section 295 (*Chapter 11*).

Disqualification from working with children

A highly specific new power introduced by section 299 CJA 2003 (introducing Schedule 30) is that whereby certain offenders can be disqualified from working with children. Part 2 Criminal Justice and Court Services Act 2000 already requires such an order on conviction of 'an offence against a child' (as defined in section 26 of that Act by reference to a list in Schedule 4 of that Act), where a sentence of imprisonment or detention for 12 months or more is imposed. In relation to adults, such an order must be made unless the court is satisfied that it is unlikely that the individual will commit any further offence.[36] Schedule 30 inserts new sections 29A and 29B into the 2000 Act.

Section 29A extends the court's powers by adding a discretion to make a disqualification order if it is satisfied that it is likely that a further offence against a child will be committed, even though the sentence threshold specified in the 2000 Act is not met. The test whether the order should be made is whether the court is satisfied, having regard to all the circumstances, that it is likely that the individual will commit a further offence against a child. If so, and the court makes an order, the court must give its reasons.

Under section 29B, if a court had a duty to consider a disqualification but did not do so (or give reasons), the prosecutor can apply for disqualification at any time in the future. The court will then consider (or reconsider) the criteria, seemingly taking account of the present circumstances, and make or refuse a disqualification order and give appropriate reasons. This applies where a court was obliged to consider disqualification post-implementation of these provisions on 11 January 2001.

FINES

In broad terms, the CJA 2003 restates the criteria and procedures for courts when imposing a fine. Under separate provisions, in the magistrates' court the maximum fine is set by the statute creating the offence (usually) and in most instances by reference to one of five standard levels.[37] There is no over-arching limit for multiple offences (as there is with imprisonment). The global ceiling is, in effect, determined by proportionality, the totality principle and the offender's individual financial circumstances. In general, the Crown Court can impose a fine instead of or in addition to dealing with an offender in any other way and maximum fines in that court are often not subject to any legal limit. Section 163 CJA 2003 emphasises that:

> . . . where a person is convicted on indictment of any offence, other than an offence for which the sentence is fixed by law [or required by law] the court, if not precluded from sentencing an offender by its exercise of some other power, may

---

[36] For those below 18 years of age see *Chapter 12*.
[37] I.e. Level 1 £200; Level 2 £500; Level 3 £1,000; Level 4 £2,500; and Level 5 £5,000 (March 2004). There has, in relation to existing law, been a long-running debate concerning the extent to which, if at all, a fine and a community sentence can be imposed for the same offence. If anything, the new law with its in-built flexibility appears, overall, to be less against this.

impose a fine instead of or in addition to dealing with him in any other way . . . subject, however, to any enactment requiring the offender to be dealt with in a particular way.

Fixing the amount of a fine

Under the CJA 2003, the fining process is re-enacted in section 164 which sets out the following steps:

- before fixing the amount of any fine on an individual the court must inquire into his or her financial circumstances;
- the amount of any fine must reflect the seriousness of the offence;
- the court must take into account the circumstances of the case, including, among other things, the financial circumstances of the offender so far as they are known or appear to the court - and this applies whether it has the effect of increasing or reducing the amount of the fine; and
- where (for one of a variety of reasons) the court has insufficient information to make a proper determination it may make such determination as it thinks fit.

Financial circumstances

'Financial circumstances' are not defined by the CJA 2003 but as under existing law and practice these appear to cover not only direct income but also, e.g. savings, investments, endowment policies and valuable possessions, as well as permitting a court to consider the position of, say, an offender with no apparent income but who is living a fairly lavish lifestyle, based possibly on a partner's support—which thereby reduces the need for personal expenditure. In the case of people on state benefits the amount of each instalment may well have to be kept to the minimum and the number of instalments reduced to enable payment over a matter of weeks.

Financial circumstances order
Under section 162 CJA 2003, once an individual stands convicted of an offence, the court may, before sentence, make a financial circumstances order. The offender must then, within a period set by the court, provide 'such a statement of his financial circumstances as the court may require' (section 162(4)). In practice, this may be by way of written details or in answer to inquiries in court where the offender is present. An offender who without reasonable excuse fails to comply with such an order is liable on summary conviction to a Level 3 fine (up to £1,000). If he or she knowingly or recklessly furnishes a statement that is false in a material particular, or knowingly fails to disclose any material fact, he or she is liable on summary conviction to a Level 4 fine (£2,500) (the CJA 2003 removing the former alternative of three months imprisonment).[38] Similarly, under the Courts Act 2003 *the justices' chief executive* will be able to require such details and furthermore at any time *after charge* - in readiness for the court to set an appropriate fine and payment terms if there is a conviction (and with similar offences and penalties for failure or a false return): section 95 Courts Act 2003.[39]

---

[38] The usual six months time limit for starting proceedings is extended to two years (section 162(6)).
[39] Query whether such a demand made *pre-conviction* potentially contravene Article 8 of the European Convention On Human Rights (right to private and family life).

The Department for Constitutional Affairs (DCA) has encouraged courts to adopt a standard 'means form' through which can be obtained not only actual income and expenditure, etc. but also, e.g. the defaulter's National Insurance number (for the purpose of attaching benefits or earnings) or vehicle registration number (for clamping where a vehicle is to be seized and sold so that the proceeds can be used to settle the financial order).

Remission and alteration of fines[40]

A later court has a general power to remit a fine, in whole or in part, in the light of any *subsequent* change in circumstances. A specific power in section 165 CJA 2003 allows a later court to remit all or part of a fine where it was originally fixed in the offender's absence or without an adequate statement of financial circumstances if information before the later court suggests that, had the original court had that information, it would have fixed a lower fine or no fine at all. However, it is not possible to substitute a different type of penalty even if such new information suggests that a fine was not appropriate in the first place (i.e. the court can only vary the amount of the fine and set a new rate of payment). In extreme cases, section 142 of the Magistrates' Courts Act 1980 (rectification of decisions) might be used to alter sentence.

Fine enforcement

As part of a general 'firming up' in relation to enforcement of sentences generally, the CJA 2003 re-enacts (with modifications) two mechanisms for enforcing fines:[41]

Unpaid work requirement

Section 300 CJA 2003 replaces the default provisions in section 35 Crime Sentences Act 1997 whereby - when a court is considering whether to commit an offender to custody in default of payment by activating a committal warrant - it is given an alternative power, i.e. to order that the defaulter perform unpaid work (as now defined by section 199 CJA 2003) or to impose a curfew requirement (as defined by section 204 CJA 2003) (see section 300(2)). This is called a 'default order' (section 300(3)). Under further provisions of section 300, the requirements can be made subject to electronic monitoring and the default order can be postponed until such time as the court thinks fit. The section also provides for breach and enforcement of the default order. There is thus a kind of 'snowball' effect: fine, default, committal to custody (almost); unpaid work; breach; enforcement. If the defaulter wishes to pay all or part of the fine, his or her obligation to perform requirements is reduced in proportion.

Driving disqualification

Similarly, section 301 re-enacts section 40 Crime Sentences Act 1997 so as to allow the court to disqualify from driving for up to 12 months a fine defaulter,

---

[40] The DCA has restricted the extent to which it will normally sanction writing off a fine administratively, emphasising the need for courts to consider the correct level of fine at the outset or where appropriate formal remission at a later stage.

[41] The provisions apply to juveniles aged 16 upwards (notwithstanding restrictions on custodial sentences for people under 18 years of age): section 300(1)(b) and 301(1)(b).

i.e. instead of sending him or her to custody. If the fine is then paid, the order ceases to have effect, or if part is paid the disqualification is reduced by a corresponding proportion. The Secretary of State is given power to alter the period of 12 months by order.[42]

DEFERMENT OF SENTENCE

Section 278 together with Schedule 23 CJA 2003 introduces replacement provisions concerning deferment of sentence. Schedule 23 inserts new provisions into the Powers of Criminal Courts (Sentencing) Act 2000 (PCC(S)A). As under existing law, the new provisions allow a court to defer sentencing an offender for the purpose of allowing it to have regard to the conduct of the offender and any change in his or her circumstances. However, the CJA 2003 strengthens this process by providing for reparative or similar activity to be undertaken during the period of deferment, and extends 'conduct' to mean 'how well the offender complied'.[43] Thus, good progress on the part of the offender will continue to operate as a mitigating factor with regard to his or her eventual sentence. Sentence can be deferred only if the offender consents; and also undertakes to comply with any requirements laid down by the court - and only where it considers that deferment is in the interests of justice. The court cannot remand an offender when it defers sentencing; and sentencing cannot be deferred for more than six months. The new section 1(5) PCC(S)A states who should receive a copy of the deferment order. The court can later issue a summons or a warrant if the offender does not appear for sentencing at the end of the deferment period, as required.

Under new section 1A PCC(S)A, the court can include requirements about an offender's residence. If he or she is to undertake requirements, it may appoint a supervisor to monitor compliance (an officer of the local probation board or anyone else the court thinks fit). He or she must consent to this; and provide the court with information about the offender's compliance if the court so wishes. Under new section 1B PCC(S)A, the court can deal with the offender before the end of the period of deferment if satisfied that he or she has failed to comply with one or more requirements. Under existing law there are no requirements as such attached to deferment and the offender can only be returned to court early if he or she commits another offence. Section 1B(2) sets out circumstances in which he or she will be liable to be returned early (including for breach of undertakings); whilst section 1B(3) gives the court power to issue a summons or warrant for this purpose. As already indicated, but worthy of emphasis, monitoring of deferment will be in place where there are undertakings.

Under new section 1C PCC(S)A, the court may deal with an offender before the end of the deferment period if he or she commits another offence. Sections

---

[42] There is power in section 146 Powers of Criminal Courts (Sentencing) Act 2000 whereby courts can disqualify from driving by way of sentence for any offence, which in practice is sometimes used instead of a fine.

[43] It remains to be asked - particularly in view of the greater flexibility of the CJA 2003 and its more stricter enforcement provisions - what can be achieved by deferment that might not in many cases be achieved by making a generic community order with appropriate requirements at the outset.

1C(2) and (3) set out the powers of the Crown Court and magistrates' court respectively. When a court deals with an offender at the end of the period of deferment (or earlier if undertakings are not complied with) it has the same powers as if the offence had just been committed. If the offender is convicted of another offence during the deferment period, the court may deal with the offence in respect of which sentencing was originally deferred at the same time as sentencing for the new offence. If the original sentence was deferred by the Crown Court, the Crown Court must pass sentence for both offences. If originally deferred by a magistrates' court and the offender is brought before a Crown Court to be sentenced for the two offences, the Crown Court cannot pass a sentence greater than a magistrates' court could have done, i.e. usually up to 12 months (above). Generally speaking, however, magistrates will deal with the sentence where they originally deferred matters.[44] The court may issue a summons to someone appointed as a supervisor if that person refuses to appear before the court when the court wants to consider an offender's failure to comply with the requirements of the deferment or anything to do with the original offence.

A new section 1D PCC(S)A clarifies the legal status of deferment, i.e. it is 'an adjournment', and if the offender does not appear before the court on the due date he or she is to be dealt with accordingly.

THE SENTENCING GUIDELINES COUNCIL (SGC)

An important development brought about by the CJA 2003 in relation to the new sentencing framework and its practical deployment by judges and magistrates is the creation of a Sentencing Guidelines Council (SGC). Traditionally, magistrates have set their own guidelines and these have been published under the auspices of the Magistrates' Association (though latterly with the involvement of other parties). Overall, the most significant source for sentencing guidance has been Court of Appeal guidance in 'guideline cases', albeit not covering the full spectrum of sentencing or readily transposed to 'common starting points' in summary cases. Sentencers also rely on reported judgements from a myriad of individual appeal outcomes in cases that have reached the Court of Appeal, together with (infrequent) *Practice Directions*.[45] In future, the SGC will be the ultimate authority in terms of sentencing guidelines and once these are 'definitive' courts must have regard to them and give their reasons for any departure from them (section 172), i.e. at every level from the magistrates' court to the Court of Appeal and House of Lords (Supreme Court).

---

[44] According to the Home Office guidance notes, this includes committing the offender to the Crown Court for sentence, but this would be wholly inconsistent with the fact that a magistrates' court will of necessity have assumed jurisdiction. Deferment can hardly operate to 'turn back the clock' to before that point (see under the heading *Committal for sentence*, above). And why else would the Crown Court's powers be restricted where the new offence occurs in that court?

[45] There is some debate about how long this will continue, but it may need to for a time - alongside the work of the SGC - unless the SGC is to perform a Herculean, all-embracing task overnight. There is room for reflection about the exact future relationship between the SGC, Court of Appeal/House of Lords (or Supreme Court) and Secretary of State. These and some further thoughts concerning the strategic importance of the SGC are noted in *Chapter 14*.

Creation and make-up of the SGC

The Sentencing Guidelines Council is created under section 167 CJA 2003.[46] It consists of the Lord Chief Justice (who is designated as chairman by the statute), seven judicial members and four non-judicial members. The provisions set out the basis upon which both kinds of member are eligible for appointment and are to be appointed (see, generally, section 167(2) to (6)). Whereas judicial members are to be selected from the various ranks of the judiciary (and by the Lord Chancellor/Secretary of State for Constitutional Affairs) so as to reflect the views of people regularly dealing with criminal cases, non-judicial individuals are only eligible for appointment if they appear to the Secretary of State (in this case the Home Secretary who has the general responsibility in relation to such members: see section 168(2)) to have experience in one or more of the following areas: policing; criminal prosecution; criminal defence; and the promotion of the welfare of victims of crime. People 'eligible by virtue of experience' include the Director of Prosecutions (section 167(5)). The non-judicial appointees must include at least one person appearing to have experience in each of the areas mentioned above (section 167(6)). The Home Secretary can also appoint an observer with experience of sentencing policy and administration of sentences and he or she may attend and speak at meetings (section 167(9)).[47]

The Lord Chief Justice must appoint a deputy chairman from the judicial members (section 167(7)), and can nominate an eligible judicial 'substitute' to attend when he or she is absent. The SGC must make an annual report to Ministers on the exercise its functions (section 173).

The Sentencing Advisory Panel

The SGC will be supported by the Sentencing Advisory Panel (SAP) set up under the Crime and Disorder Act 1998. The SAP is expressly continued by section 169 CJA 2003 but with the creation of the SGC the SAP is no longer confined, as previously, to suggesting approaches to particular kinds of offences. The SAP is constituted by the Lord Chancellor/Secretary of State for Constitutional Affairs (after consultation with the Lord Chief Justice and Home Secretary) who also appoints its chairman. It is responsible for research into sentencing and producing reports and information. The 'constitutional' position is that the panel will continue with its research, discussions, outside consultations and analysis of information concerning sentencing matters. The outcome of its deliberations will be communicated to the SCG for consideration alongside other information, data and relevant materials. This may also be by way of a proposal to the SGC pursuant to section 171 CJA 2003, which the SGC is then duty bound to consider. Conversely, the SGC must notify the SAP about any other proposed or revised guidelines and as part of that process the SAP must also in turn (and except in cases of urgency) consult with people stipulated by the SGP and, in effect, respond to the SGC.

---

[46] At the time of writing, a secretariat was in place and advertisements had appeared in the national press seeking applications by people wishing to be appointed as non-judicial members.

[47] Earlier proposals, e.g. that Parliament should have a role in the framing of guidelines or that a Home Office official should sit as a member of the SGC were not pursued.

Guidelines

Perhaps the key aspect of the new law is that in section 170 CJA 2003 whereby the SGC may from time to time consider whether to frame sentencing or allocation (see *Chapter 4)* guidelines and under which the Home Secretary may propose to the council that sentencing or allocation guidelines be framed or revised by it in respect of:

- offences or offenders of a particular category; or
- a particular matter affecting sentencing (i.e. going beyond the SAP's original scope).

The SGC must consider such proposals (plus any from the SAP (above)) and, in effect, whether or not to act upon them. This discretion represents a critical buffer in terms of preserving the independence of the judiciary. There are the following statutory criteria when considering the issue of sentencing guidelines:

- the need to promote consistency in sentencing;
- the sentences imposed by courts in England and Wales;
- the cost of different sentences and their relative effectiveness in preventing offending;
- the need to promote public confidence in the criminal justice system; and
- the views communicated to the SGC by the SAP (see section 170(5)).

With regard to allocation guidelines the SGC's considerations must include 'consistency' and the views of the SAP (section 170(6)).

The SGC is free to act of its own motion to create guidelines; and there are various provisions aimed at keeping SGC guidelines current and up-to-date. As intimated above, the SGC must consider whether to frame guidelines if it receives a guidelines proposal from the SAP (as it must where this stems from the Home Secretary: above). Guidelines must be kept under review and the SGC must revise them if appropriate (section 170(5)); and there is a statutory process of drafts, consultation and eventual publication (section 170(8), (9)). As already indicated above, courts will have to follow the definitive guidelines of the SGC.

Already in this chapter, examples have been suggested of areas that the SGC might usefully address: the weight to be given to any previous convictions in relation to the seriousness of the present offence (as, in fact, is required by section 170(7)); consistency of discounts for a timely plea of guilty; the appropriate reduction in a community sentence to reflect time spent in custody on remand (i.e. what might be ordered to be treated as 'time served'. in relation to custody). There is similarly an urgency concering the operation of the new-style sentences introduced by the CJA 2003 and also allocation and sending guidelines (see also section 170(6)) which will replace the existing National Mode of Trial Guidelines (last revised in 1995 and now showing their age).

PUBLICATION OF SENTENCING INFORMATION

Running alongside the work of the Sentencing Guidelines Council is the duty of the Secretary of State to publish information about sentencing. Section 175 CJA

2003 extends section 95 Criminal Justice Act 1991 under which the Secretary of State is under a duty to publish information to people engaged in the administration of justice concerning the costs of sentences and a range of discrimination issues. Such people are now to receive information so as 'to become aware of the relative effectiveness of different sentences - (i) in preventing re-offending, and (ii) in promoting public confidence in the criminal justice system'. Reconciling (i) with (ii) may require a degree of ingenuity if the reputed effectiveness of well-run community schemes is to counter the simplistic solutions of many a political 'sound-bite'.

REASONS FOR SENTENCE DECISIONS

Section 174 CJA 2003 contains a general duty - other than where a sentence is mandatory, fixed or otherwise required by law - for a court to give reasons for and to explain the effect of a sentence in 'ordinary language and in general terms', and in particular for departure from any sentencing guidelines which may be applicable. Section 174 - which also sets out certain specific situations where an explanation is required, e.g. why an offence is 'serious enough' for a community sentence (excluding where it is already required to explain itself under another provision where such a sentence is being used for a persistent offender instead of a fine) - is reproduced in the *Appendix* to this work.

Requirements that can be used re a generic community sentence/suspended sentence (GS/SS) or as licence conditions for custody plus or for intermittent custody (CP/IC)		
Unpaid work	'New' 40 to 300 hour limit (compared with 240 hours for existing community punishment order). Offender must be suitable for work and court should normally hear from an officer of the local probation board (OLPB).	GS/SS/CP/IC
Activity	Court must consult OLPB and obtain consent from anyone else whose co-operation is needed.	GS/SS/CP/IC
Programme	Accredited programmes as recommended by OLPB. Programme and a place on it must be available locally. Court must obtain consent if co-operation is needed by another. Places of attendance must be approved by LPB.	GS/SS/CP/IC
Prohibited activity	Court must first consult OLPB. CJA 2003 expressly states may prohibit possessing, carrying, using firearm.	GS/SS/CP/IC
Curfew*	Court must consider information about place or places and attitudes of people involved (consent not strictly necessary). NB: There is a six months/180 day limit.	GS/SS/CP/IC
Exclusion*	Enables flexible requirements concerning the exclusion of the offender from specified places at specified times.	GS/SS/CP/IC
Residence	Recommendation by OLPB needed if hostel/institution.	GS/SS
Mental health treatment	May be as a resident or non-resident patient. Exact treatment a matter for the doctors etc., not the court. Various pre-conditions apply: see text. Offender must express 'willingness' to comply.	GS/SS
Drug rehabilitation	Order includes regular drug testing and is reviewable by the court under special procedures. Resident or non-resident. OLPB must recommend. Exact treatment is for the doctors etc., not the court. Offender must express 'willingness' to comply. Other pre-conditions: see text.	GS/SS
Alcohol treatment	Dependency must be susceptible to treatment which must be available. Resident or non-resident. Offender must express 'willingness' to comply.	GS/SS
Supervision	To promote the offender's rehabilitation.	GS/SS/CP/IC
Attendance centre	Under 25s only. The centre must be accessible: see text.	GS/SS/CP/IC
Electronic monitoring requirement can be added and normally *must* be where an asterix appears.		

CHAPTER 8

The Generic Community Order

As noted in *Chapter 7*, section 148(1) CJA 2003[1] states that a community sentence must not be passed (the new and strategic emphasis being on the words *must not*) unless the court is of the opinion that the offence[2] was serious enough to warrant such a sentence. Discounting this change of emphasis, the threshold test for a community sentence thus reflects existing law.

Under section 148(2): the requirement (or requirements 'taken together') in a community order must be the most suitable for the offender; and the restrictions of liberty which they entail must be commensurate with the seriousness of the offence - again familiar territory for sentencers and practitioners alike.

What *is* new and different about the CJA 2003 provisions, is that a court will be able to make just one kind of community sentence, the 'generic community order' - for offenders aged 16 years or over[3] - and within which it will be possible for there to be various components, styled 'requirements'. The new-style requirements[4] broadly reflect what under existing law are community orders in their own right - such as the community punishment order (in future reflected in an 'unpaid work requirement'), attendance centre order ('attendance centre requirement') - or what have been called 'conditions' as currently attached to community rehabilitation orders (such as 'supervision', 'activities' or 'residence' requirements). Courts will thus need to adjust to the idea of building a single generic order from a 'menu' of requirements and whilst ensuring - given a potential for excess - that the order remains 'commensurate' with (or proportionate to) the seriousness of the offence. The real strength and potential - or 'teeth - of the generic order lies not just in the restriction of liberty it imposes on the offender but also in the increased severity of the breach and associated provisions (see later in the chapter).

The Secretary of State is given extensive powers to regulate the supervision of offenders and a range of associated matters (section 222 CJA 2003); as well as to amend certain limits relating to orders (section 223).

Requirements in practice

Requirements themselves may begin to take a different shape according to the arrangements for dealing with offenders emanating from a new National Offender Management Service (NOMS), together with nationwide accreditation of schemes, programmes and facilities. Also, the Secretary of State is empowered to make rules in relation to various aspects of requirements (section 222); an expansion of authority - in that this would seemingly allow a higher degree of control from the centre of what sentences comprise in practice than hitherto, and especially if viewed in conjunction with further powers allowing him or her to

---

[1] The relevant part of section 148 CJA 2003 is set out in that chapter.
[2] Or the combination of the offence and one or more offences associated with it. All references to 'the offence' in this chapter should be so read.
[3] For juveniles, see *Chapter 12*.
[4] Note that requirements are also available in other contexts as described in *Chapter 7*.

amend the statutory maxima for various requirements (and thereby override substantive provisions of the CJA 2003) (see section 223). As is explained in *Chapter 14*, what community sentences comprise - and thus what sentences are actually available to courts - may well depend on a mix of strategies from the centre and the resulting 'capacity of the [correctional] services' to deliver (or put another way, what government allows them to deliver).

Linked to this, there are provisions whereby arrangements for orders must be available locally before certain requirements can be used (section 218); for copies of relevant orders to be supplied to certain people;[5] and placing a duty on an offender to keep in touch with the responsible officer (section 220). Mostly, these aspects of the CJA 2003 reflect existing law, procedure and practice.

Scope of the requirements

When making a generic community order the court can choose from any of the 12 basic requirements set out in sections 199 to 223 CJA 2003. This 'menu' has already been outlined in *Chapter 7* and the nature of each of the individual requirements contained in it is described below. As part of a renewed emphasis on electronic monitoring there is a further requirement enabling this: further, such a requirement *must* be added whenever a court orders a curfew or exclusion requirement (unless it is legally prevented from doing so, or in the circumstances it considers that such monitoring would be inappropriate) (section 177(3)). In all other situations the court has a discretion to do so, i.e. in relation to requirements of unpaid work; activities; programmes; prohibited activities; residence; mental health; drug rehabilitation; alcohol treatment; supervision; and attendance centre (section 177(4)). Electronic monitoring cannot be used on its own.

In certain situations consultation with third parties, and in some circumstances their agreement to a particular course of action, is a pre-requisite to adding a requirement. Similarly, an indication from the offender of his or her willingness to comply with a given requirement may be needed. All these situations are noted in the descriptions of individual requirements below.

The community order must set a date - not more than three years beyond the date of when made - by which the requirements in it must have been complied with; and an order that specifies two or more different requirements may set an earlier date or dates in relation to compliance with any one or more of them (section 177(5)). There are certain further time-related provisions tied to specific orders, e.g. 'unpaid work' must normally be completed within 12 months and an exclusion requirement can only extend for a maximum two years (below).

Where there are two or more requirements these must be compatible (section 177(6)), something that the court must consider before including them alongside one another. Neither must requirements (nor directions given during an order by a responsible officer[6]) conflict with an offender's religious beliefs, any existing requirements of other orders, or the offender's work or education (section 217). The Secretary of State is given power to regulate these matters. In practical terms, both courts when sentencing and probation officers when writing PSRs will, in practice, need to take reasonable steps to avoid the disproportionate loading of

---

[5] With separate provisions for juveniles contained in section 219: see, generally, *Chapter 12*.
[6] For an explanation of 'responsible officer' see later in the chapter.

requirements on an offender (what used to be described as 'setting the offender up to fail), particularly now in view of the severity of the breach provisions (see later).

Other general provisions and terminology
Section 216 CJA 2003 deals with the petty sessions area to be specified in a community order - the court must specify the petty sessions area[7] where the offender resides or will reside. It is also necessary to be familiar with certain basic terminology used in relation to the community sentence provisions. The term 'relevant order' is employed throughout the 2003 Act as a reference mechanism - and, under section 196 CJA 2003, means, in the present context, a 'community order'. Similarly, 'responsible officer' is a device for referring to the individual responsible for certain functions in relation to a given type of order or requirement. Section 197 CJA 2003 gives a range of definitions: if an order imposes only a curfew or exclusion requirement, and if that curfew or exclusion order is electronically monitored, the responsible officer is the person responsible for the monitoring (currently private sector contractors to the Home Office); if an offender is 18 or over and under 25 and is subject only to an attendance centre requirement the responsible officer will be the officer in charge of the attendance centre; in all other situations in the case of an adult, the responsible officer is an officer of the local probation board.[8] Again, the Secretary of State can amend these provisions by order (subject to affirmative resolution by Parliament) including so as to allow a court to determine for itself which description is to apply in a given situation.

Respective duties of the responsible officer and the offender
Section 198 CJA 2003 casts duties on the responsible officer as follows (except where he or she is responsible only to the extent of electronic monitoring):

Where a relevant order has effect, it is the duty of the responsible officer -
   (a) to make any arrangements that are necessary in connection with the requirement imposed by the order,
   (b) to promote the offender's compliance with those requirements,
   (c) where appropriate, to take steps to enforce those requirements.

Under section 220 CJA 2003, the offender must keep in touch with his or her responsible officer and in accordance with any instructions given by the latter. The offender must notify the officer of any change of residence; and if he or she does not keep in touch as required, or changes residence without notifying the officer, the offender is liable to breach proceedings (see later in the chapter).

REVIEW OF COMMUNITY SENTENCES BY A COURT

By way of significant modification of and extension to existing arrangements, section 178 CJA 2003 allows the Secretary of State (by statutory instrument) to:

---

[7] Petty sessions areas will be replaced by local justice areas under the Courts Act 2003.
[8] For the position in relation to juveniles see *Chapter 12*.

- enable or require a court making a community order to provide for the community order to be reviewed periodically by that or another court;
- enable a court to amend a community order so as to include or remove a provision for review by a court; and
- make provision as to the timing and conduct of reviews and as to the powers of the court on review.

Thus, the Secretary of State would be able to allow a court to attach or remove a review provision from a community order, and regulate the timing of reviews. The Home Office guidance notes indicate that 'such an order may in particular contain provisions similar to those applying to reviews of suspended sentences [see *Chapter 9*] . . . It is intended that the decision to extend reviews to community orders would be based on consultation with the courts.'

UNPAID WORK REQUIREMENT

Under sections 199 to 222 CJA 2003 this is a requirement that the offender perform unpaid work in the community for the number of hours specified by the court and within set limits. In practice, such work is carried out on projects set up by the probation service and which may involve consultation with judges, magistrates and the local community. The aggregate hours of work must not be below 40 nor above 300.[9] If there are two or more offences, consecutive orders are possible if the court deems this appropriate, but subject to the same 300 hours aggregate limit; or such requirements can be ordered to operate concurrently. The court may only impose an unpaid work requirement where it is satisfied that the offender is a suitable person to perform work under such a requirement and - 'if the court thinks necessary' - after hearing from an appropriate officer.[10]

The offender is obliged to perform for the number of hours specified in the order 'such work at such times' as he or she is instructed by the responsible officer[11] - and usually within 12 months (although there is power to extend this 'in the interests of justice': see paragraph 20 of Schedule 8 to the Act). However, unless revoked the order remains in force until the hours of work are completed.

ACTIVITY REQUIREMENT

Under section 201 CJA 2003 an activity requirement is one that the offender present himself or herself to a specified person, at a specified place, for a certain number of days, and/or take part in specified activities for a certain number of days.[12] It may involve tasks designed to help with future employment, or group work focusing on particular problems. Reparative activities are one aim of such requirements. In the case of an adult, the court must consult an officer of a local

---

[9] A rise from 240 hours under existing law concerning community punishment orders.

[10] Meaning, here, an officer of a local probation board in the case of an adult; the same, a social worker, or member of a youth offending team in the case of a juvenile: section 199(4) CJA 2003. This is analogous to the existing (but currently mandatory) 'community service assessment'.

[11] For the meaning of 'responsible officer', see earlier in the chapter.

[12] Section 201 is based on the existing requirements concerning activities contained in Schedule 2 to the Powers of Criminal Courts (Sentencing) Act 2000.

probation board before making such an order; and the court must not impose an activity requirement before obtaining the consent of any other person whose co-operation is needed. Under section 201(5) the maximum number of days of activity is 60. The offender must present himself or herself at a place or places specified by the responsible officer on the number of days specified in the order, and comply with instructions given by or under the authority of the person in charge of that place. If the place is a community rehabilitation centre, the offender must attend elsewhere if the person in charge of that centre so instructs.

PROGRAMME REQUIREMENT

Under section 202 CJA 2003, a programme requirement is one that the offender participate in an accredited programme at a place and on a number of days as specified by the court. A programme is defined as 'a systematic set of activities', in effect, a type of course that seeks to address offending behaviour, e.g. anger management, sex offending, substance misuse. 'Accredited programme', 'programme' and 'accreditation body' are defined by the section and the Secretary of State may by order designate accreditation bodies so that changes in the list can be accommodated from time-to-time. In the case of an adult,[13] an officer of a local probation board must recommend that the specified programme is suitable for the offender before the court imposes a programme requirement. The court must also be satisfied that a place on the programme is available and must not impose a programme requirement on an offender before obtaining the consent of any person (other than the offender or responsible officer) whose co-operation is necessary. The offender must participate in the programme as specified in the order and in accordance with instructions given by the responsible officer; and he or she must also comply with any instructions given by, or under the authority of, the person in charge of the programme. A place must not be specified unless it has been approved by the local probation board.

PROHIBITED ACTIVITY REQUIREMENT

Under section 203 CJA 2003 this is a requirement that the offender refrain from taking part in activities specified in the order on a day or days specified by the court, or during a specified period. The requirement cannot be included in the case of an adult[14] unless the court has first consulted an officer of a local probation board. Expressly, requirements may provide 'that the offender does not possess, use or carry a firearm within the meaning of the Firearms Act 1968'.[15]

CURFEW REQUIREMENT

Under section 204 CJA 2003[16] this is a requirement that the offender remain for periods specified by the court at a place or places specified in the order. The

---

[13] For juveniles, see *Chapter 12*.

[14] For juveniles, see *Chapter 12*.

[15] He or she would, of course, usually commit a firearms offence if he or she did so, in any event.

[16] Re-enacting with modifications section 37 Powers of Criminal Courts (Sentencing) Act 2000.

order may specify different places or different periods for different days, but not periods of less than two hours nor more than 12 'in any day'. Before making the order the court must obtain and consider information about the place proposed to be specified in the order including information about the attitude of people likely to be affected by the enforced presence there of the offender (although that person's agreement or consent is not strictly required, even if in all practical terms it may be wholly desirable).

As already noted, an electronic monitoring requirement (see later) *must* be added unless the court is prevented from doing so or in the particular circumstances considers that this is inappropriate (section 177(3)). It should be noted that section 204(3) to (5) (which limits curfew periods for different types of orders) restricts the length of curfews under a community sentence to six months from the date of the order.

EXCLUSION REQUIREMENT

Under section 205 CJA 2003[17] an exclusion requirement is one prohibiting the offender from entering a place or places specified in the order for a period specified by the court but not exceeding two years.[18] The exclusion requirement may provide 'for the prohibition to operate only during the periods specified during the order' or specify 'different places for different periods or days'. An area can be specified rather than a specific place, such a football ground on match-days or a town centre at night. As noted earlier, an electronic monitoring requirement (see later) *must* be added unless the court is prevented from doing so or in the particular circumstances considers this inappropriate (section 177(3)).

RESIDENCE REQUIREMENT

Under section 206 CJA 2003[19] this is a requirement that during the period set by the court the offender must reside at a place specified by the court in the order. If the order so provides, a residence requirement does not prohibit the offender from residing, with the prior approval of the responsible officer, at a place other than that specified in the order. The court must first consider the home surroundings of the offender. It may not specify a hostel or other institution for residence except on the recommendation of an officer of a local probation board.

MENTAL HEALTH TREATMENT REQUIREMENT

Under sections 207 to 208 CJA 2003[20] this is a requirement that the offender must submit, during a period or periods specified by the court in the order, to

---

[17] Re-enacting with modifications the unimplemented section 40A Powers of Criminal Courts (Sentencing) Act 2000 (the non-implemented inserting provision was section 46 Criminal Justice and Court services Act 2000).

[18] There are, in practice, different limits in relation to custodial scenarios: *Chapter 9.*

[19] Based on existing provisions in relation to community rehabilitation orders contained in the Powers of Criminal Courts(Sentencing) Act 2000, Schedule 2, paragraph 1.

[20] Based on the existing Powers of Criminal Courts(Sentencing) Act 2000, Schedule 2 paragraph 5.

treatment by or under the direction of a registered medical practitioner or chartered psychologist with a view to the improvement of his or her mental condition. The treatment must be one of the following as specified in the order:

- as a resident patient in an independent hospital or care home within the meaning of the Care Standards Act 2000 or a hospital within the meaning of the Mental Health Act 1983 (but not in hospital premises where high security psychiatric services within the meaning of that Act are provided);
- as a non-resident patient at such institution or place specified in the order;
- by or under the direction of such registered medical practitioner or chartered psychologist (or both) as may be specified in the order.

The nature of the treatment is not to be specified except as above. Various pre-conditions apply, including the need for the court to be satisfied on the basis of a report from an approved registered medical practitioner concerning the susceptibility to treatment of the offender's mental condition and that it is not such as to warrant a hospital order or guardianship order[21] - as well as that arrangements have been made for the treatment 'intended to be specified in the order' (including arrangements for reception as a resident patient where applicable)[22] and also that the offender has expressed his or her willingness to comply with the requirement. There are also provisions concerning treatment at a place other than that specified in the order being arranged by the practitioner mentioned above with the consent of the offender. Where treatment is residential the offender's responsible officer supervises him or her only to the extent of revocation or amendment of the order.

DRUG REHABILITATION REQUIREMENT

Under sections 209 to 211 CJA 2003 this is a requirement that during a period specified by the court in the order (and known as 'the treatment and testing period' in relation to controlled drugs) the offender:

(a) must submit to treatment by or under the direction of a specified person having the necessary qualifications or experience with a view to the reduction or elimination of the offender's dependency on or propensity to misuse drugs, and

(b) for the purposes of ascertaining whether he has any drug in his body during that period, must provide samples of such description as may be so determined, at such times or in such circumstances as may (subject to the provisions of this order) be determined by the responsible officer or by the person specified as the person by or under whose direction the treatment is to be provided.

Under the remainder of section 209, the court cannot impose such a requirement unless satisfied that the offender is dependent upon or has a propensity to misuse drugs, and that his or her dependency is such as requires and may be susceptible to treatment. It must also be satisfied that arrangements have been or can be made for the treatment intended to be specified in the order (including arrangements for reception where the offender will be a resident); and

---

[21] As to which see, e.g. *The Sentence of The Court*, Watkins M, Edn.4 (www.watersidepress.co.uk).
[22] When further provisions also come into play.

the requirement must have been recommended as being suitable for the offender by an officer of a local probation board in the case of an adult.[23] The offender must also express his or her willingness to comply with the requirement.

The treatment and testing period of at least six months (section 210(3)) must be as a resident in the institution or place specified in the order, or as a non-resident there - and at such intervals as are specified - but the *nature* of the treatment is not to be further specified. The Secretary of State will have power to regulate 'the function of making a determination as to the provision of samples'. Tests results are communicated to the responsible officer under the requirement.

Review by the court of drug rehabilitation requirements

There is provision for periodic review by the court (independent of and separate to the general community sentence review provisions in section 178 CJA 2003 (above): which are inapplicable to drug rehabilitation requirements). These are sometimes compulsory and at other times discretionary. Thus:

> (1) A community order . . . imposing a drug rehabilitation requirement may (and must if the treatment and testing period is more than 12 months) -
>> (a) provide for the requirement to be reviewed periodically at intervals of not less than one month,[24]
>> (b) provide for each review of the requirement to be made . . . at a hearing held by the court responsible for the order ('a review hearing'),
>> (c) require the offender to attend each review hearing,
>> (d) provide for the responsible officer to make to the court responsible for the order, before each review, a report in writing of the offender's progress under the requirement, and
>> (e) provide for each such report to include the test results communicated to the responsible officer . . . and the views of the treatment provider as to the treatment and testing of the offender.

Section 211 sets out flexible arrangements concerning review processes and hearings. It allows for amendment of the order (with the offender's consent, but not so as to reduce the rehabilitation period below six months). Always the responsible officer's report is central to the court's decision. Subsequent reviews to be ordered with or without the offender's attendance (i.e. 'without a hearing' and provided progress is satisfactory). However, if progress is *not* satisfactory, 'active' reviews may be reinstated; and where an offender fails to express willingness to an order being amended he or she may be dealt with in any way that the court could have dealt with him or her at the outset. There is no mention of 'reasonableness' but on general principle a court must act thus in formulating amendments (as it should when formulating the original requirements: see earlier). If re-sentencing, a court must allow for the extent to which there has been compliance with requirements (including, it seems, other community requirements). Nonetheless, a court can pass a custodial sentence - provided that the original order relates to an imprisonable offence - *notwithstanding anything in*

---

[23] Or in the case of a juvenile an officer of a local probation board or YOT: see, generally, *Chapter 12*.
[24] Meaning a calendar month under the Interpretation Act (a relevant point for listing officers).

section 152(2) CJA 2003 (i.e. without reference to the usual 'so serious' custodial sentencing threshold as described in *Chapter 7*).[25]

ALCOHOL TREATMENT REQUIREMENT

Under section 212 CJA 2003[26] this is a requirement that the offender must submit during a period specified by the court in the order to treatment by or under the direction of a person specified in the order who has the necessary qualifications or experience with a view to the reduction or elimination of the offender's dependency on alcohol. The court may not impose such a requirement unless it is satisfied that the offender is dependent on alcohol, and that his or her dependency is such as requires and may be susceptible to treatment. It must also be satisfied that arrangements have been or can be made for the intended treatment (including for reception where the offender is to be a resident). The period for which the treatment 'has effect' must be not less than six months and the offender must express his or her willingness to comply. It must be:

- as a resident in such institution or place as may be specified in the order;
- as a non-resident in or at such institution or place, and at such intervals, as may be so specified; or
- by or under the direction of such person having the necessary qualification or experience as may be so specified.

The nature of the treatment cannot be specified, except as above. Electronic monitoring is discretionary (section 177(4) CJA 2003).

SUPERVISION REQUIREMENT

Under section 215 CJA 2003 this requirement (reflecting what was formerly a basic requirement of a community rehabilitation order, or before that the probation order)[27] is one under which the offender must attend appointments with his or her responsible officer or another person determined by that responsible officer, at such time and place as may be determined by that officer. The statutory purpose for which such a requirement may be imposed is 'that of promoting the offender's rehabilitation'. In practice this will involve formulating a supervision plan, confronting offending behaviour, discussion of daily practicalities such as finances and employment, monitoring general progress and generally holding the offender to account. The supervision requirement stays in force for the period for which the community order remains in force. Electronic monitoring is discretionary (section 177(4) CJA 2003).

---

[25] Note that, in contrast, if there is a de facto breach of the order and 'wilful failure' is established imprisonment can be used even where the original offence was not imprisonable: see Footnote 31. There are special provisions for people who were juveniles when originally sentenced: *Chapter 12*.

[26] Based on the existing Powers of Criminal Courts (Sentencing) Act 2000, Schedule 2, paragraph 6. Despite the more or less self-contained code for drug rehabilitation orders in section 212 CJA 2003, some aspects of the amendment provisions in Schedule 8 also apply (see paragraphs 17, 18 and 19).

[27] For the existing provisions, see section 41 Powers of Criminal Courts (Sentencing) Act 2000.

ATTENDANCE CENTRE REQUIREMENT

Under section 214 CJA 2003[28] this requirement can be imposed only in relation to offenders under 25 years of age.[29] An attendance centre requirement is one whereby the offender must attend at an attendance centre specified in the order for such number of hours as may be specified: not less than 12 nor more than 36 in aggregate. The court can only impose such a requirement if satisfied that the attendance centre to be specified in the order is reasonably accessible to the offender having regard to the means of access available to him or her and any other circumstances - thereby largely reflecting existing law and practice. The time for the first attendance is notified to the offender by the responsible officer (in practice in liaison with the centre), and thereafter attendance instructions for 'subsequent hours' are fixed by the officer of the centre. The offender cannot be required to attend more than once a day, nor for over three hours at a time. Electronic monitoring is discretionary (section 177(4) CJA 2003).

ELECTRONIC MONITORING REQUIREMENT

As already explained above, electronic monitoring must normally be added to curfew and exclusion requirements and may be added to other requirements. The relevant provisions are contained in section 215 CJA 2003. They define the requirement as one 'for securing the electronic monitoring of the offender's compliance with other requirements imposed by the order during a period specified in the order, or determined by the responsible officer in accordance with the relevant order'. Electronic monitoring cannot be ordered standing alone, only to reinforce compliance with another requirement. Also, it can only be imposed where the consent of any person - other than the offender - 'without whose co-operation it will not be practicable to secure the monitoring' is first obtained.

Where a monitoring requirement is to take effect during a period determined by the responsible officer, he or she must notify the offender of this, and also the person responsible for the monitoring and anyone whose consent is needed at the time when the period is to begin. The order must include provision for making someone responsible for the monitoring and who is of a description specified in an order of the Secretary of State. Home Office guidance states:

> In almost all cases of electronic monitoring, the technical equipment . . . consists of a transmitter (the 'tag'), which is usually worn round the ankle, and a receiver unit which is either connected to a landline telephone or incorporates mobile phone technology. The receiver unit communicates with a central computer system at a monitoring centre. The transmitter sends signals to the receiver at regular intervals and these are sent on to the central computer . . . The transmitter can be removed only by breaking its strap. This interferes with the fibre-optic circuitry inside the strap and is immediately registered as a tamper . . . generating follow-up action.

---

[28] Largely replicating provisions of the Powers of Criminal Courts (Sentencing) Act 2000.
[29] Representing an upwards shift. Under existing law the limit is age 21, except for fine etc. default.

BREACH OF COMMUNITY ORDERS

Non-compliance with a generic community order is dealt with by section 179 CJA 2003 which invokes Schedule 8 to the Act, under which there is an initial duty to warn an offender before taking action, the outcome of which is likely to be more punitive than under existing law. Thus, under paragraph 5:

(1) If the responsible officer is of the opinion that the offender has failed without reasonable excuse to comply with any of the requirements of a community order, the officer must give him a warning under this paragraph unless -
(a) the offender has within the previous twelve months been given a warning under this paragraph in relation to a failure to comply with any of the requirements of the order, or
(b) the officer causes an information to be laid before a justice of the peace in respect of the failure.
(2) A warning under this paragraph must -
(a) describe the circumstances of the failure,
(b) state that the failure is unacceptable, and
(c) inform the offender that, if within the next twelve months he again fails to comply with any requirement of the order, he will be liable to be brought before a court.
(3) The responsible officer must, as soon as practicable after the warning has been given, record that fact.
(4) In relation to any community order which was made by the Crown Court and does not include a direction that any failure to comply with the requirements . . . is to be dealt with by a magistrates' court, the reference in sub-paragraph (1)(b) to a justice of the peace is to be read as a reference to the Crown Court.[30]

Where non-compliance follows such a warning, paragraph 6(1) provides that if:

(a) the responsible officer has given a warning [as described above], and
(b) at any time within the twelve months beginning with the date on which the warning was given, the responsible officer is of the opinion that the offender has since that date failed without reasonable excuse to comply with any of the requirements of the order,
the officer must cause an information to be laid before a justice of the peace [or as appropriate the Crown Court] in respect of the failure in question.

Schedule 8 largely reproduces (with modifications) Schedule 3 to the Powers of Criminal Courts (Sentencing) Act 2000 (which will continue post-CJA 2003 in relation to young offenders).

Once magistrates are satisfied as to non-compliance 'without reasonable excuse' the court - by way of 'incremental sanctions' - *must*:

---

[30] The general approach of the breach, revocation etc. provisions is for the 'appropriate court' to deal with a matter, i.e. normally the level of court that imposed the original requirement, except where the Crown Court has indicated that such matters be determined by magistrates (but when there may still be power for magistrates to return the case to the Crown Court after certifying a breach etc.). If the Crown Court is 'seized' of a magistrates' court level matter (e.g. where it has just convicted the offender of a fresh offence) it can re-sentence within magistrates' maximum powers. Special considerations apply to drug rehabilitation requirement reviews which are dealt with by the court responsible for that review: see further in the text.

- **amend** the order by imposing *more onerous* requirements (e.g. by extending the period of a requirement, but not beyond the statutory limits for a certain requirement, nor the three year term of a community order); or
- **revoke** it and re-sentence the offender as if he or she had just been convicted of the original offence (but without reference to the usual custody threshold in section 152(2) (*Chapter 7*); or
- even if the original offence was *not punishable with imprisonment* but the offender has wilfully and persistently failed to comply with the order, **revoke the order and re-sentence** to custody, but limited to 51 weeks.[31]

Nothing in the CJA 2003 requires a court to start at the least severe response, or to approach the three mandatory options in any particular order. But the court must take into account the extent to which the offender has complied with an order. If the order is revoked and the offender re-sentenced, he or she can appeal against that new sentence. The Crown Court's powers when a breach occurs are analogous to those of magistrates, except that it can exercise its own wider sentencing powers if re-sentencing (i.e. it is not limited to 51 weeks). It is for the judge to determine whether a breach has occurred, not a jury. Where the original order was made by the Crown Court and that court directed that failures to comply be dealt with by the magistrates' court, the magistrates can remand the offender to appear before the Crown Court to be dealt with for it after certifying breach. If an offender has failed to comply with a mental health treatment, drug rehabilitation or alcohol treatment requirement, this is not to be treated as a breach 'on the ground only that he refused to undergo any surgical, electrical or other treatment' if the court concludes that the refusal was reasonable in the circumstances (and a court may not amend such requirements unless the offender expresses his or her willingness to comply with the proposed new requirement). The schedule also covers the situation whereby an offender attains the age of 18 between the original order and breach proceedings and where the offence would have been indictable only in the case of an adult (see *Chapter 12*).

REVOCATION AND AMENDMENT

Schedule 8 also deals with the revocation and amendment of community orders whilst they are in force. The offender or his or her responsible officer might wish to apply to the court (and either usually can do so) to revoke or change the terms of a community order for valid reasons, e.g. where the offender has become ill or is otherwise unable to cope with a given order or requirement, or to complete it,

---

[31] These provisions contained in paragraph 9(1) of Schedule 8 to the CJA 2003 represent a critical facet of the generic order provisions. Once any 'reasonable excuse' is discounted by the court, there is a significant and 'incremental shift' towards one of the three mandatory outcomes. Further, no longer will 'wilful etc. failure' then be a pre-requisite for custody (provided that the original offence was imprisonable); nor will the 'so serious' threshold test (*Chapter 7*) apply; and - subject to wilful etc. failure - there will be power to use imprisonment *even when that offence did not attract imprisonment* in the first place. It must be borne in mind that a generic community sentence will in future be available for *any* offence (subject to the 'serious enough' test). But a prison sentence of 'below 12 months' can be suspended as described in *Chapter 9*. Also, requirements could then be imposed as part of that sentence, but with the underlying 'threat' of actual imprisonment by activation of the suspended sentence in the event of non-compliance. For juveniles, see *Chapter 12*.

or complete it on time. The provisions contemplate that magistrates will deal with most such applications, at least to begin with - in the petty sessions area named in the order (including if a Crown Court has directed that such matters be dealt with by magistrates in relation to an order of that court). Generally, also, the offender has a right of appeal against any revised requirements; and in general, if a court is dealing with revocation, amendment etc. and the application is not by the offender, the court must summon the offender to court and can issue a warrant for non-attendance. This obligation does not apply, e.g. if the court is simply cancelling a requirement or reducing the period of a requirement.

Revocation

If it appears to the court to be in the interests of justice, it can revoke the order or revoke it and deal with the offender 'in any way in which he could have been dealt with . . . by the court which made the order had that order not been made',[32] but taking account of the extent to which the offender has complied with requirements. It is specifically provided that an order can be revoked for 'good progress' or 'responding satisfactorily to treatment' (when the re-sentencing provisions would be otiose). Again, special rules apply where the offender attains the age of 18 between the original order and the revocation proceedings and the offence is indictable only in the case of an adult (*Chapter 12*).

Amendment

All amended requirements are subject to the same legal provisions and constraints as for an original community order. Change of residence by an offender may necessitate amendment to reflect a new petty sessions area. If such an application is made by the responsible officer the court must cancel or change any requirements that are not available in the area to which the offender wishes to move - in other words, accredited programmes must be available in the new area.

The court cannot add a requirement of a different kind, e.g. exchange a curfew for a programme. Otherwise, it can cancel a requirement or adjust it, e.g. alter the hours of a curfew or substitute comparable activities. But it *can* add electronic monitoring to any existing requirement. It cannot amend a mental health treatment, drug rehabilitation or alcohol treatment requirement without the offender expressing his or her willingness to comply with the proposed amendment; but if the offender fails do so, it can revoke the order and re-sentence him or her. It must then take into account the extent of compliance with the original requirements. Again, special rules apply to indictable only offences if the offender has become 18 since the order was made (*Chapter 12*).

Further provisions apply where a community order includes a drug rehabilitation, alcohol treatment or mental health treatment requirement, the medical practitioner (or other person responsible for the treatment) is of the opinion that the treatment should be extended beyond the period specified in the order; that the offender should receive different treatment; or that he or she is not susceptible to treatment or does not require further treatment. He or she must

---

[32] The revocation provisions do not create 'incremental sanctions', i.e. do not dispense with the threshold test for custody (*Chapter 7*) or an originally imprisonable offence before custody is used (which will not be required for a generic community order): contrast non-compliance, Footnote 31.

then make a report to the responsible officer and can also state that he or she is not prepared to continue treatment of the offender (or its direction). The responsible officer must then apply to the court to have the requirement amended or revoked. See also the special review etc. arrangements for drug rehabilitation orders above.

The court can extend an unpaid work requirement beyond the 12 months limit specified in section 193 CJA 2003 if it believes this to be in the interests of justice having regard to circumstances that have arisen since the order was made.

CONVICTION OF A FURTHER OFFENCE

By way of a major and 'incremental'[33] change to existing sentencing law, schedule 8 to the CJA 2003 deals with the position where the offender is subsequently convicted of a further offence whilst a generic community order is in force. A magistrates' court may, if it appears to be in the interests of justice having regard to circumstances that have arisen since the order was made, revoke the order (e.g. if it is imposing a custodial sentence for the new offence), or revoke it and re-sentence the offender for the original offence as if he or she had just been convicted of it. If it re-sentences the offender, the court must take into account the extent to which the offender complied with the order. If a magistrates' court is dealing with a new conviction but the original community order was made in the Crown Court it can commit the offender to appear at the Crown Court to be dealt with. On convicting of a new offence (or where the case has been committed back to the Crown Court by the magistrates' court), the Crown Court can impose any sentence that it could have done for the original offence.

---

[33] However, whilst the 'further offence' provisions create an extra (and thus incremental basis) for re-sentencing, they do not - with regard to the offence for which the community order was originally made - dispense with the threshold test for custody (*Chapter 7*) nor the requirement for an imprisonable offence. Contrast non-compliance, Footnote 31.

CHAPTER 9

Prison Sentences: The New Varieties

If there are aspects of the sentencing provisions of the CJA 2003 that have attracted particular interest they are perhaps those for the 'generic community sentence' and recurring menu of requirements (*Chapter 8*), the 'dangerous offender' provisions (*Chapter 10*) and the new short forms of discretionary custody for adults outlined in this chapter.

The new forms of sentence are:

- **custody plus;**
- **intermittent custody;** and the
- **suspended sentence.**[1]

All three forms are - as categorised by the CJA 2003 itself - 'prison sentences of less than 12 months'.[2] Post-CJA 2003 a discretionary custodial sentence *must not* be passed unless the court is of the opinion that the offence was so serious that *neither a fine alone nor a community sentence can be justified* (section 152(2)).[3] As also explained in *Chapter 7*, the new statutory purposes of sentencing and approach to the seriousness of offences have a direct bearing on such sentences.

CUSTODY PLUS

'Custody plus' is a term used by the CJA 2003 to describe the *licence component* of a term of imprisonment of less than 12 months (this according to the definition in section 181(4) CJA 2003). Under the Act and in broad terms, all sentences of less than 12 months will consist of two components:

- a short 'custodial period' (in 'weeks': below), normally spent in prison; and
- a longer 'licence period', spent in the community following release and during which - by way of an innovation - the offender must comply with requirements set by the court at the time of and as part of the sentence.

This new-style approach involves several distinct stages:

- first the court must set an **overall term of imprisonment;**
- it must then specify the **'custodial period'** - at the end of which the offender will, other things being equal, be released on licence;
- it must also specify the **'licence period';** and

---

[1] Sometimes called 'custody minus' (as explained in *Chapter 7*) but in fact a variant of custody plus.

[2] And thus all capable of being passed by magistrates' courts whose maximum power is 12 months: *Chapter 7*. Seemingly, magistrates could pass a discretionary custodial sentence of exactly 12 months (i.e. as an 'ordinary' sentence of imprisonment) that would be unaffected by the provisions outlined here. The provisions also have the effect of creating new minimum custodial sentences based on an overall term of 28 weeks as already noted in *Chapter 7*.

[3] The relevant part of section 152(2) CJA 2003 is set out in *Chapter 7*. All references in this chapter to 'the offence' should be read as meaning the offence and any offences associated with it.

- it must set **licence conditions** to be observed on release from prison, i.e. at the time of sentence, the court must add one or more requirements from the relevant statutory 'menu' (thereby creating the 'custody plus' element).

At the end of his or her actual time spent in prison, an offender who is subject to custody plus will be obliged to comply throughout the licence period (or any part of it as determined by the court) with the requirement or requirements added by the court when sentencing. This dividing-up by the court of a sentence into separate components is wholly novel, as is setting licence conditions by a court - and as with the generic community order discussed in *Chapter 8* the strength and significance of custody plus (and other new forms of sentence) lie partially in the legal provisions for and practical application of enforcement sanctions linked to such requirements.[4] The mechanisms for ensuring compliance with licence conditions are dealt with in *Chapter 11*.

The key to understanding custody plus thus depends on a knowledge of the legal rules in relation to: the overall term of imprisonment; the 'custodial period'; and the 'licence period'; and of the requirements that may be added to the licence element. All these aspects are further outlined below.

Exceptions to the general rule
It should be noted that although the overall term of intermittent custody is the same as for custody plus, i.e. 28 to 51 weeks (section 183(4) CJA 2003) the standard custody plus provisions *do not* apply to intermittent custody (section 181(1)) concerning which there are dedicated provisions (see below). Neither does the duty to set licence conditions at the point of sentence apply to the *suspended sentence* (section 181(9)) (although the sentencing court does have a discretion to add requirements at that point in time and which would then take effect if the suspended sentence were later to be activated: see, further, below).[5]

The overall term of imprisonment
Section 181 CJA 2003 provides:

(1) Any power of a court to impose a sentence of imprisonment for a term of less than 12 months on an offender may be exercised only in accordance with the following provisions . . . unless the court makes an intermittent custody order [see below].
(2) The term of the sentence -
   (a) must be expressed in weeks,
   (b) must be at least 28 weeks,
   (c) must not be more than 51 weeks in respect of any one offence, and
   (d) must not exceed the maximum term permitted for the offence.

It is this overall sentence of 28 to 51 weeks that must be commensurate with and justified by the seriousness of the offence, rather than just the custodial part of that sentence (a minimum of two weeks: see below).

---

[4] The approach also contrasts with that in relation to sentences of imprisonment for 12 months or more where the Parole Board or Secretary of State sets licence conditions: see *Chapter 11*.
[5] By necessary implication the remainder of section 181 *does* apply to suspended sentences (or looked at another way, but for setting licence conditions, they are a species of custody plus: see later in the chapter). If licence conditions are not set by the court at the time of passing a suspended sentence they will be set later by any court that determines to activate it.

Section 181(6) makes clear that in determining the overall term (including the licence period: below) the court must ensure that the latter is at least 26 weeks long. Thus, e.g. the minimum sentence of 28 weeks equates with the minimum custodial period (i.e. two weeks: see next heading) plus the minimum licence period of 26 weeks set by section 181(6).

The custodial and licence periods
Under section 181(3) CJA 2003, the court must specify both a custodial and a licence period:

The court, when passing sentence, must -
(a) specify a period (. . . 'the custodial period') at the end of which the offender is to be released on a licence, and
(b) by order require the licence to be granted subject to conditions requiring the offender's compliance during the remainder of the term (. . . 'the licence period') or any part of it with one or more requirements falling within section 182(1) [see below] and specified in the order.

Section 181(5) provides that the length of the custodial period:

(a) must be at least 2 weeks, and
(b) in respect of any one offence, must not be more than 13 weeks.

Thus, e.g. with a maximum overall term of imprisonment of 51 weeks, the custodial period would be for a maximum of 13 weeks (the most allowed by section 181(5)) and the licence period 38 weeks (or proportionately more if the custodial period was set at below 13 weeks). But each of the three elements is variable (yet inter-related) in terms of its extent: the statutory mimima/maxima must be adhered to and the overall term must equal the sum of its constituent parts. What will be important is to ensure that the sentence is proportionate overall in that the full term must correspond with *the shortest term commensurate with the seriousness of the offence* (see section 153 CJA 2003 set out in *Chapter 7*). No such constraints are attached to the licence component, but on general principle licence conditions should not be allowed to become disproportionately punitive.[6]

Aggregate terms of imprisonment and multiple requirements
Concerning aggregate terms of imprisonment, section 181(7) states that:

(7) Where a court imposes two or more terms of imprisonment in accordance with this section to be served consecutively -
(a) the aggregate length of the terms of imprisonment must not be more than 65 weeks, and
(b) the aggregate length of the custodial periods must not be more than 26 weeks.

At 65 weeks, the aggregate sentence with regard to sentences of below 12 months is thus in line with the new general aggregate sentencing powers of

---

[6] In contrast to requirements of community sentence (*Chapter 8*). Without guidelines, the situation could lead to injustice/inconsistency, suggesting a task for the Sentencing Guidelines Council.

magistrates' courts as described in *Chapter 7*. There are also rules to be observed in relation to multiple requirements:

(8) A custody plus order which specifies two or more requirements may, in relation to any requirement, refer to compliance within such part of the licence period as is specified in the order.

Requirements that can be used in relation to custody plus
The 'menu' of requirements that may be used for custody plus is contained in section 182(1) CJA 2003. This menu is shorter than that in relation to a generic community sentence as described in *Chapter 8*. The nature of individual requirements that do appear in the custody plus list are as already explained within that chapter. For present purposes it will therefore suffice to list the possible custody plus requirements, which are as follows:

• unpaid work requirement;
• activity requirement;
• programme requirement;
• prohibited activity requirement;
• curfew requirement;
• exclusion requirement;
• supervision requirement; and
• attendance centre requirement (under 25 years of age only).

Under section 182(2) CJA 2003 it is essential that arrangements are available locally and the court must be satisfied concerning the suitability of the offender for a particular requirement. In certain instances (equating to situations already described in *Chapter 8*) there is a need to consult other people or to ensure that there is a willingness to comply on the part of the offender or to obtain the consent of other individuals before adding the requirement. Multiple requirements must be compatible with one another and avoid conflict with work and education times. It should also be noted that section 204(3) to (5) CJA 2003 (which limits curfew periods) restricts curfews under a custody plus order to six months beginning with the start of the licence period.

A requirement for electronic monitoring must be added whenever the court orders a curfew requirement or exclusion requirement unless the court is prevented from doing this or in the particular circumstances considers that it is inappropriate (182(3)). In other situations, listed in section 182(4), there is a discretion to order electronic monitoring.[7] Under section 216 CJA 2003 the petty sessions area to be specified for the purpose of requirements in a custody plus order is that where the offender will reside during the licence period.

---

[7] This is quite separate to the arrangements for home detention curfew (HDC) that allow certain (currently longer term) offenders to be released early. Some 3,500 offenders have been released on HDC and that scheme looks set to expand alongside the situations described in this chapter.

INTERMITTENT CUSTODY

Again in relation to sentences of under 12 months only and in broad terms, intermittent custody[8] means 'part-time custody', e.g. at weekends or at other times fixed by the court, rather than continuous imprisonment from the beginning to the end of the custodial portion of a term of imprisonment. The offender presents himself or herself at the prison at times laid down by the court in the sentence. The underlying rationale is to enable the offender, e.g. to retain employment (or try to obtain it) and/or community and family ties (where these exist or to try to develop them). Intermittent custody is also intended to effect a saving on the high cost of actual imprisonment and a reduction in the UK prison population that was over 75,000 at the time of writing. Similar schemes have operated abroad for some years, including in Germany, Portugal and Spain.

Intermittent custody in outline
The intermittent custody provisions are contained in sections 183 to 186 CJA 2003. Section 183 starts by providing that:

(1) A court may, when passing a sentence of imprisonment for a term complying with subsection (4) [as to which *see the first bullet point below*] -
   (a) specify the number of days that the offender must serve in prison under the sentence before being released on licence for the remainder of the term, and
   (b) by order -
      (i) specify periods during which the offender is to be released temporarily on licence before he has served that number of days in prison, and
      (ii) require any licence to be granted subject to conditions requiring the offender's compliance during the licence periods with one or more requirements falling within section 182(1) and specified in the order.

The following summarises the overall sentencing process:

- first, the court sets an overall prison term which as with custody plus must correspond, in terms of its length, with the seriousness of the offence and:
  —must be expressed in weeks;
  —must be for at least 28 weeks;
  —must be for not more than 51 weeks in respect of any one offence; and
  —must not exceed the maximum sentence for the offence in question (section 183(4));[9]
- it then specifies the number of days - called 'custodial days' (see section 183(3)) - that the offender must serve in prison under the sentence of intermittent custody before being released on licence for the remainder of the overall term (section 183(1)(above)). The 'custodial days' must number at least 14; and, for a single offence, must not exceed 90 (section 183(5));
- the court then specifies periods when the offender is to be released at intervals from prison temporarily and on licence before he or she has

---

[8] The CJA 2003 (Commencement No. 1 Order) (SI 2003, No. 3282) activated the intermittent custody provisions which are being piloted in a modified form in certain areas. For the adjustments/details of the scheme see Home Office/NPS circular 'Intermittent Custody', 18 November 2003.

[9] Thus corresponding to the same basic 'overall term' requirements as for custody plus, above.

served the full number of custodial days to which he or she has been sentenced, together with an order that any licence granted must be subject to conditions requiring the offender's compliance with one or more requirements (section 183(1) (above)). The imposing of such requirements follows the same pattern, procedures and qualifications as described above in relation to custody plus[10] and in particular the requirements attached to the licence parts of the sentence must be compatible, must not conflict, and they must or may include electronic monitoring according to the requirement under consideration question (see the outline in relation to custody plus). Similarly, different requirements may be imposed with regard to different time limits (section 183(9));

- there are certain restrictions relating to four requirements - unpaid work, activities, programmes and prohibited activities (see section 185(1)) - when the court must be satisfied that arrangements are available locally and as to the suitability of the offender for the particular requirement;
- under section 216 CJA 2003, the petty sessions area to be specified for the purpose of requirements in an intermittent custody order is the place where the offender will reside during the licence periods;
- it should be noted that section 204(3) to (5) (which limits curfew periods for different types of orders) restricts curfews under an intermittent custody order so that the court must not specify a period if to do so would cause the aggregate number of days on which the offender is subject to the requirement for any part of the day to exceed 182; and
- the court cannot make the intermittent custody order unless the offender expresses his or her willingness to serve the custodial part of the sentence intermittently (section 183(6)).

Further key points
In contrast to custody plus, there is no minimum or other specific licence period at the end of the sentence that has to be ordered by the court at the point of sentence. With intermittent custody, the licence period - and thus the period to which requirements can be attached - means whatever is left of the sentence after the full number of days ordered to be served in prison have been completed together with the periods of release under the order of the court (the effect of section 183(3) and (4)).

With consecutive terms of intermittent custody, the aggregate imprisonment must not exceed 65 weeks nor the aggregate number of custodial days 180 (section 183(7)).

Under section 183(8) the Secretary of State is given delegated power to prescribe times, periods and 'parts of the week', etc. for the purpose of release during the custodial part of the sentence. The Home Office guidance states:

He may make provision about the length of licence periods (e.g. 86 or 120 hours) which enables the custodial days to be served during the week or weekend; particular days of the week on which licence periods may begin or end (to restrict custodial periods to weekends, for example); and periods including or not including specified parts of the week (e.g. 'not Fridays').

---

[10] The nature of individual restrictions are likewise described in *Chapter 8*.

There are certain prerequisites or restrictions. Arrangements must exist for intermittent custody in the local area; such an order cannot be made without consulting an officer of a local probation board (seemingly with regard to the offender's suitability for intermittent custody); suitable prison accommodation must be available during the custodial periods and it must appear to the court that the offender will have suitable accommodation available to him or her in the community during the licence periods (section 184(1) to (2) summarised).

There are corresponding amendments concerning arrangements for expenses and, e.g. the Prisoner (Return to Custody) Act 1995 is changed so that someone who is released temporarily under intermittent custody is guilty of an offence if, without reasonable excuse, he or she remains unlawfully at large beyond the periods stated in the order. The offender is not entitled to be conveyed to prison or to be reimbursed his or her costs of getting to or from prison, e.g. during an interval of temporary release. However, the Secretary of State may determine to pay expenses incurred 'in travelling to and from prison during licence periods' (section 186(2)).

REVOCATION, AMENDMENT AND TRANSFER

Section 187 CJA 2003 invokes Schedule 10 CJA 2003 that contains provision for revocation or amendment of custody plus and the amendment of intermittent custody. In either case, the prison sentence itself is unaffected, but Schedule 10 provides for the court to revoke the custody plus element of a sentence and to remove licence requirements from intermittent custody on the application of the offender or responsible officer[11] where the court considers this to be 'in the interests of justice'. The schedule also allows the court to amend the order to refer to a different petty sessions area (e.g. on change of residence and provided a requirement - particularly, in practice, an accredited programme requirement - is available in the new area, or a similar, available requirement can be substituted).

Similarly, the court can amend custody plus or intermittent custody by cancelling a requirement or replacing it with another of the same type (i.e. from within the same sub-section of section 177(1) CJA 2003) and subject to the same restrictions. The court can change the release periods of intermittent custody if suitable prison accommodation is available or remove them, e.g. if the underlying reason changes (such as loss of employment) - as where an offender may simply wish to 'get his or her custodial days over'; where he or she has proved unsuitable for release intermittently.

An application is barred if an appeal is pending. If a court amends an order other than on the application of the offender it must require him or her to appear before the court by summons and can issue a warrant if he or she does not appear (but not if the court is simply cancelling a requirement).[12]

---

[11] See *Chapter 8.*

[12] Section 188 CJA 2003 and Schedule 11 to the Act lay down procedures for transferring orders to Scotland or Northern Ireland where intermittent custody does not exist.

THE NEW-STYLE SUSPENDED SENTENCE

Before describing the new-style suspended sentence further it may be helpful to emphasise certain points:

- first, the relevant provisions are, in effect, superimposed on the underlying arrangements for custody plus described earlier in this chapter including for a sentence of 28 to 51 weeks. In concept and basic structure the suspended sentence thus comprises a sentence of custody plus, but one that is subject to:
  - the immediate suspension of the custodial part of the sentence so that the offender will not go to prison straightaway (and without any need here for the court to find 'exceptional circumstances' for that suspension, as there is under existing law);[13]
  - requirements being added at the court's discretion to be carried out in the community during the 'operational period' of the suspended sentence. Such requirements are implemented and performed in a similar way to those under a generic community order and broadly speaking subject to the same supplementary considerations that are described in *Chapter 8*. Note however that requirements *need not* be added to a suspended sentence. This will depend on the court's assessment of the overall facts and circumstances;
  - with no obligation on the sentencing court (as there is with custody plus) to set any licence conditions at the time of sentencing. In practice, it seems, such conditions will normally only be set at a later stage, if and when the suspended sentence is activated, i.e. by the offender actually being sent to prison under it - and by the activating court;[14] and
- enforcement of a suspended sentence will, post-CJA 2003 arise in two quite different contexts: either due to the commission of a further offence (when there will no longer be any requirement that this further offence is an imprisonable offence); or due to non-compliance with any community requirements set at the time when the suspended sentence was imposed.

The term 'custody minus'

Whereas 'custody plus' and 'intermittent custody' are terms adopted by the CJA 2003 itself, 'custody minus' is one that came to be applied informally to the new-style suspended sentence and which gained currency in certain circles during the consultation processes which preceded the 2003 Act. It does not appear in the Act or, e.g. in the Home Office guidance notes. Indeed, although 'custody plus' may still be used as a term of convenience, the suspended sentence is - as is perhaps most visible at the 'activation' stage (see later) - a variant of custody plus.

---

[13] Now that 'exceptional circumstances' will no longer be a pre-requisite, guidance by the Sentencing Guidelines Council (*Chapter 7*) would be helpful - and on other aspects of the new-style sentences.

[14] It is important not to confuse requirements ordered to be performed in the community during the operational period of a suspended sentence with licence conditions (since, at least in theory, both could be set by the sentencing court). Both varieties can be correctly described as 'requirements' and, as noted in *Chapter 7*, find their origins within the same overall 'menu'. But both the range of choice and their enforcement provisions differ. Breach of a requirement of a suspended sentence may lead to activation of that sentence as described in the text of this chapter and following which those requirements 'evaporate'. For the enforcement of licence conditions see *Chapter 11*.

Further general points
Post-CJA 2003, in practice it may become virtually automatic for requirements to be added, to be complied with in the community whilst the suspended sentence is running. The offender would thus no longer appear to have 'got away with his or her offence' (a frequent popular reaction) and the latent nature of the sentence will serve both to discourage future offending and to ensure compliance with community-based requirements. This latter aspect represents a considerable strengthening of such sentences. However, it should be emphasised that - as under existing law - the 'so serious' custody threshold will normally need to be met[15] before a suspended sentence can be considered, including the new 'must not' emphasis that affects discretionary custodial sentences: see *Chapter 7.*

Key provisions
The main statutory provisions concerning suspended sentences are contained in section 189 CJA 2003 under which a court that passes a term of imprisonment of at least 28 weeks but not more than 51 weeks pursuant to section 181 CJA 2003[16] has a discretion to order that:

- the offender comply for a period specified in the order with one or more of the requirements noted below;[17] and that
- the sentence of imprisonment is not to take effect unless during the supervision period
  — he or she fails to comply with such requirements as are ordered; or
  — during a period specified in the order he or she commits in the UK another offence whether or not punishable by imprisonment[18]
  unless - in either case - a court having power to do so (see below) subsequently orders that the original sentence is to take effect.

It should be emphasised that by virtue of section 181 CJA 2003 the court will, as with custody plus, need to set an overall term of imprisonment, a 'custodial period' (limited to between two and 13 weeks) and a licence period (of at least 26 weeks); and where two or more sentences are imposed on the same occasion and ordered - at the court's discretion - to be served consecutively, the aggregate of the overall custodial terms must not exceed 65 weeks (section 189(2)) (when the aggregate custodial period will be limited to 26 weeks: section 181(7)).

The period of suspension and the bar on combination with other sentences
Having determined the overall term and the custodial and licence periods the following rules apply:

- the supervision period and the operational period must each be a period of not less than six months and not more than two years beginning with the date of sentence (section 189(3));

[15] But not in other situations where that test is dispensed with: see, e.g. *Chapter 8*, Footnote 31.
[16] Which obliges courts passing sentences of less than 12 months to set an overall term of imprisonment, a 'custodial period' and a 'licence period' as described earlier in this chapter in relation to custody plus.
[17] See the text above concerning the need to distinguish these requirements from licence conditions.
[18] A significant, 'incremental' change. Under existing law the new offence must be imprisonable.

- the supervision period must not end later than the operational period (section 189(4)); and
- a suspended sentence cannot be combined with a separate, free-standing community sentence on the same sentencing occasion (section 189(5)).

Under existing law a suspended prison sentence cannot be combined with other orders (except for a fine,[19] compensation and ancillary orders such as costs or disqualification) or further obligations of the kind envisaged by the CJA 2003.

Requirements
The requirements that may be attached to a suspended sentence are identical in nature to those for the generic community order as described in *Chapter 8*. Any of the 12 basic requirements described in that chapter can be used and subject largely to similar qualifications concerning consultation, 'willingness to comply', compatibility of multiple requirements, presumptive electronic monitoring of curfew and exclusion orders (and discretionary use of monitoring in all other situations). Similarly and in general terms the same revocation and amendment provisions as for the generic community order contained in Schedule 8 to the CJA 2003 apply (see *Chapter 8*). But there are certain modifications:

- the unpaid work requirement must normally be performed within 12 months; and the supervision period continues until the work is complete but not beyond the operational period of the suspended sentence (section 200 CJA 2003). However, note that under paragraph 20 of Schedule 8 to the Act a court may subsequently extend this 12 months limit if it is in the interests of justice to do so; and
- section 204(3) to (5) (which limit curfew periods for different types of orders) restrict curfews as a requirement of a suspended sentence to six months from the date of the order.

Under section 216 CJA 2003 the petty sessions area to be specified for the purpose of requirements is that where the offender will reside.

Licence conditions
With regard to any requirements to be attached to the licence period (rather than the suspended sentence itself), section 181(9) expressly states that the original sentencing court 'need not' set these, i.e. at the point of sentence - though it can if it wishes to do so. Where it does not - the normal practice it seems to be anticipated by government - there is provision for the conditions to be set by the court that activates a suspended sentence (see Schedule 1 CJA 2003, paragraph 9).

Periodic review
Importantly - and again by way of innovation - there are arrangements for review by the court in relation to the suspended sentence. Section 191 CJA 2003 confers a discretion on a court when imposing such a sentence to provide for the order to be reviewed periodically at specified intervals, i.e. at a 'review hearing'. Section 191(2) excludes the situation where an offender is subject to a drug

---

[19] Under existing law such *a fine must be considered*. This requirement disappears under the CJA 2003.

rehabilitation requirement.[20] Review hearings are held by the court responsible for the suspended sentence within the meaning of section 191(3) and (5) (broadly speaking, the court that made the order, the court for some other area as specified in the order, or the Crown Court where the order was made on appeal from that court).

The resulting powers and procedures are prescribed by section 192 CJA 2003. Under section 192(1) the court can, after considering the responsible officer's report, amend a community requirement. But section 192(2) limits this, in effect, to imposing amended requirements only if the offender expresses his or her willingness to comply with them, although the court can impose fresh requirements without such consent provided that they are not different in kind (i.e. fall within the same subparagraph of section 190(1)). The 'willingness' of the offender is also a pre-requisite in the case of certain requirements (mental health treatment, drug rehabilitation and alcohol treatment); and the offender's consent is required if an appeal is pending. An electronic monitoring requirement can always be added to other requirements (being 'of the same kind': see section 192(3)(a)).

The court may extend the supervision period, but not so that this lasts for longer than two years nor ends later than the operational period. It cannot change the operational period.

A review hearing can be dispensed with for 'satisfactory progress' in complying with requirements as evidenced by the responsible officer's report. The court may also amend the order so that subsequent reviews can be held without a hearing, i.e. so as to dispense with attendance at court by the offender and enable the review to take place at a hearing but on the basis of the paperwork only; or at different intervals. There are flexible provisions for reversing such arrangement, e.g. if matters deteriorate. A review hearing can be adjourned, e.g. if the court wishes to deal with the offender formally for breach of a requirement.

Breach, revocation and amendment

Section 193 CJA 2003 invokes Schedule 12 of the Act which relates to breach, revocation and amendment of suspended sentences (including following an adjournment for this purpose from a review hearing: see above). Schedule 12 adopts a similar approach to Schedule 8 (in relation to the generic community order: see *Chapter 8*) but with dedicated, not exactly replicated, provisions in relation to certain aspects. There are thus analogous arrangements:

- for the responsible officer to warn the offender and for record keeping;
- concerning breach where a warning is not heeded, including a duty to begin proceedings if that officer considers that the offender has again failed without reasonable excuse to comply with the order; and
- about which court should deal with the breach (and for the reviewing court to do so where apposite) and the issuing of process for this purpose.

---

[20] Drug rehabilitation requirements are subject to review under the scheme described in *Chapter 8*.

Powers of the court on breach or the commission of a fresh offence

Paragraph 8 of Schedule 12 outlines the court's powers where it is satisfied that the person who is subject to the suspended sentence has failed *without reasonable excuse* to comply with a community requirement; or has committed a further offence anywhere in the UK. The overall effect is to create a presumption that a suspended sentence must be ordered to take effect (i.e. be 'activated') unaltered unless the court finds that it would be unjust to follow this course (when it must give reasons for this).[21] Otherwise, it enables the court to modify the sentence by setting a shorter custodial term or lesser custodial period (within the ordinary limits for a suspended sentence as described above). Alternatively, it can leave the sentence suspended to run but may, when doing so, amend it so as to make requirements 'more onerous', or extend either the supervision or operational periods (again within the original limits for a suspended sentence). It must also take into account the extent to which the offender has complied with requirements and the facts of any subsequent offence.

A magistrates' court can send the offender to the Crown Court to be dealt with in relation to orders made by the latter court but which included a direction that any failures to comply with the community requirements of the order be dealt with by a magistrates' court. In the Crown Court breach matters are determined by a judge of that court (i.e. a opposed to a jury).

Finalising the underlying 'custody plus' order

Under paragraph 9 of Schedule 12, when a suspended sentence *is* activated (with or without variation), the activating court must, in effect, finalise the underlying custody plus order by dealing with the licence conditions. The custodial and licence periods will already have been set by the original sentencing court (see above), but the activating court will normally need to set requirements that will apply on the offender's release from custody at the end of the custodial period.[22] It can also order that the sentence is to take effect immediately or on the expiry of some other sentence of imprisonment passed by that or another court.[23] For all legal purposes, an activated suspended sentence is treated as having been imposed by the court that originally ordered the suspended sentence.

Treatment and rehabilitation requirements

Paragraph 10 of Schedule 12 deals with the situation where an offender has failed to comply with a mental health treatment, drug rehabilitation or alcohol treatment requirement, or refused to undergo any surgical, or electrical or other treatment, and in the opinion of the court that refusal was reasonable having regard to all the circumstances. That situation is not to count as breach. Also, such a requirement may not be amended in response to a breach unless the offender expresses his or her willingness to comply with the amended requirement as proposed by the court.

---

[21] Seemingly, a 'softening' of the existing position whereby there must be 'exceptional circumstances'.

[22] Assuming that these were not set by the original sentencing court: see earlier in the chapter.

[23] And subject to a restriction on consecutive sentences in relation to sentences from which prisoners have been released early: see section 265 CJA 2003.

Jurisdiction

Schedule 12 also designates the court that is to deal with matters where an offender is convicted of a further offence. If the original sentence was passed by the Crown Court and the subsequent conviction was dealt with by magistrates, the magistrates' court can remand the offender to appear in the Crown Court to be dealt with for the breach, or can give written notice to the Crown Court of the subsequent conviction. If it becomes apparent that a court has somehow missed dealing with a suspended sentence in a situation where the offender has committed a fresh offence, the court that originally imposed the suspended sentence (it seems to be anticipated), where it learns of this, can remedy the situation by issuing a summons or warrant to the offender to appear before it.[24] A magistrates' court may not issue a summons except on information and may not issue a warrant except on information in writing and on oath.[25]

Amendment of suspended sentences

Schedule 12 also deals with the amendment of suspended sentences (other than at a review hearing: above). The appropriate court can cancel community requirements on the application of the offender or his or her responsible officer. Overall, the considerations here are similar to those in relation to community orders (*Chapter 8*), so that, e.g. a requirement may be cancelled for 'good progress';[26] a programme requirement must be available before a new petty sessions area is specified in relation to it; the court is restricted to replacement requirements 'of the same kind'; and electronic monitoring can always be added to existing requirements. Similarly, a court can only amend a mental health treatment, drug rehabilitation or alcohol treatment requirement if the offender expresses his or her willingness to comply with the amended requirement, as proposed by the court; and if the offender fails to do so, the court can revoke the suspended sentence order and re-sentence the offender as if he or she had just been convicted of the original offence - and taking into account the extent to compliance with requirements. There is no provision concerning making requirements 'more onerous' as there is when a suspended sentence order is altered following breach (above).

Where the order includes a drug rehabilitation, alcohol treatment or mental health treatment requirement and the medical practitioner or other person responsible for treatment considers that it should be extended beyond the period specified in the order, that the offender should receive different treatment, or is not susceptible to treatment or does not require further treatment, that person must make a report to the responsible officer. He can also report that he is unwilling to continue to treat (or direct treatment) of the offender. The responsible officer must then apply to the court to have the requirement amended or cancelled. Where the order contains a drug rehabilitation requirement, the officer can apply to change a 'review without a hearing' to a 'review with a hearing', and vice versa.

---

[24] There are special provisions for enforcement as between different parts of the UK.

[25] Both, seemingly, inconsistent with changes elsewhere in the 2003 Act dispensing with informations in the case of public prosecutors and removing the oath requirement for some warrants (*Chapter 4*).

[26] The Act uses 'satisfactory progress' (periodic reviews) and sometimes 'good progress' (discharge of community sentence/suspended sentence requirements). Presumably this is intentional.

The offender or responsible officer can apply to extend the 12 months limit on an unpaid work requirement if in the interests of justice.

Applications to cancel or amend requirements cannot be made if an appeal against the order is pending, except in the case of treatment requirements which the responsible officer has applied to the court to alter. Where a court is amending an order, and the application is not by the offender, the court must summon him or her to appear before it and may issue a warrant if he or she does not appear; but not if the court is merely cancelling a requirement.

Transfer of suspended sentence orders to Scotland or Northern Ireland
Provisions for transfer within the UK are contained in Schedule 13.

CHAPTER 10

Dangerous Offenders

Even with discretionary sentences of 12 months or more, the question whether prison is the appropriate response is answered by application of the standard threshold test for custody set out in *Chapter 7* - i.e. a court must not pass such a sentence unless the offence is 'so serious' that neither a fine alone nor a community sentence can be justified for it. Similarly, the length of the term will be determined by what is proportionate. Other things being equal, the more serious the offence the longer the resulting prison sentence (and always provided that this falls within the maximum sentence available for a particular offence). With such sentences there are no further complications of the kind described in relation to the new-style sentences described in *Chapter 9*. The offender will normally have certain automatic entitlements concerning the date of his or her release from prison and the Secretary of State will set the licence conditions[1] (see *Chapter 11*).

The CJA 2003's 'dangerous offender' provisions create exceptions to (or in one instance modify) the above rules, broadly speaking in the interests of protecting the public from people who present certain risks. The provisions concern:

- **life imprisonment** (other than for murder: see below);[2]
- certain required sentences for **public protection**; and
- **extended sentences** for certain violent and sexual offences.

Under these provisions the normal custodial threshold is otiose because once the respective criteria are met the court is obliged to pass a custodial sentence. However, aspects of commensurate sentencing - those whereby the *length* of a sentence falls to be determined by the seriousness of the offence - may remain relevant, e.g. when *choosing between* a discretionary life sentence and a lesser indeterminate sentence for public protection; or when setting the 'appropriate custodial term' of an extended sentence (but not the 'extension period' itself); or simply where the dangerous offender criteria are not met.[3]

The special significance of the dangerous offender provisions lies in the arrangements for the offender's eventual release from prison. In broad terms, these are designed to ensure public safety by minimising the risk of future harm to members of the public. Where any court sentences an offender to a term of imprisonment of 12 months or more it can recommend licence conditions to the Secretary of State (who must then consider that recommendation), but this is not part of the sentence. All matters affecting release are explained in *Chapter 11*.

KEY TERMINOLOGY

It is first necessary to understand certain concepts employed by the CJA 2003:

---

[1] Although the court can recommend such conditions to the Secretary of State: *Chapter 11*.
[2] Similar but modified provisions apply to detention for life in relation to juveniles: see *Chapter 12*.
[3] See, particularly, Footnote 10.

- **specified offence** Under section 224(1) a specified offence is either a:
  - *specified violent offence* This is any one of a number of listed offences ranging from manslaughter, kidnapping, riot and affray to offences involving actual or grievous bodily harm to explosives offences, aggravated burglary, hostage-taking, endangering safety, hijacking, possession of a firearm with intent to endanger life and female genital mutilation. The list includes aiding and abetting such offences or conspiring or attempting to commit them. The full list of specified violent offences (all of which carry a maximum sentence of two years or more) is contained in Part 2 of Schedule 15 to the CJA 2003; or a
  - *specified sexual offence* This is any one of a number of listed offences ranging from rape and indecent assault upon a female or a male, to abduction of a woman, procuring, unlawful sexual intercourse, grooming, child prostitution and child pornography offences (commonly called 'paedophile offences'), living off immoral earnings, importation of obscene articles, trafficking for sexual exploitation, voyeurism, bestiality and necrophilia. Again, the list includes aiding and abetting, and conspiracy or attempts. The full list of specified sexual offences (all of which carry a maximum sentence of two years or more and which include certain offences created by the Sexual Offences Act 2003) is contained in Part 2 of Schedule 15 to the CJA 2003.[4]
- **serious offence** This is a specified offence (within the meaning outlined above) but one punishable by a maximum sentence of either life imprisonment or a determinate period of imprisonment for ten years or more (section 224 (2)). It should be noted that any resulting imprisonment for 'public protection' (below) will be *indeterminate* (below).
- **relevant offence** This is a device that is sometimes used by the CJA 2003 to refer to a specified offence (within the meaning outlined above) as well as certain offences under the laws of Scotland and Northern Ireland (section 229(4)). The definition comes into play in relation to the risk assessment criteria for assessing dangerousness (see later in the chapter). There is provision for a court to certify that it has previously convicted someone of a relevant offence: see section 230 CJA 2003.
- **serious harm** This means 'death or serious personal injury, whether physical or psychological' (section 224(3)). The term serious harm is relevant in relation to public protection.

LIFE IMPRISONMENT AND 'PUBLIC PROTECTION'

Section 225 CJA 2003 applies to adults[5] convicted of serious offences (as defined above)[6] where the court is 'of opinion that there is a significant risk to members of the public of serious harm occasioned by the commission by [the offender] of further specified offences'. Under section 225, the court must pass one of the following sentences, both of which are indeterminate in nature:

---

[4] Sex offenders are also placed on the Sex Offender Register under independent provisions.
[5] The special provisions of section 226 CJA 2003 apply to juveniles see *Chapter 12.*
[6] Committed after the relevant provisions of the CJA 2003 are in force: section 225(1) CJA 2003.

- a discretionary **life sentence**, i.e. where the offence carries such a sentence and provided that the seriousness of the offence - together with any associated offences - justifies such a sentence (section 225(2)); and
- in every other case caught by section 225(1), a sentence of **imprisonment for public protection** (section 225(3)).[7] When passing such a sentence the court must also set the relevant part of the sentence that is to be served in custody for the purposes of punishment and deterrence and following which the Parole Board may make its recommendation for release.

EXTENDED SENTENCES

The term 'extended sentence' is employed by the CJA 2003 to signify a sentence comprising an appropriate period in custody followed by an extended period of supervision in the community, this extended period being set by the court at the time of sentence. Under section 227 CJA 2003 'extended sentence' means:

. . . a sentence of imprisonment the term of which is equal to the aggregate of -
(a) the appropriate custodial term, and
(b) a further period ('the extension period') for which the offender is to be subject to a licence and which is of such length as the court considers necessary for the purposes of protecting the public from serious harm occasioned by the commission by him of further specified offences.

The provisions apply only to adults[8] convicted of specified violent or specified sexual offences other than those serious offences which attract the sentences of life imprisonment or for public protection described under the last heading (and see the definitions above) (section 227(1)).[9] As noted in *Chapter 7* in relation to the overall sentencing framework, the existing 'protection of the public' basis for imposing a custodial sentence - or a longer than usual custodial sentence - linked to the fact that an offence is a sexual or violent one (as originally enacted by the Criminal Justice Act 1991) will be removed post-CJA 2003 in favour of the extended sentence provisions.[10] The new provisions contemplate:

- a custodial term that is initially the shortest commensurate with the seriousness of the offence (section 227(3)(applying section 153(2)[11]);
- but which if it is below 12 months becomes 12 months (see below);
- to which is added an extended period of supervision in the community following release (which may well be substantial: below). During this extension period, the offender is liable to be recalled to prison for any breach of the conditions of his or her licence as devised by the Secretary of

---

[7] Further defined as subject to the provisions of Chapter 2, Part 2 of the Crime (Sentences) Act 1997.
[8] The special provisions of section 228 CJA 2003 apply to juveniles see *Chapter 12*.
[9] Committed after the relevant provisions of the CJA 2003 are in force: section 227(1) CJA 2003.
[10] The new measures replace, modify and extend those in section 85 Powers of Criminal Courts (Sentencing) Act 2000. A side effect of removing the 'protection of the public' ground for custody from the basic sentencing framework is that violent or sexual offences not caught by the extended sentence (e.g. where a court is *not* satisfied that there is a significant risk of further specified offences) or by other dangerous offender provisions fall to be dealt with by way of the standard sentencing criteria described in *Chapter 7* (and possibly even by way of a non-custodial sentence).
[11] As in other section 153(2) situations, certain offences, including firearms, offences are excluded.

State/National Offender Management Service and including both standard and any special conditions designed to avert risk:[12] see *Chapter 11.*

Criteria for an extended sentence

The extended sentence provisions can thus be summarised as applying when an offender is:

- convicted of a specified violent or specified sexual offence;
- other than a serious offence (to which the life sentence or public protection provisions outlined earlier will generally apply); and
- where the court 'considers that there is a significant risk to members of the public of serious harm occasioned by the commission by [the offender] of further specified offences'. For the meaning of 'serious harm' see the definitions at the beginning of this chapter.

As already intimated, the main difference between the extended sentence provisions and those for life sentences or public protection (above) is that with extended sentences there is no requirement that the offence be a 'serious offence': so that, in effect, the extended sentence provisions apply to specified violent or sexual offences that do not in themselves attract sentences of ten years or more.

Measuring the appropriate custodial term and extension period

As already indicated, 'appropriate custodial term' means a term of imprisonment (not exceeding the maximum permitted by the offence) that would apart from the extended sentence provisions be imposed under the standard provisions concerning the *length of imprisonment* contained in section 153(2) CJA 2003 (i.e. the shortest term commensurate with the seriousness of the offence). However, where in the court's assessment that term is less than 12 months, appropriate custodial term is defined as meaning 12 months (section 227(3)(b)). Thus, if a court concludes that an extended sentence is the correct outcome, but then considers that the commensurate term would be below 12 months, that term automatically rises to 12 months.[13] During the second half of his or her appropriate custodial term the offender may be released on licence on the recommendation of the Parole Board (section 247 CJA 2003 and see *Chapter 11*).

The maximum extension periods are five years in relation to a violent offence and eight years for a sexual offence (section 227(4)); and always provided that the overall term - i.e. the custodial part plus the extension period - does not exceed the maximum sentence available for the offence in question (section 227(5)). There are no special statutory criteria for the extension period.

ASSESSING DANGEROUSNESS AND RISK

The CJA 2003 sets out criteria that come into play where someone has been convicted of a specified offence and it falls to the court to assess - under any of the

---

[12] When there will, in effect, be an 'incremental' sanction as there is in relation to certain other aspects of sentencing under the CJA 2003 as noted elsewhere in this book.
[13] There is a temptation for courts to rationalise matters. If the 'correct' term would have been below 12 months, the court is bound to question whether it was correct in finding a future risk of serious harm, i.e. whether the criteria are satisfied at all - especially if 12 months is seen as unjust.

dangerous offender provisions described above - whether there is a significant risk to members of the public of serious harm from the offender due to further offences - and which therefore affects both the eligibility of the offender for one of the above kinds of sentence and the duty of the court to pass whichever sentence is applicable. Where at the time when the present offence was committed the offender did not stand convicted in the UK of a previous relevant offence[14] or was then aged under 18 the court, under section 229(2):

- must take into account all such information as is available to it about the nature and circumstances of the offence;
- must take into account any information that is before it about any pattern of behaviour of which the offence forms part; and
- may take into account any information about the offender that is before it.

Otherwise, if the offender is an adult and has been previously so convicted this presumption is, in effect, reversed and the court is required 'to assume that there is such a risk' unless, after taking into account all available and appropriate information of the same kind as that set out above it considers that it would be unreasonable to conclude that there is such a risk (section 229(3) and (4) summarised).

Ongoing arrangements for assessing risk

Section 325 CJA 2003 re-enacts section 67 Criminal Justice and Courts Services 2000 (with amendments) so as to place a duty on the 'responsibility authority' (the chief officer of police, local probation board and prison service) to establish and keep under review arrangements for assessing and managing the risks posed by 'relevant sexual and violent offenders'[15] or other offenders who may cause serious harm to the public.

In practice such arrangements take the form of multi-agency public protection panels (or MAPPs). The various constituent bodies must co-operate with one another and the responsible authority to enable it to perform its duty and a memorandum outlining this process must be produced. The Secretary of State is given power to amend the list of specified bodies by addition or removal. Section 326 requires the authority to keep the effectiveness of these arrangements under review and to change them as necessary. The review must be conducted in consultation with two lay advisers to be appointed for each area by the Secretary of State. The authority must also publish an annual report.

---

[14] Meaning, so far as sentencing in England and Wales is concerned a specified violent or sexual offence, including a conviction under service law: see section 233 CJA 2003.

[15] As defined in section 327 CJA 2003.

CHAPTER 11

Release and Post-custody Supervision

Readers will now be familiar with the fact that under the CJA 2003 the new short forms of prison sentence of 'below 12 months' outlined in *Chapter 9* (custody plus, intermittent custody and suspended sentence) have 'built-in' release and licence arrangements by virtue of the terms of the original sentence and/or in the case of the suspended sentence decisions of the 'activating' court. Court-ordered licence conditions will be in addition to 'standard' conditions set by the Secretary of State (section 250 CJA 2003). Again, if short sentence offenders need to be recalled to prison following release, the Secretary of State is given power to re-set licence conditions in the light of current circumstances (section 244 CJA 2003).

Recommending release conditions

Where a sentence is for 12 months or more, fixed-term prisoners will normally be released at the half-way point of their sentence and stay on licence until the end of the full term of their sentence (as distinct from the half-way or two-thirds point under existing arrangements depending on length of sentence and/or Parole Board decisions). Here, the Secretary of State sets the licence conditions, subject to considering any recommendations by the court. Section 238 states:

> (1) A court which sentences an offender to a term of imprisonment of twelve months or more in respect of any offence may, when passing sentence, recommend to the Secretary of State particular conditions which in its view should be included in any licence granted to the offender . . . on his release from prison.
>
> (2) In exercising his powers . . . the Secretary of State must have regard to any recommendation under subsection (1).
>
> (3) A recommendation under subsection (1) is not to be treated for any purpose as part of the sentence passed on the offender.[1]

The Parole Board

Section 239 CJA 2003 provides for the continuation of the Parole Board which will have functions in respect of certain fixed term prisoners, and also life sentence prisoners within the meaning of Part 2 of the Crime (Sentences) Act 1997 (i.e. discretionary lifers and mandatory lifers unless sentenced to life imprisonment for murder or offences involving murder[2]). The Board is given a duty 'to advise the Secretary of State with respect to any matter referred to it by him concerned with the early release or recall of prisoners. It must, under that section, when dealing with cases in respect of which it makes a recommendation, consider '(a) any documents given to it by the Secretary of State, and (b) any other oral or written information obtained by it; and if in any particular case the Board thinks it necessary to interview the person to whom the case relates before reaching a decision, the Board may authorise one of its members to interview him and must consider the report of the interview made by that member'.

---

[1] The provision does not apply to juveniles: see section 238(4).
[2] To which the provisions in section 269 CJA 2003 apply (see later in the chapter).

The Board must also deal with cases in respect of which it makes any direction under Part 12 CJA 2003 or the 1997 Act (below) 'on consideration of all such evidence as shall be adduced before it'. The Secretary of State can make rules and give directions concerning matters to be taken into account having regard to:

- the need to protect the public from serious harm from the offender; and
- the desirability of preventing further offences by him or her and of securing his or her rehabilitation (section 239(5), (6) CJA 2003 summarised).

Schedule 19 CJA 2003 contains various supplementary provisions including those affecting the Parole Board's status, constitution, powers and proceedings.

MATTERS AFFECTING RELEASE AND SUPERVISION

Part 12 CJA 2003 contains a range of provisions affecting various aspects of release on licence, supervision and breach of licence.

Time spent on remand
Section 240 re-enacts section 87 PCC(S)A 2000 (with modifications),[3] so as to make custodial remand time count as time served; but only in connection with the same or a related offence. The court must state in open court the number of days spent on remand and those counting towards sentence. It can decline to do so 'in the interests of justice' - but must give reasons if not awarding full credit. Section 241 ensures that custodial remand time counts towards time served for the purpose of calculating whether or not an offender has completed a proportion or period of a sentence, including *vis-à-vis* intermittent custody; whilst section 242 lists the sentences where crediting applies and defines 'remand in custody'. Time in PACE detention does not count (but being held on remand in police cells in an emergency to relieve prison overcrowding would).

People extradited to the UK
Section 243 CJA 2003 re-enacts section 47 CJA 1991 (with modification) so that extradited prisoners receive credit for time spent in custody awaiting extradition.

Duty to release prisoners and the offender's obligation
Section 244 CJA 2003 contains a general duty to release prisoners. All prisoners to whom the section applies must serve a 'requisite custodial period' and then the Secretary of State must release them on licence. That period depends on the particular sentence. For all prisoners serving 12 months or more (excluding dangerous offenders and life sentence prisoners) the Secretary of State must release them at the half-way point of their sentence. Whatever the length of sentence, section 252 CJA 2003 requires the offender to comply with any conditions attached to his or her licence, failing which he or she is recalled.

Restrictions in relation to intermittent custody
With intermittent custody release is at the end of each custodial period. Section 245 provides that an intermittent custody prisoner who has been returned to

---

[3] I.e. modifying provisions not yet in force and stemming from the CJA 1991. Piloting suggested that the process was somewhat unwieldy. Implementation may well depend on technological advances.

custody following a period of being unlawfully at large (which he or she is deemed to be by not returning to prison as required by the order) does not have to be released under section 244(1). He or she can be held whilst an application is made to a court to alter the pattern of intermittence under paragraph 6(1)(b) of Schedule 10 (see *Chapter 9*). The Secretary of State must apply within 72 hours, or release the offender to continue his or her sentence intermittently. If whilst so held, the offender's custodial days expire, he or she must be released (section 245(1)(b)). A recalled intermittent custody prisoner does not then fall to be released until the Parole Board directs otherwise.

Power to release prisoners on licence before required to do so
The Criminal Justice Act 1991 (as amended) allows certain prisoners, following risk-assessment, to spend the final portion of their sentence on home detention curfew (HDC). Under section 34A CJA 1991, a suitable offender may be released up to 135 days early. A curfew is imposed plus electronic monitoring to ensure compliance. If the offender breaches that curfew - or other licence conditions - he or she is recalled. The curfew condition will in future be imposed under section 253 CJA 2003 (below). Under section 246, the maximum period of HDC remains 135 days (but the Secretary of State is given power to alter this). Only certain prisoners are eligible, excluding dangerous offenders; those liable to deportation; or with less than 14 days to serve (e.g. due to remand time being credited: above). Also, HDC is 'tapered' in line with length of sentence; and with intermittent custody the offender spends a number of days on HDC, matching custodial days.

Release of extended sentence prisoners
Section 247 makes special provision in relation to extended sentences (*Chapter 10*). Once the offender has served half of the 'appropriate custodial term', then subject to the recommendation of the Parole Board he or she may be released on licence. Once the entire 'appropriate custodial term' has been served he or she must be released but they will remain on licence until the extension period expires (and thus be subject to possible recall for a substantial period).

Power to release prisoners on compassionate grounds
Section 248 re-enacts section 36 Criminal Justice Act 1991 concerning the release of fixed-term prisoners on compassionate grounds. The Secretary of State may only release prisoners on this basis under the CJA 2003[4] where exceptional circumstances exist (e.g. terminal illness). The Parole Board must be consulted unless circumstances render this impracticable.

Duration of a licence
Section 249 provides that, after release, all prisoners serving determinate sentences must remain on licence for the remainder of their sentence. Special provision is made for intermittent custody, reflecting the fact that an offender must return to prison following each licence interval before final release. In either case, the provisions as to duration of licence are subject to the fact that the offender may be recalled with regard to breach of a licence condition (below).

---

[4] Although it may be that the Secretary of State has a wider discretion under the Prerogative powers.

Licence conditions and breach

Section 250 deals with the conditions that can be attached to a licence. For sentences below 12 months, licences must include court-ordered conditions plus 'standard conditions' (i.e. as prescribed by the Secretary of State: section 250(1)) and insofar as the latter are not inconsistent with the former. Standard conditions will vary according to the sentence. They apply in conjunction with any electronic monitoring or drug-testing conditions under the Criminal Justice and Court Services Act 2000 (section 259(2)(a)) or prescribed for public protection (section 250(2)(b)). Any court-ordered licence conditions (except curfew and electronic monitoring of a court-ordered curfew) will also apply where a prisoner is released on compassionate grounds or on HDC (above).

For prisoners serving more than 12 months conditions will be set by the Secretary of State (in practice by NOMS). These will comprise standard conditions plus any others that are prescribed and specified in the licence. Again, electronic monitoring and drug-testing conditions can be added. If a court-ordered licence has a curfew condition, this cannot operate alongside HDC. Section 250(7) sets out arrangements in relation to consecutive or concurrent terms; section 250(8) requires the Secretary of State to consider certain factors, including the protection of the public and preventing re-offending, when creating new conditions.

Licence conditions on re-release of prisoner serving under 12 months

Section 251 deals with re-release where an offender is serving a sentence of less than 12 months (*Chapter 9*) but is recalled to prison, when his or her court-ordered licence conditions may be disrupted. Following the recall, the Secretary of State can re-set the conditions before re-release. In effect, following recall, conditions are imposed as they are for sentences of 12 months or over.

Curfew condition to be included in licence under section 246

Section 253 specifies the curfew condition (as attached to early release on HDC (above)). It must specify periods during which the offender must remain in a specified place and include a requirement of electronic monitoring. It can specify more than one place and/or more than one period. Except for the first and last days, a curfew cannot last for less than nine hours in any one day. It lasts until the date when the offender would have been released from prison but for early release. Section 253(4) makes provision in relation to intermittent custody.

Power to recall prisoners

Section 254 CJA 2003 allows the Secretary of State to revoke an offender's licence and recall him or her to prison. A recalled prisoner must be informed of the reason or reasons for this and can make written representations. The Parole Board must consider all recalls. If it decides that the person should be released, the Secretary of State must release him or her. If it immediately re-releases an intermittent custody prisoner he or she continues with his or her sentence on an intermittent basis. If a prisoner on licence is recalled, he or she can be detained and if at large is treated as unlawfully at large. Section 254 does not apply to offenders recalled from HDC (see section 254(7) and the next heading).

Power to recall prisoners released under HDC

Section 255 enables the Secretary of State to revoke the licence of an offender on HDC and recall him or her to prison if he or she has failed to comply with licence conditions or if his or her whereabouts can no longer be tracked. The recalled prisoner must be informed of the reason, and can make written representations. The Secretary of State can then decide to cancel such a revocation. This has the effect that the licence is treated as not having been revoked. Offenders whose HDC licence is revoked become 'unlawfully at large' and can be arrested.

Further release after recall

Under section 256 CJA 2003 - after a prisoner is recalled - arrangements are made with a view to further release. The Parole Board must set a date for future release or for it to review the offender's case within a year. A date need not be fixed if the offender is due for release within 12 months. If the Board decides on a future release date, the offender must be released on that date. At a review, the Board can recommend immediate release, or fix a future release or review date.

Disciplinary offences: 'Added days'

Section 257 re-enacts section 42 Criminal Justice Act 1991, which enables prison rules pursuant to the Prison Act 1952 to provide for days to be added to a prisoner's sentence if he or she is found guilty of disciplinary offences in custody.

Early release of fine defaulters and contemnors

Section 258 re-enacts section 45 Criminal Justice Act 1991 (as amended: with modifications), that sets out release provisions for people committed to custody in default of payment of a fine or contempt of court, which are not 'sentences'. The new section provides for unconditional release at the half-way point of the default term whether under or over 12 months. Fine defaulters and contemnors can be released on compassionate grounds.

People liable to removal from the UK

The CJA 2003 deals with various matters concerning removal from the UK of people so liable as defined in section 259. Under existing law, short-term foreign national prisoners (i.e. serving less than four years) who are liable to removal from the UK are automatically released and liable to be removed at the half-way point of their sentence. They are excluded from HDC (section 34A(e) CJA 1991 as amended). Long-term foreign national prisoners (i.e. serving a determinate sentence of four years or more) are considered for early release at the half-way point of their sentence (known as their 'parole eligibility date'). Release decisions are based on risk assessments. Those thought to be an unacceptable risk remain in custody until their automatic release date, i.e. the two-thirds point of their sentence. Both short-term and long-term foreign national prisoners released from prison are liable to be held under immigration law until removed from the UK.

Section 260 CJA 2003 introduces a new scheme whereby eligible prisoners may be removed up to 135 days earlier than their normal release date. There will be a minimum custodial period before removal is possible and certain prisoners are excluded. Section 260 also ensures that prisoners remain liable to be detained in pursuance of their sentences if they remain in the UK so that if, e.g. a released prisoner makes an application for asylum he or she will be returned to prison to continue with his or her sentence. The Secretary of State can change 'eligibility' and set minimum sentence and custodial periods.

Section 261 deals with the arrangements in the case of a prisoner who returns to the UK following removal. If this is before his or her sentence expires, he or she will be detained under that sentence for a period equal to the outstanding custodial period, or until the sentence expiry date whichever comes first.

Section 262 invokes Schedule 20 to the CJA 2003, which provides for a similar scheme to apply under the CJA 1991 pending commencement of the CJA 2003.

Concurrent terms of imprisonment

Section 263 concerns release where there are concurrent terms. The offender must serve the longest custodial period of the sentences passed. He or she will remain on licence until the expiry of the longest sentence. In cases where sentences of more than and less than 12 months were ordered concurrently, the Secretary of State (in practice NOMS) may set licence conditions without regard to court-ordered conditions in relation to the shorter sentence.

Consecutive terms of imprisonment

Section 264 concerns release in relation to consecutive terms. The offender must serve a period equal to the aggregate of the custodial periods before being released. Where sentences of less than 12 months and more than 12 months (including an extended sentence) are passed at the same time, or where more than one sentence of more than 12 months is involved, the offender will remain on licence for a period equal to the aggregate of the lengths of the individual licence periods. Where sentences of under 12 months are to be served consecutively, the offender will remain on licence until he or she has served an overall term equal in length to the longest licence period. The term will be the aggregate of the custodial periods plus the longest licence period.

Restriction on consecutive sentences for already released prisoners

Section 265 re-enacts section 84 Powers of Criminal Courts (Sentencing) Act 2000 (with modifications) so as to provide that if the offender is sentenced to imprisonment for a new offence while on licence, the prison term for that new offence starts immediately, not after the first term expires.

Drug-testing requirements

Section 266 amends section 64 Criminal Justice and Court Services Act 2000. It provides that should a responsible officer (as defined in section 299(6)) be of the opinion that the offender has a propensity to misuse any specified Class A drugs, that such misuse has caused or contributed to any offence of which he or she was convicted, or that it is likely to cause or contribute to him or her committing further offences, then the offender must provide, when requested, a sample to ascertain whether he or she has a specified Class A drug in their system. The existing requirement for a 'trigger' offence to have been committed is removed.[5]

---

[5] For the implications in relation to juveniles see *Chapter 12*.

Power to amend by order the 'relevant proportion' of a sentence

Section 267 gives the Secretary of State power to amend by order the proportion of a custodial sentence of 12 months or more that must be served in prison before release. It also enables him or her to amend the proportion of an extended sentence for certain sexual and violent offences (*Chapter 10*) to be served before a prisoner is eligible for release on the recommendation of the Parole Board.[6]

Minimum terms in relation to mandatory life sentences

Section 269 CJA 2003 relates to mandatory life sentences (i.e. for murder and certain offences involving murder). The court must make an order specifying a period that the prisoner will have to serve before the Parole Board can consider release on licence under section 28 Crime (Sentences) Act 1997 (i.e. a 'minimum term'). There is an exception if the offender was 21 or over at the time of the offence and the court considers that the murder was so grave that he or she ought to spend the rest of his or her life in prison, when it can order that the early release provisions are not to apply (see section 269(4)). In relation to adults, 'life sentence' is defined as one of imprisonment for life imposed on someone convicted of murder who is 21 years of age or more, or a sentence of custody for life if aged 18, 19 or 20 years of age (section 277).

The court must set the minimum term by reference to the seriousness of the offence, taking into account time spent on remand. Whole life, 30 year and 15 year 'starting points' are contained in Schedule 21 and the court must have regard to the principles set out in that schedule and any guidelines issued by the Sentencing Guidelines Council (*Chapter 7*).[7] Section 270 CJA 2003 requires a clear explanation to be given (and see section 174 CJA 2003 in the *Appendix*).

Section 271 CJA 2003 ensures that the opportunity to apply to the Court of Appeal or House of Lords in order to appeal against a minimum term is open to prisoners in respect of whom an order under section 269 is made following sentence in the Crown Court; and also in relation to sentences by courts-martial.

Section 275 deals with the release of mandatory life prisoners so as to bring the arrangements for release into line with those for discretionary life sentence prisoners under the Crime (Sentences) Act 1997. The amendments ensure that a mandatory lifer will be able to require the Secretary of State to refer his or her case to the Parole Board once he or she has served the minimum term. Once a case is referred to it, the Parole Board will decide whether a prisoner should be released and may direct this only if satisfied that the prisoner's continued detention is no longer necessary for the protection of the public. The Secretary of State then comes under a duty to release the prisoner on life licence.

Section 276 CJA 2003 invokes Schedule 22 which deals with existing lifers; and section 273 contains special provisions concerning life sentence prisoners transferred from other parts of England and Wales.

---

[6] Either of which measures could, e.g. be used to deal with prison overcrowding.

[7] Provided they are compatible: Schedule 21. Which rather begs the question of 'who knows best'. The Secretary of State can amend Schedule 21 by statutory instrument (subject to the affirmative resolution procedure). He or she has a duty to consult the SGC before doing so.

CHAPTER 12

Juveniles: A Note

As noted in *Chapter 1*, it would be impossible in a work of this kind to deal with every conceivable effect that the CJA 2003 might have in relation to adults, even more so with people below the age of 18 - and still less to place the 2003 Act within a full youth justice context. This chapter is therefore intended as a guide to key aspects of that Act as they concern juveniles rather than as a definitive treatment of a subject that represents a specialist area of study.[1] One notable feature of the CJA 2003 is that its statutory purposes of sentencing (*Chapter 7*) will *not* apply to juveniles - even if much of the new sentencing framework (including its sentencing thresholds, with their revised emphases) will do so. The principal purpose of youth justice will continue to be 'the prevention of offending by children and young persons' as required by section 37 Crime and Disorder Act 1998 (whilst the 'welfare principle' in section 44 Children and Young Persons Act 1933 will continue to signal a distinctive approach towards juvenile offenders). Similarly, many everyday processes of youth justice are unaffected by the CJA 2003 and general responsibility will continue to fall on the Youth Justice Board and local youth offending teams (YOTs).

INDIVIDUAL SUPPORT ORDER

Section 322 CJA 2003 inserts a new section 1AA into the Crime and Disorder Act 1998 so that if an adult court[2] makes an anti-social behaviour order (ASBO)[3] in respect of a juvenile it may also make an 'individual support order' (ISO). Section 1AA provides:

(1) Where a court makes an anti-social behaviour order in respect of a defendant who is a child or young person when that order is made, it must consider, whether the individual support conditions are fulfilled.

(2) If it is satisfied that those conditions are fulfilled, the court must make an order under this section ('an individual support order') which -
    (a) requires the defendant to comply, for a period not exceeding six months, with such requirements as are specified in the order; and
    (b) requires the defendant to comply with any directions given by the responsible officer[4] with a view to the implementation of the requirements under paragraph (a) above.

(3) The individual support conditions are -
    (a) that an individual support order would be desirable in the interests of preventing any repetition of the kind of behaviour that led to the making of the anti-social behaviour order;
    (b) that the defendant is not already subject to an individual support order . . .

---

[1] See *Introduction to Youth Justice* or *Child Law* (details at www.watersidepress.co.uk).
[2] See Home Office guidance notes on ASBOs and Acceptable Behaviour Contracts (2003).
[3] Seemingly, an ISO cannot be linked to a criminal anti-social behaviour order (or 'CRASBO'), even though a CRASBO will often have the same basic intent, content and effect as an ASBO.
[4] Specified in the order and being a social worker, someone nominated by the chief education officer or a member of a YOT: section 1AA(10) of the 1998 as inserted by section 322(10) CJA 2003.

Additionally, arrangements for ISOs must be available in the area in which it appears that the defendant resides or will reside, but otherwise under section 1AA(2) above the court *must* make the ISO (even if certain judgements concerning its 'desirability in the interests of justice' do fall to be made when considering the underlying criteria in that subsection). If the court is not satisfied that the conditions in section 1AA(3) are met, it must state this in open court and say why (section 1AA(4)). The requirements that may be specified are those the court considers desirable in the interests of preventing any repetition of the behaviour that led to the ASBO (section 1(5)), requiring the juvenile to:

- participate in activities or directions; and/or
- present himself or herself to someone at a given place and time; and/or
- comply with any arrangements for his or her education.

As specified in the ISO, the juvenile cannot be required or directed to attend on more than two days a week (meaning within 'a period of seven days beginning on a Sunday') at the same or different places. So far as practicable, requirements must not conflict with religious belief or interfere with work, schooling or education times. Before making the ISO, the court must obtain from a social worker or YOT member any information it thinks necessary in relation to the statutory conditions or requirements and consider these. It can be noted that this will not be by way of a 'pre-sentence report' (PSR) or 'specific sentence report', an ISO being a civil matter such that some new form of *ad hoc* report would appear to be in contemplation.

Explanation, breach, variation and discharge of an ISO

Before making an ISO, the court must explain its effect, requirements, the consequences that flow from non-compliance and the court's powers to review the order on the application of the juvenile or responsible officer (new section 1AB(1) of the 1998 Act[5]). The Secretary of State can prescribe exceptions or situations where explanations may be given in writing. Failure without reasonable excuse to comply with a requirement renders the juvenile guilty of an offence and liable to a fine of up to £1,000 (or £250 if under 14). No referral order (i.e. referring the juvenile to a youth offending panel) can be made (new section 1AB(4)). If the underlying ASBO ends, so does the ISO (if it has not already expired). The juvenile or responsible officer can apply for the ISO to be varied or discharged; or this can happen if the ASBO itself is varied or discharged.

PARENTING ORDERS AND REFERRAL ORDERS

Section 324 CJA 2003 invokes Schedule 34 CJA 2003 which makes provision about the interaction between parenting orders under sections 8 to 10 Crime and Disorder Act 1998 and referral orders under the Powers of Criminal Courts (Sentencing) Act 2000. Schedule 34 removes the existing restrictions whereby a court cannot make a parenting order alongside a referral order, and makes it possible to make both orders for the same offence. It also ensures that the normal

---

[5] Compare the general such duty in relation to *sentencing* in section 174 CJA 2003 in the *Appendix*.

duty on the court to make a parenting order where a juvenile under the age of 16 is convicted of an offence (or to explain why it has not done so) will not apply if the court makes a referral order in respect of the offence.

Under a newly inserted section 22(2A) Powers of Criminal Courts (Sentencing) Act 2000, a court making a referral order may require a parent or guardian to attend meetings of the youth offending panel[6] under section 20 of that Act. Where the parent or guardian fails to comply, the new provisions give power to the panel to refer the case back to the youth court. This would allow the court the opportunity to decide whether it should impose a parenting order.

New provisions are inserted into section 28 Powers of Criminal Courts (Sentencing) Act 2000 and Schedule 1 to that Act. These set out the arrangements when a youth offending panel refers a parent or guardian to the appropriate youth court using the new power in section 22(2A) (above). The panel must make a report to the court explaining why the parent is being referred to it and the court can require the parent to appear before it. The youth court may then make a parenting order if:

- the court is satisfied that the parent has failed without reasonable excuse to comply with an order made by the court to attend as required; and
- it believes that the parenting order is desirable in the interests of preventing further offences by the offender.

The provisions also clarify which of the provisions of the Crime and Disorder Act 1998 relating to parenting orders apply to such an order made in these circumstances and provide for a right of appeal to the Crown Court.

OTHER KEY POINTS

Other key points concerning juveniles and the CJA 2003 can be summarised as follows:

- **indication of plea** Juveniles will be able to 'indicate' their plea in relation to certain serious allegations or where being tried alongside an adult, along the lines of the existing 'plea before venue' arrangements for adults (Schedule 3 CJA 2003, paragraph 10 inserting new sections 24A to 24D MCA 1980). The idea is to avoid cases being sent to the Crown Court for trial (in those situations where that is possible) and, of course, a juvenile would normally expect the full sentence discount for a guilty plea intimated at this early stage;
- **drug-testing** Various testing provisions apply to juveniles: section 5 CJA 2003 amends PACE so as to allow the police to detain a juvenile aged 14 years or over after charge to test for specified Class A drugs, subject to conditions set out in a new section 63B of PACE; and there is similar provision in relation to pre-sentence drug-testing at the behest of the court (section 161) (and see *Chapter 13*). An appropriate adult must be present during the testing. The Secretary of State may alter that minimum age by order. Further provisions concern juveniles released on licence (see section

---

[6] In practice as set up and managed by the YOT.

266(2), (3) CJA 2003 which amends section 64 Criminal Justice and Court Services Act 2000), including with regard to release from long term detention imposed under sections 226 or 228 CJA 2003 (below). Section 279 CJA 2003 invokes Schedule 24 to the Act which enables a requirement for drug-testing to be included in an action plan order or a supervision order.[7]

- **bail** Changes to the Bail Act 1976 whereby a court must normally refuse bail if a defendant is alleged to have committed an offence whilst on bail, or absconds, apply only to adults (see *Chapter 4*). Nonetheless, when considering *whether a juvenile would commit an offence* if released on bail, particular weight must be given to the fact that he or she was on bail at the time of the newly alleged offence (section 14(2) CJA 2003). Similarly, when considering whether he or she would fail to surrender to custody, to the fact that he or she had previously absconded (section 15(2)). The new restrictions on bail for certain drug users (section 19) apply only to adults.

- **conditional cautions** Juveniles remain subject to the special scheme of warnings and reprimands established by the Crime and Disorder Act 1998 and are unaffected by the adult scheme for conditional cautions described in *Chapter 3*;

- **reports** As under existing law, post-CJA 2003 a court must not form an opinion that a pre-sentence report (PSR) is 'unnecessary' (*Chapter 7*) in the case of a juvenile unless 'there exists a previous pre-sentence report obtained in respect of the offender, and . . . the court has had regard to the information contained in that report . . . or the most recent report' (section 156(3)(b)CJA 2003). Under section 159(6)) where a local authority has parental authority and the offender is in care or provided with local authority accommodation pursuant to 'social services functions',[8] that authority must be given a copy of the report. In relation to juveniles, the terms 'appropriate' officer and 'responsible officer' have separate meanings from those same terms when used in relation to adults. Thus, e.g. the compiler of a report will be a probation officer, social worker of a local authority social services department or a member of a youth offending team (YOT) (section 158(2)); there are similar modifications where someone is to be consulted, made responsible, allowed to give instructions or agree to a requirement of an order (see, e.g. sections 201 (activities), section 322 (ISOs); or is to be given copies of orders etc. (see, e.g. section 219). The precise rules vary: it is essential to be alert to this fact.

- **previous convictions** Evidence of offences by a defendant aged 21 or over *committed when he or she was still under 14 years of age* will be admissible under the general new provision concerning evidence of 'bad character' described in *Chapter 5* and 'for the purposes of evidence relating to previous convictions', but only where both the new and earlier offences are triable on indictment and the court is satisfied that the interests of justice require the evidence to be admissible (section 108 CJA 2003: in part altering section 16 Children and Young Persons Act 1963). Disclosure must still be appropriate within the general restrictions of section 101 (see *Chapter 5*);

---

[7] For an explanation of these underlying orders see works on youth justice such a *Introduction to Youth Justice* or *Child Law* (www.watersidepress.co.uk)

[8] See Local Authority Social Services Act 1970.

- **sentencing generally** Schedule 8 to the CJA 2003 largely reproduces (but with modifications) Schedule 3 to the Powers of Criminal Courts (Sentencing) Act 2000 (which will continue post-CJA 2003 in relation to young offenders);

- **fine enforcement** The CJA 2003 enforcement mechanisms of unpaid work, a curfew or driving disqualification (*Chapter 7*) will apply to defaulters aged 16 or over notwithstanding restrictions on custodial sentences for people under 18 years of age (sections 300(1)(b) and 301(1)(b));

- **generic community sentence/youth community orders** The generic community order (*Chapter 8*) applies to juveniles aged 16 and above only. But there is a 'merging' of old and new provisions in relation to juveniles below that age. It will thus be possible for CJA 2003-style requirements to be attached to certain existing 'youth community orders' (made under existing legislation), i.e. in relation to curfew orders, exclusion orders, attendance centre orders, supervision orders and action plan orders (see sections 147 and 148 CJA 2003).[9]

- **re-sentencing following a community order** Schedule 8 to the CJA 2003, paragraph 12 provides that where a community order was made by magistrates in the case of a juvenile but in respect of an offence triable only on indictment in the case of an adult, any re-sentencing powers in respect of the offender after he or she attains the age of 18 are powers to do either or both of the following: impose a fine not exceeding £5,000 for the offence in respect of which the order was made; or to deal with the offender for that offence in any way in which a magistrates' court could have done if it had just convicted the offender of an offence punishable with imprisonment for not beyond 51 weeks.[10]

- **custodial sentencing** The new-style short adult custodial sentences (*Chapter 9*) will not apply to juveniles, but certain of the dangerous offender provisions (*Chapter 10*) will do so in a modified form (below). In relation to the existing detention and training order (DTO), the term of the DTO - where the offence is a summary offence and the maximum term of imprisonment for an adult is 51 weeks - 'may not exceed six months' (section 298 CJA 2003).

- **dangerous offenders** Sections 226 and 228 CJA 2003 provide for sentences for juveniles of detention for public protection or for life and for extended sentences. Minor subtleties apart, the provisions approximate to those for adults (*Chapter 10*). However, in the case of detention for public protection or for life there are special criteria geared to certain existing provisions in relation to juveniles and for the court to expressly eliminate the possibility of an extended sentence before progressing to these more severe sentences (see, particularly, section 226(1), (3)). The 'whole life', 30 year and 15 year starting points for life sentences in Schedule 21 to the CJA 2003 (as invoked by section 269) (*Chapter 11*) are inapplicable in the case of a juvenile: in comparable circumstances, all juveniles have a starting point of 12 years.

- **disqualification from working with children** There is a slightly different emphasis where a court comes to consider such a disqualification in the

---

[9] Further changes have been suggested in the consultation paper, *Youth Justice: The Next Steps*.

[10] Another example of 'incremental sentencing', i.e. juvenile crimes attracting adult punishments.

case of a juvenile, compared to that in relation to an adult offender (*Chapter 13*). With juveniles, the court must make such an order if satisfied that *it is likely* that a further offence against a child will be committed.

- **firearms** The new minimum sentence in the freshly inserted section 51A Firearms Act 1968 (which applies to people aged 16 and over) is set at three years for juveniles (in England and Wales)[11] as opposed to five years for adults (*Chapter 13*) (section 287 CJA 2003). Otherwise, section 289 amends section 91 Powers of Criminal Courts Act 2000 so as to ensure that someone aged 16 or 17 can be sentenced to the minimum term of detention required by section 51A of the 1998 Act. Section 291 gives the Secretary of State power to exclude the application of the minimum term in relation to juveniles.

---

[11] In Scotland the minimum sentence is three years for offenders *below 21 years of age* (section 287(5)). See also section 290 CJA 2003 which equates with section 289 as it applies to England and Wales.

CHAPTER 13

Miscellaneous and General Changes

Beyond its central provisions, the CJA 2003 contains a significant number of what are variously described as 'miscellaneous', 'other', 'supplementary' or 'general' provisions, of which the following items - not dealt with elsewhere in this book - deserve mention due to the significance of the changes that they introduce.

FIREARMS

Section 287 CJA 2003 inserts a new section 51A Firearms Act 1968 to provide for a minimum custodial sentence for unauthorised possession of certain types of firearm. Section 51A(1) lists the offences to attract that sentence and applies the provisions to people aged 16 years or over at the time of the offence. New section 51A(5) sets the minimum sentence at five years for adults in England and Wales.[1] Under section 51A(2) courts must impose the minimum sentence unless there are exceptional circumstances relating to the offence or offender. Home Office guidance instances, e.g. inadvertent failure to renew a firearms certificate, or 'where a war trophy is discovered among a deceased person's effects'.

Section 288 amends Part 1 of Schedule 6 to the Firearms Act 1968 so as to increase the status of all offences to which the minimum sentence applies to indictable only; whilst section 293 amends the Customs and Excise Management Act 1979 so as to increase the maximum penalty for smuggling prohibited weapons covered by the minimum sentence provisions from seven to ten years imprisonment. The offences are improper importation (section 50 of the 1979 Act), exportation of prohibited or restricted goods (section 68 of the 1979 Act) and fraudulent evasion of duty etc. (section 170 of that Act).

DRUG-RELATED MATTERS

Various provisions of the CJA 2003 address areas of concern in relation to drugs. There are arrangements to test people in police detention (*Chapter 2*) and at other points in the criminal process, including where a court is considering passing a community sentence - particularly with a view to a drug rehabilitation requirement under section 209 (*Chapter 8*) or as part of a suspended sentence under section 161 (*Chapter 9*) with regard to Class A drugs. As already noted in *Chapter 2*, section 11 CJA 2003 makes possession of a Class C drug an arrestable offence (thereby, among other things, enabling the police to arrest people for possession of cannabis which is simultaneously downgraded from a Class B to a Class C drug).[2] There are new restrictions on certain drug-users being granted

---

[1] See the Act for the position in Scotland and *Chapter 12* for juveniles. Section 292 CJA 2003 invokes Schedule 29 CJA 2003 which makes similar provision for Northern Ireland. In particular, it applies the minimum sentence provisions to handguns, currently not prohibited there.

[2] Contrary to many a media report that the police cannot now arrest people for possession of cannabis. It has been indicated by the police that in practice this power will only be relied on if

bail (*Chapter 2*) and penalties for many drug-related offences are increased (see sections 284, 285). There are also provisions relating to drug-testing whilst on licence following release from prison etc., breach of which will lead to recall as described in *Chapter 11* (section 266). Section 284 invokes Schedule 24 so as to increase the maximum penalty for trafficking in Class A drugs to 14 years imprisonment.

DISQUALIFICATION FROM WORKING WITH CHILDREN

Section 299 CJA 2003 invokes Schedule 30 which contains amendments to the Criminal Justice and Court Services Act 2000 concerning disqualification orders under Part 2 of the 2000 Act, i.e. in relation to working with children. A new section 29A of the 2000 Act provides that where someone is convicted of an offence against a child (whether committed as an adult or juvenile), he or she is convicted by a senior court, and no qualifying sentence is imposed, then:

> . . . if the court is satisfied, having regard to all the circumstances, that it is likely that the individual will commit a further offence against a child, it may order the individual to be disqualified from working with children.

If the court makes such an order it must state its reasons for doing so and cause these to be included in the record of the proceedings. Schedule 30 makes provision for related situations, including where an application is made for a disqualification order when a court has not previously made one.

ATTENDANCE CENTRES

Section 214 CJA 2003 contains provisions in relation to attendance centres (see attendance centre 'requirements' (as they will become in relation to offenders aged 16 and over) in *Chapter 8*). These restate that the aggregate number of hours of attendance are not less than 12 nor more than 36 - and reflect other aspects of existing law, e.g. that a court may not impose the requirement unless satisfied that the centre to be specified is reasonably accessible to the offender, having regard to the means of access available to him or her and any other circumstances. The offender first attends as notified by the responsible officer and subsequent hours are arranged by the officer in charge. Traditionally, 'reasonably accessible' has been accepted as meaning up to an hour's travelling time each way (not deductible from the hours to be served) and/or 'up to 15 miles - depending, e.g. on transport links and the age of the offender. As with all matters affected by the CJA 2003, fresh guidance can be expected.

there are aggravating features. But soon after implementation it became clear that practice varied from one police area to another.

TERRORISM

Section 306 CJA 2003 concerns detention under Schedule 8 to the Terrorism Act 2000 and relates to suspected terrorists arrested under section 41 of that Act. The changes confer on the 'judicial authority' (as defined in paragraph 29 of Schedule 8) the power to extend the period of detention for up to (a total of) 14 days from the existing starting times in paragraphs 29(3) and 36(3) of the schedule - if the conditions in paragraph 32 are met, i.e. there must be reasonable grounds for believing that further detention is necessary to obtain relevant evidence; and the investigation must be being conducted diligently and expeditiously. Under paragraph 37, the detainee must be released immediately if the grounds for detention cease to apply.

It is not possible for the 14 days to be granted in one block, and the judicial authority can only extend the detention period for more than seven days if the order already authorises detention for the existing maximum of seven days. Otherwise, detention can be extended - but only within the original seven day limit. But the CJA 2003 amendments do not prevent an application for an extension for longer than seven days being made before seven days has expired (and so long as the warrant already authorises detention for a full seven days). The procedures are contained in paragraphs 30(3) and 31 to 34 of Schedule 8 and are as for existing applications.

CRIMINAL CASES REVIEW COMMISSION

Section 313 CJA 2003 amends the Criminal Appeal Act 1968 so as to allow the Court of Appeal to direct the Criminal Cases Review Commission (CCRC) to investigate and report on any matter where the defendant is *applying for leave to appeal* against conviction, as well as *on appeal* against conviction. Under existing law, section 23A Criminal Appeal Act 1968 allows that court (where a defendant *has been given leave* to appeal against conviction) to direct that the CCRC investigate and report to it on any matter relevant to the determination of the case and likely to assist in resolving it. Section 313 also inserts a new subsection 23A(1A) into the 1968 Act, so as to clarify that a direction to the CCRC to investigate may not be given by a single judge - the purpose being to require the full court to consider any such directions and to ensure that they are used sparingly.[3]

Appeals following a reference by the CCRC
Section 315 CJA 2003 adds a new section 14(4A) to the Criminal Appeal Act 1995. Under section 14(5) of the 1995 Act, an appellant whose case is referred to the Court of Appeal by the CCRC may introduce any number of additional grounds of appeal, including those that may bear no real relationship to the CCRC's original reasons for referral. The new section 14(4A) of the 1995 Act

---

[3] Section 314 makes similar provision in relation to Northern Ireland. Section 315 also extends to Northern Ireland.

means that, in future, leave will be required before the appellant can add any grounds unrelated to such reasons.

OTHER CHANGES

Other significant changes brought about by the CJA 2003 and not mentioned elsewhere in this book can be summarised as follows:

- **disqualification of magistrates** The existing bar on magistrates sitting to hear a case after having learned of details of an offender's previous convictions etc. during a bail application is removed (section 42 MCA 1980 as deleted by Schedule 3, para. 14, CJA 2003);[4]
- **plea befoe venue and allocation** Both these matters will be capable of being conducted by a single lay justice - whether in relation to an adult or a juvenile - but it is expressly provided that he or she may not hear the trial of a not guilty plea or impose sentence when sitting alone, for which two lay justices are required as a minimum (Schedule 3, paras 3, 4 and 10);
- **process** There is provision for summonses and warrants issued in England and Wales under the sentencing provisions of the CJA 2003 to be served or executed in Scotland (section 302);
- **written pleas of guilty** In relation to the 'paperwork' procedures in section 12 Magistrates' Courts Act 1980 whereby the offender can be given an opportunity to plead guilty in writing, at the instigation of the prosecutor, the existing restriction confining this process to offences punishable by imprisonment for not more than three months is removed (section 308);[5]
- **preparatory hearings before judges** In relation to preparatory hearings for serious offences not involving fraud, section 309 CJA 2003 amends section 29 Criminal Procedure and Investigations Act 1996 (which sets out the circumstances in which a statutory preparatory hearing may be held concerning such cases). Under existing law, preparatory hearings can be held in such cases where it appears to the judge that the case is of such complexity or length that holding a preparatory hearing is likely to bring substantial benefits. Section 309 adds 'seriousness' as a further criterion. Similarly, with preparatory hearings to deal with the severance or joinder of charges, section 310 CJA 2003 amends sections 7(1), 9(3) and 9(11) Criminal Justice Act 1987 and sections 29(2) and 31(3) Criminal Procedure and Investigations Act 1996. This serves to add issues of severance and joinder issues to those for which preparatory hearings may be held; and the changes also provide that the judge may make rulings on severance and joinder at a preparatory hearings;[6]

---

[4] But this cannot override the right to a fair trial as guaranteed by Article 6 of the European Convention On Human Rights - and it can hardly be argued that this change is an integral part of previous convictions becoming more relevant during the preliminary stages of a case or the loosening of the rules whereby they can be given in evidence (*Chapter 5*), since this would be to presuppose their relevance in a particular trial.

[5] A provision with potentially far-reaching effects.

[6] Such rulings can be appealed to the Court of Appeal under the 1987 or 1996 Acts either by the prosecutor or defendant, subject to the leave of that court or the judge; and there are related costs

- **alternative verdict on appeal from the Crown Court** Section 316 CJA 2003 inserts a new section 3A Criminal Appeal Act 1968 giving the Court of Appeal power to substitute a conviction of an alternative offence where the defendant appeals against conviction after pleading guilty and where the facts admitted by virtue of the guilty plea justify such a conviction.[7]
- **rights of appeal from decisions of the Crown Court** Under existing law, section 10 Criminal Appeal Act 1968 gives certain defendants who have not been tried in the Crown Court, but are sentenced there, a right of appeal to the Court of Appeal against sentence. But there is no such right where the offender is sentenced to less than six months' imprisonment, unless he or she receives certain specified kinds of sentence (described in the 1968 Act, e.g. a driving disqualification). Section 319 CJA 2003 simplifies section 10 by removing the six months limitation and its exceptions. The overall effect is that post-CJA 2003 anybody committed to the Crown Court for sentence (or dealt with by that court under other circumstances described in section 10(2) of the 1968 Act), will have a right of appeal to the Court of Appeal.
- **outraging public decency** Section 320 reclassifies the common law offence of 'outraging public decency' so as to make this an offence triable either way (as opposed to indictable only) and thus punishable on summary conviction with up to six months' imprisonment (rising to 12 months once section 282 CJA 2003 is in force) and/or a maximum fine of £5,000;[8]
- **criminal record certificates** Section 328 CJA 2003 and Schedule 35 make extensive provision in relation to the disclosure of criminal record certificates - largely by way of amendment to Part 5 of the Police Act 1997 - which governs disclosure of these and other records by the Criminal Records Bureau (CRB). The changes follow on from an independent review for the Home Office and include enabling legislation for regulations to be made prescribing the manner in which an application for disclosure must be made, either for standard or enhanced disclosure (and associated matters such as fees), the intention being to require applications to be submitted to the CRB via a registered body - as under the existing practice and, in due course, electronically. The CRB will be able to decide to make standard disclosure even though enhanced disclosure was applied for, with criteria being specified in regulations. Special provisions will apply to applications for enhanced disclosure in relation to judicial appointments and Crown employment. The CRB will set standards for registered bodies, particularly concerning validation of the identity of applicants for disclosure, and will be able to grant registration (subject to revised criteria), suspend or cancel it on various grounds.
- **civil proceedings by offenders against their victims** Section 329 makes new provision in relation to civil proceedings for trespass to the person *brought by an offender convicted of an imprisonable criminal offence* who takes civil action for damages against his or her victim or against a third party

---

provisions (section 312). Reporting restrictions concerning preparatory hearings are extended to Northern Ireland (section 311 CJA 2003).
[7] Section 317 makes similar provision in relation to Northern Ireland and section 318 where the appeal is from a court-martial.
[8] See section 32 Magistrates' Courts Act 1980.

who intervened, e.g. to protect the victim or to protect or recover property. Under section 329(1) this will apply where the claimant has been convicted in the UK of an imprisonable offence committed on the same occasion as that on which the victim's act of trespass allegedly occurred. In such circumstances, proceedings may only be brought with the leave of the court which may only be given if there is evidence that the condition set out in subsection (5) is not met, or if there is evidence that in all the circumstances the victim's act was grossly disproportionate. If the court does give permission and the proceedings are brought, the defendant will not be liable if he or she can prove that the condition set out in subsection (5) is met, and that in all the circumstances his or her act was not grossly disproportionate. Section 329(5) sets out that condition, i.e. that the victim only did the act amounting to trespass to the claimant's person because he or she believed that (a) the claimant was either about to commit an offence, in the course of committing an offence, or had committed an offence immediately beforehand; and (b) the act was necessary to defend himself or herself or another person; protect or recover property; prevent the commission or continuation of an offence; apprehend or secure the conviction of the claimant after he or she had committed the offence; or that the act was necessary to assist in achieving any of those things. Other provisions ensure that the statutory defence available to the victim (above) does not prejudice his or her ability to rely on any other defence; and that it applies under services legislation. 'Trespass to the person' comprises assault, battery, or false imprisonment and the references in the CJA 2003 to the victim's belief are to his or her honest belief, whether or not it was also reasonable.[9]

- **release of prisoners who have been transferred to hospital** In relation to mental patients, section 295 inserts a new section 74(5A) into the Mental Health Act 1983. This change concerns transferred prisoners who are detained in hospital beyond their release date and whose detention in hospital has been found by a mental health review tribunal to be no longer justified on grounds of mental disorder, but who the tribunal has recommended should remain in hospital rather than be returned to prison in the event that the Secretary of State does not agree to discharge them from hospital. Section 74(5A) provides that the fact that restrictions under the Mental Health Act 1983 remain in force does not prevent an application or reference to the Parole Board for release; and that if the Parole Board directs or recommends release, the restrictions cease to have effect at the time when the prisoner is entitled to release. The overall effect is that a prisoner who has been transferred to hospital is assured access to the Parole Board, and the possibility of release on licence, once he or she has reached his or her release date and the mental health review tribunal has found that he or she is no longer appropriately detained in hospital.

---

[9] It may be that these provisions are in part a response to the Tony Martin *cause célèbre* where there were civil cross-actions as between the offender (Tony Martin, a householder who claimed to be defending his property) and his victim (a burglar). The case involved a shooting in which one burglar was killed and the other injured.

CHAPTER 14

The Act in Context: A Brave New World?

As will now be evident, the CJA 2003 touches upon every aspect of criminal justice. Indeed, the Act is more far reaching, perhaps, than many people might have anticipated - not just in relation to sentencing, but also in the way it affects other stages of the criminal process. What seems clear is that a great deal of thought, planning and effort must have gone into its preparation.[1] The CJA 2003 is not 'just another Criminal Justice Act' but represents a new landmark. If deciphering its often complex provisions (a central task in writing this book) is one challenge for practitioners, similar decoding in relation to the backdrop against which it became law also seems essential for a full understanding.

CHANGES ACROSS THE CRIMINAL JUSTICE SYSTEM

For a long time now, structural changes have been taking place in the way that criminal justice is provided in England and Wales - and in the way the criminal justice agencies (or 'services') function, or are allowed to function. These changes are ostensibly designed to guarantee improved efficiency and effectiveness in a sphere where public confidence is a prime consideration. But they are also intermingled with political aims and objectives and hardly a week goes by without some new development being announced as part of this process of change. To the extent that developments are a reaction to the uncontrolled, often idiosyncratic and occasionally dubious approaches of the past - and somewhat vague notions of accountability - they are to be welcomed. But when viewed as a mechanism whereby Ministers are better able to respond to the short-term demands of popular opinion there is a need for caution. The CJA 2003 confers considerable powers on the Secretary of State at a number of points, whilst he or she has also acquired, through this backdrop of change and development, considerable sway in relation to several of the agencies involved - and at certain key points. Whatever else, it will be essential to keep checks and balances under review. It is one thing to create a more effective system with improved procedures for arresting, trying and convicting the guilty, but there must also be fair treatment at all points and the acquittal of the innocent.

'Firming up' law and order arrangements
It is instructive to note some of these developments. They have included, e.g.:

- notable advances in law enforcement generally, including in relation to the individual or joint activities of the police, Customs and Excise, Serious Fraud Office and the Health and Safety Executive;

---

[1] This seems to go beyond anything that might have been predicted solely on the basis of the Auld and Halliday reports or *Justice For All* (mentioned in the *Preface*). The scale, breadth and implications of the Act are enormous - and what is striking is the way in which 'big issues' and countless lesser, individual items that have been 'in need of repair' for some time are dealt with simultaneously. A corresponding investment might be anticipated *vis-à-vis* implementation.

- reforms to policing (including a Police Reform Act 2002), with more promised including, e.g. a National Crime Squad to tackle organized crime, increased numbers of community support officers who work with police officers in a supporting role, and major advances in the use of technology to detect and solve crimes;
- crime prevention responsibilities being placed on police and local authorities (and both increasingly required to deal with anti-social behaviour also) with crime prevention also becoming a performance indicator for several agencies - and a 'statutory purpose' under both the Crime and Disorder Act in relation to juveniles and now, under the CJA 2003, one of the statutory purposes of sentencing to which all courts will be obliged to have regard (*Chapter 7*);
- the creation of Criminal Justice Boards both nationally and locally, whereby the various agencies meet to discuss matters of common interest and in some instances adopt joint strategies, approaches or protocols;[2]
- a 'joining up' of various aspects of the criminal justice process, co-ordinated strategies, 'partnerships' and bringing into line of the geographical boundaries of the different services (e.g. Criminal Justice Units made up of police and Crown[3] prosecutors);
- a move away from using the criminal courts at all for lesser matters (but including an increasingly wide range of gradually more serious ones), through the deployment of fixed penalties;
- a simultaneous move to bring more forms of disruptive, irresponsible or anti-social behaviour[4] within the scope of the umbrella of the criminal law and criminal justice processes;
- the creation of a Department for Constitutional Affairs in place of the Lord Chancellor's Department and the planned abolition of the office of Lord Chancellor and creation of a Supreme Court;[5]
- a 'reordered' Courts Service within which the criminal courts will have seamless management arrangements (under the Courts Act 2003) and changed jurisdictional boundaries (under the CJA 2003);
- the 'revitalising' of the Judicial Studies Board to ensure enhanced arrangements for judicial training (including for the CJA 2003);
- the creation of a National Offender Management Service (NOMS) as part of a 'reconstruction' of HM Prison Service and the National Probation Service (itself a recent innovation) - with separate but co-ordinated arms for commissioning and for providing accommodation and facilities - to ensure the effective implementation of sentences (with a Chief Executive, originally styled 'Commissioner for Correctional Services', in overall charge);

---

[2] Often, again, against a background of similar aims, targets and priorities in relation to which central government will often have had an input - and there are inevitably funding and resource implications for government and the Treasury.

[3] There has also been a move to exchange the word 'Crown' for 'Public' (though seemingly shelved for the time being) and speculation about the removal of 'Her Majesty's' from HM Prison Service.

[4] Anti-social behaviour may attract civil and/or criminal processes/powers.

[5] At the time of writing the House of Lords had just voted to refer these plans to a Select Committee (what has been described by certain commentators as 'a Constitutional crisis').

- a national Accreditation Board in relation to programmes for offenders (a side effect of which will be greater control of what sentences are actually available for courts to pass);
- the switch to a Criminal Defence Service (CDS) and corresponding changes in the way that legal advice is provided to defendants (and funded); and
- a growing emphasis on key underlying causes of crime evidenced by the introduction of drug-testing at key points in the criminal process, increased reliance on electronic monitoring under court orders and following release from prison (including on home detention curfew) and an emphasis on confronting persistent offenders (themes taken up within the CJA 2003).

These items are just part of the 'firming up', 'coming together' and 'streamlining' of the criminal process onto which the CJA 2003 will be grafted. Others could be mentioned, such as the Assets Recovery Agency, an improved Forensic Science Service, Drug Action Teams, Independent Monitoring Boards[6] and, of course, the Youth Justice Board and local youth offending teams (YOTs) in relation to juveniles. There have been comparable advances in the non-statutory and voluntary sectors, not least in relation to victims of crime. This is the 'new world' of criminal justice, though how 'brave' still remains to be seen - especially perhaps while prison overcrowding and prison building remain major pre-occupations.

Within the field of sentencing, the CJA 2003 arrangements described in *Chapters 7* to *11* of this book presuppose a certain capacity to deliver on the part of NOMS and some kind of tie in between what courts do and the facilities and resources that will be available. The creation of NOMS is based on the independent Carter Report[7] commissioned by the Home Office. A central argument of Carter is that, if sentences are to be effective, sentencing practice must take account of a capacity to deliver those sentences that are imposed. Under the heading 'New Role for the Judiciary', the report states:

> Roles and responsibilities need to be clarified for the judiciary . . . Judges and magistrates need to be able to make entirely independent sentencing decisions in individual cases . . . The judiciary needs to ensure the consistent and cost-effective use of prison and probation capacity and to ensure a clear link between the sentence given and the sentence served.

The report concludes that 'The new Sentencing Guidelines Council provides an immediate opportunity to improve the effectiveness of sentencing'. It will also provide a fresh opportunity for addressing roles and responsibilities overall.

A KEY ROLE FOR THE SGC

The statutory role of the SGC has already been outlined in *Chapter 7*, and the Carter Report indicates how the council might operate in practice. Critically, it is seen in the CJA 2003 as enabling courts to pass sentences which will be

---

[6] Replacing Boards of Visitors in relation to prisons and prisoners.
[7] *Managing Offenders, Reducing Crime* ('The Carter Report', January 2004).

'effective', presumably in reducing crime; and in the report as providing the link between appropriate sentencing decisions and the availability and deployment of penal resources. It might thus be suggested that the success or otherwise of the CJA 2003 - and the value of the building blocks for criminal justice that are already in place as intimated by the list of developments given above - will, ultimately, depend on what definitive guidelines the SGC provides to criminal courts (all of which are duty bound to follow these or give sound reasons for departing from them). Even assuming that the SGC accepts that its role extends to matching sentences to resources it faces other challenges. Not least among these is the extent of the range of items that will need attention - and relatively soon - in terms of timely training for and implementation of the CJA 2003, so that the new law can be applied in a coherent and consistent way. Even with the support of the Sentencing Advisory Panel and input from the Home Office[8] this will be no mean feat. Suggestions of the kind of areas requiring immediate attention have already been mentioned in *Chapter 7*. It is not simply a question of guidance in relation to individual sentences, but also about how each of the new-style sentences and other approaches created by the 2003 Act is to operate in practice. It is about how the in-built flexibility of parts of the Act (what the Home Office would describe as fitting the sentence to the offender) can lead to fair and consistent outcomes; how one type of sentence, requirement or programme is to be measured against another in terms of its weight so as to ensure that sentences remain broadly proportionate to the seriousness of the offence; and all the nuances of sentencing in relation to dangerous offenders (which can be typified by asking, e.g. how long the extension period of an extended sentence should be)(*Chapter 10*).

REDUCING CRIME

All the strategies now in place have a central aim of reducing crime. One less encouraging aspect of this has been an increase in the prison population to over 75,000 with its consequent impact on the capacity of the prison service to deliver safe regimes, effective strategies and high quality offending behaviour and resettlement programmes. This is illustrative, perhaps, of the kind of tensions that may occur when sentencing and enforcement processes are 'stepped up a

---

[8] The relationship between the SGC and the Court of Appeal/Supreme Court on the one hand and the SGC and Home Secretary on the other represent a new area for constitutional debate. The Home Secretary has no direct say in the SGC's deliberations but can both propose guidelines and send an observer who is entitled to speak at meetings. The scenario in which the SGC is overwhelmed by its tasks but the Home Office able to 'assist' cannot be discounted. Neither can the Court of Appeal, it seems, be expected to refrain from guidance in the general sense where the SGC has not yet issued it - even if guideline judgements as they are styled (where general principles are abstracted, usually by dealing with a number of comparable appeal cases simultaneously) will of necessity become a thing of the past. Individual cases can hardly be halted and then held up to await guidelines, imminent or otherwise. All this only serves to emphasise the importance - but also the sheer scale - of the SGC's role. It also highlights the vulnerability of the judiciary to political pressure. Much will no doubt depend on the Lord Chief Justice of the day - as head of the SGC - and whether he or she is convinced that the SGC represents the right or an adequate mechanism for resolving the myriad issues that could potentially arise in a sentencing context. It may also depend on whether he or she remains comfortable that sentencing is still a truly judicial function and to an extent on his or her personal reaction to the kind of ideas expressed in Carter.

gear' - as they will be by the CJA 2003.[9] This said, many features of the Act offer a more constructive approach, depending on how new powers are used. Various provisions could have the effect of taking people out of prison. But fresh and 'enticing' powers to construct burdensome community requirements in relation to various types or stages of a sentence could also lead to 'escalation', i.e. many more people in prison - or back in prison after being recalled (*Chapter 11*) - as such orders are seen to 'fail', and with the tolerance of (and alternative options for) courts exhausted. As Nacro commented on welcoming the White Paper, *Justice For All* with its emphasis on focusing imprisonment on serious cases and improving the rehabilitation of all prisoners:

> The sentencing proposals would create a more rational framework for using prison and community penalties . . . However, there is a risk that some of these measures could backfire if courts misuse them. While the custody plus sentence could shorten the periods offenders spend in prison, courts could alternatively decide to use it for offenders who at present receive community sentences. While custody minus[10] and intermittent custody could replace jail sentences, courts could alternatively use them instead of non-custodial penalties.

It might be suggested that the history of criminal justice is littered with missed opportunities and unintended effects as judges, magistrates, police, prosecutors, probation officers and others have applied their own legitimate discretion and interpretations. One hope for the CJA 2003 is that the enhanced mechanisms for 'working together' and similar building blocks now in place - alongside the work of the SGC - will lead to a more positive and constructive outcome this time around. It is within some of the Act's more enlightened aspects, such as the momentum that it creates in relation to the use of community sentences in a broader range of situations that do not truly merit custody that signs of the Government's often expressed commitment to restorative justice and rehabilitative approaches is most visible. But there is also the risk of an escalating prison population due to a potential for more onerous treatment in certain other situations - not only due to sentence levels but also the 'incremental' nature of the various enforcement provisions and the longer-term character of the obligations that many offenders could find themselves under. Ultimately, successful implementation of the Act may depend as much on a preparedness to rethink the appropriate response in a given context as on an understanding of its often complex yet innovative measures.

---

[9] Including due to the incremental nature of certain aspects of the provisions as noted in the text.

[10] What became the new-style suspended sentence described in *Chapter 8*.

Appendix **Reasons for Decisions**

The giving and recording of reasons and explanations is now a familiar process for courts, other criminal justice decision-makers and practitioners but the CJA 2003 significantly extends such duties, which will demand yet closer attention to detail by all concerned.

New general duty on sentencers
Section 174 CJA 2003 places a general duty on a court to give reasons and explanations for all sentences as follows:

(1) Subject to subsections (3) and (4), any court passing sentence on an offender -
  (a) must state in open court, in ordinary language and in general terms, its reasons for deciding on the sentence passed, and
  (b) must explain to the offender in ordinary language -
    (i) the effect of the sentence,
    (ii) where the offender is required to comply with any order of the court forming part of the sentence, the effects of non-compliance with the order,
    (iii) any power of the court, on the application of the offender or any other person, to vary or review any order of the court forming part of the sentence, and
    (iv) where the sentence consists of or includes a fine, the effects of failure to pay the fine.
(2) In complying with subsection (1)(a), the court must -
  (a) where guidelines[1] indicate that a sentence of a particular kind, or within a particular range, would normally be appropriate for the offence and the sentence is of a different kind, or is outside that range, state the court's reasons for deciding on a sentence of a different kind or outside that range,
  (b) where the sentence is a custodial sentence and the duty in subsection (2) of section 152 is not excluded by subsection (1)(a) or (b) or (3) of that section, state that it is of the opinion referred to in section 152(2)[2] and why it is of that opinion,
  (c) where the sentence is a community sentence and the case does not fall within section 151(2)[3] state that it is of the opinion that section 148(1) applies and why it is of that opinion,
  (d) where as a result of taking into account any matter referred to in section 144(1), the court imposes a punishment on the offender which is less severe than the punishment it would otherwise have imposed, state that fact, and
  (e) in any case, mention any aggravating or mitigating factors which the court has regarded as being of particular importance.

Subsection 174(1)(a) (above) does not apply: where the sentence is fixed by law (separate provision for this being made by section 270); or in various situations where the court must pass a custodial sentence. The Secretary of State may prescribe cases where the duty does not arise, or in which reasons or explanation can be given in the absence of the offender or in writing. If a magistrates' court passes a custodial sentence, it must repeat its reasons in the warrant of commitment and court register (the effect of section 174(5)).

New specific duties
The CJA 2003 also adds to the individual situations in which reasons etc. must be given. Thus, they must normally be announced and recorded - and may become particularly significant later, e.g. for appeal, review or assessment purposes - where:

---

[1] Meaning definitive sentencing guidelines issued by the SGC (section 174(6)). See also *Chapter 7*.
[2] I.e. that the offence is 'so serious' as to meet the custodial sentencing threshold.
[3] I.e. where a community sentence is used instead of a fine for a 'persistent offender': *Chapter 7*.

- a police officer declines to allow 'street bail' but delays taking the arrested person to a police station. The reason for that delay must be recorded when the person first arrives at the station (section 4(5) CJA 2003 amending section 30 PACE) (*Chapter 2*);
- a decision is made to hold a judge-alone trial (section 48 CJA 2003) (*Chapter 5*);
- in relation to certain evidential rulings. The judge or magistrate must state in open court (but in the absence of the jury where applicable) the reasons for the ruling. A magistrates' court must cause such rulings and the reasons for them to be entered in the court register. 'Relevant rulings' for this purpose are those whether: an item of evidence is evidence of a person's bad character; an item of evidence is admissible under section 100 or 101 ('bad character') (and including a ruling on a defence application under section 101(3) ('fairness')); and a ruling under section 107 (contaminated evidence) (section 110 CJA 2003) (*Chapter 5*);
- racial or religious aggravation is treated as an aggravating factor by a court in relation to sentence (section 145 CJA 2003) (*Chapter 7*);
- hostility based upon sexual orientation or disability is treated as an aggravating factor in relation to sentence by a court (section 146 CJA 2003) (*Chapter 7*);
- a court allows sentencing 'credit' to reflect time spent on remand in custody (or refuses such credit). An explanation must be given by reference to the number of days involved (section 240 CJA 2003) (*Chapter 7*);
- a court dealing with breach of a suspended sentence concludes that it would be unjust to activate a suspended sentence (para. 8(3) of Schedule 12) (*Chapter 9*);
- a court makes certain orders in relation to the minimum term to be served under a life sentence 'fixed by law' - when it must state the 'starting point' (Schedule 21) and its reasons for any departure from it as well as explaining in ordinary language its reasons for deciding upon the order made (but does not have to explain the sentence itself) (section 270 CJA 2003) (*Chapter 10*);
- the Secretary of State revokes a prisoner's licence and recalls him or her to prison (section 254 CJA 2003) (*Chapter 11*);
- a court dealing with a juvenile is *not* satisfied that individual support conditions are fulfilled, when it must state in open court that it is not so satisfied and why (new section 1AA Crime and Disorder Act 1998 as inserted by section 322 CJA 2003). Similarly, before making an individual support order, the court must explain its effect, that of the requirements in it, the consequences that flow from failure to comply with these and the court's powers to review the order (new section 1AB(1) Crime and Disorder Act 1998 as similarly inserted) (*Chapter 12*);
- the court orders (or in certain situations does not order) someone to be disqualified from working with children under section 29A Criminal Justice and Court Services Act 2000 (as inserted by section 299 CJA 2003 and Schedule 30) (*Chapter 13*).

Index

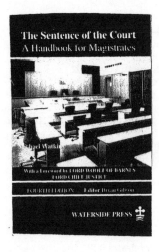